Stand-Out Shorts

Stand-Out Shorts
Shooting and Sharing Your Films Online

Russell Evans

AMSTERDAM • BOSTON • HEIDELBERG • LONDON
NEW YORK • OXFORD • PARIS • SAN DIEGO
SAN FRANCISCO • SINGAPORE • SYDNEY • TOKYO

Focal Press is an imprint of Elsevier

Focal Press is an imprint of Elsevier
30 Corporate Drive, Suite 400, Burlington, MA 01803, USA
The Boulevard, Langford Lane, Kidlington, Oxford, OX5 1GB, UK

Notices

Knowledge and best practice in this field are constantly changing. As new research and experience
broaden our understanding, changes in research methods, professional practices, or medical
treatment may become necessary.
Practitioners and researchers must always rely on their own experience and knowledge
in evaluating and using any information, methods, compounds, or experiments described
herein. In using such information or methods they should be mindful of their own
safety and the safety of others, including parties for whom they have a professional
responsibility.
To the fullest extent of the law, neither the Publisher nor the authors, contributors, or editors,
assume any liability for any injury and/or damage to persons or property as a matter of products
liability, negligence or otherwise, or from any use or operation of any methods, products,
instructions, or ideas contained in the material herein.

Library of Congress Cataloging-in-Publication Data
Application submitted

British Library Cataloguing-in-Publication Data
A catalogue record for this book is available from the British Library.

ISBN: 978-0-240-81210-6

For information on all Focal Press publications
visit our website at www.elsevierdirect.com

Printed in the United States of America

10 11 12 13 5 4 3 2 1

Working together to grow
libraries in developing countries

www.elsevier.com | www.bookaid.org | www.sabre.org

ELSEVIER   BOOK AID
            International   Sabre Foundation

Contents

For more content such as additional chapters and interviews please visit the companion site at: http://booksite.focalpress.com/companion/Evans/stand-out/

Register using the passcode: shorts106

Why Make Movies?

When George Lucas' car hit a walnut tree just after his eighteenth birthday he thought maybe he should do something with his life after all. His Fiat Bianchina left the track, he was thrown clear, and the walnut tree was shifted three feet by the impact.

What happened that June 12th 1962 changed the course of the future director's life forever, a sudden jolt that threw him out of his small-town life and into a whole new direction. And it's kind of like what happened to filmmakers when affordable digital video arrived. One minute you know where you are headed – along a familiar and well-worn road – and the next you're traveling at high speed through the air into the middle of a wide open plain. No more slow road, no more road markings and no landmarks. DV meant that you could cut to the chase, pick up your camera, no cash needed, and make that movie. Then show it around the world. Suddenly the horizon was wide open, and that old slow road looked very slow indeed.

So, if that's what today's filmmakers have at their disposal, how is it being used? Is everyone making digital masterpieces? Not quite. Some just drive round in circles with their new-found DV tools. Like any new territory, most people don't really know where to go and after a while start to long for the old certain places to go, even if it was slower traveling that way.

But you know that whatever technology you use, you still need passion and soul to make any movie. The biggest asset you have is your own unique way of seeing the world, and the more your films get shared on the web, the more you find other people who see things your way.

Thanks

There are a lot of people who have made this book possible, from the many film students I've worked with, to the filmmakers around the world who have taken time to tell me how they work and part with their hard-won tips for every aspect of making a movie. People who make films tend to be extremely generous with their time, maybe aware of how tough it was for them when they were starting out, and they responded to the request to tell what they have learned with enthusiasm. Some of them are film students themselves, others famous directors such as Nick Broomfield, but they all had the same positive response when I asked them to share their practical experiences.

A big thank you to: Preston Randolph; Nick Broomfield; Kerry David; Ben Rutkowski; Ben Winter; Derek Flagge; Gary Teperman; Nick Cox in LA; R. Gesualdo in Florida; Walter Murch; Elliot Grove; Anne Aghion; the talented Chance Brothers, Richard and John; Jason Korsner; Oscar Knott; Armen Antranikian; Blanca Escoda; Ryan Bilsborrow-Koo; Elliot Bristow; Lee Philips; Kevin Powis; Til Mustapha; Mohamed Al-Daradji; Ashvin Kumar; Dewi Griffiths; Stacey Harrison; Ray Gower; Catbus; Neville Steenson; Gus Berger. And to Gavin Evans for knowing all the good movies.

Thank you to Focal Press, and in particular Elinor Actipis for relentlessly pursuing this project with me over the last few years. Thanks for your belief! Also, editor Chris Simpson has been calm, patient and always on the end of the phone to gradually guide the project through. Thanks are due also to my editors on the several filmmaking magazines I worked on over the years, particularly *Practical DV*, for sending me great ideas to work on, some of which inspired a few chapters in this book.

Finally, a big thank you to Wendy Klein, for your constant support and inspired ideas, and to Esme, Zoe and Alfie just for being around.

Start Here

WHY READ THIS BOOK?

This book says that making movies is no different from any other creative work – you really can just pick up a camera and start to create something, just like you do with music, dancing or acting. You don't wait to be told you're good enough, you just do it. And you don't have to do things "the right way," you just have to do it *your* way. Use this book to find out what works for most people, then go ahead and add your own ideas.

The big advances we look back on as the greatest moments in the movies have only come about by people rejecting "the right way" and instead doing it "their way": special effects were invented by director Georges Méliès messing around with cameras and doing what cameras weren't supposed to do; the great Russian editors' invention of montage trashed every editing idea; and a 24-year old Orson Welles knew almost nothing about filmmaking except what he saw in his head, ending up with what was the number 1 critics' movie for half a century.

You don't have to read a dozen heavy manuals on making films, or go to film school, or be a genius director. Just find out the essential knowledge you need and start.

That's why this book is as skinny as possible. It's a distillation of the stuff you need to know, packed into a small space. Sure, you can get filmmaking advice on the web, but what this book does is use real experience, real interviews and tried and tested ideas and techniques to offer the simplest, most direct way to get started making movies. And it's all in one place, just the main stuff you need to know, nothing more, nothing less.

Once you start, your journey leads to more ambitious projects – longer movies, serials, or bigger productions. When you are through with this book, carry on by finding out more from other books, film school or jobs, and burrow deep into the world of technical and artistic knowledge. But for now, shoot your shorts and share them, finding out what sort of filmmaker you are.

Quotes

1. "Just make it."

2. "Don't worry about technical quality for your first film so much and put the emphasis on the creative aspects – the writing, the performing, the shooting. Because people are most interested in fresh voices, not whether films look expensive or not."

3. "Don't let instructors and classmates impede you from being yourself, even if your ideas defy convention."

4. "Show your film in as many places as you can and watch it with audiences in order to learn from your mistakes."

5. "Make a second film."

Nick Cox, filmmaker, Los Angeles

"Whatever part of the filmmaking process you decide is your path, only attach yourself to projects you are truly passionate about. If you are a writer, write something that captivates you, as a director take on projects that you know need your imprint. I believe that it is passion and tenacity that gets a project to the big screen and the person who has the most passion and tenacity pushes their project past the finish line.

"Enjoy the process. Relish the journey. Don't take yourself too seriously and appreciate the people around you and what they bring to the project – no film gets made alone and, take it from me, it feels much better to accept awards for your films with your friends from the project right there with you."

Kerry David, producer, *My Date With Drew,* USA

"A lot of filmmaking is putting the time in, having the patience to make it great. It's not about being a genius, it's about going that extra mile and digging as deep as you can, not giving up and being persistent."

Nick Broomfield, director, *Battle for Haditha,* UK

How to Use This Book

Stand-Out Shorts is in four parts:

- How to make movies
- How to share movies online
- What movie to make
- How to make sure your movie happens

The first part is made up of three sections (Prep, Shoot, and Cut) and has all the technical and practical stuff you need to know, and the way to make the films you want. It's designed to be accessed easily, avoiding long chunks of text, so you can quickly scan it to find out whether you even need it or not.

Right after the technical know-how, there is a section on sharing online. Whatever kind of film you make, this gives you a detailed guide to preparing your film for the web, creating a buzz around it, and making the most of what's out there, from festivals to network sites. This gives you a real-world plan to get viewers for your movies.

The next section is all about the different movies you might want to make. There's a mix of genre movies and popular online tags. Each one gives you a dip inside what that movie is and what people today expect from it, plus all the practical tips you need like what equipment to borrow, who to call up to help you and what can inspire you. There's also an outline of what that movie needs to be like to fit in with today's audiences. Movies change over time and what was OK once might be strictly passé now. Find out how to make sure your movie doesn't look dated or clichéd.

Finally, to help your stand-out short stand up, there are a few schedules. These have been put together from years of working with new filmmakers and students, looking at what people need to do and what they can ignore. There's a schedule for a quick 48-hour movie – very popular in film competitions around the world – and one-week and one-month projects. If none of those work, there's one to fit around you when you get the time to shoot.

And when you're through with the book, make sure you check out www.standoutshorts.com to get free updates and additions to the book. It'll keep the book alive and up-to-date.

A FEW MORE THINGS

There are a lot of graphic bits in the text, words in bold, and icons. Most books have straight text, but this one knows you might be in a hurry, so you can read it in two ways. First, you can go at it straight, like a regular book, and read it from start to finish. Or you can scan the page for the bold text or graphics and pick up a bare-bones version. It's like having the essentials of the essentials.

In each section you'll see interviews and quotes from people who make films. All these have been given to me personally for this book, with everyone kindly responding to questions about every aspect of making movies, sharing their real experience for other filmmakers.

There are also parts called "Second Opinion." These give you an opposite point of view about what was just said in a chapter. That's because sometimes you need to have all sides of a story, not just what some people say is the right way. In filmmaking there are big differences in the ways people do things – yes or no to tripods, storyboards, or effects, using real or artificial light and so on – and any book that says there's only one way is out of step with the real world.

Although this book takes a pop at traditional methods of filmmaking, it's not anti-film school. If you are in a film school with some great, inspirational teachers and professors, then use this book to accompany what they say. They'll also be talking from experience, just like the filmmakers in this book.

Section One: Prep

PREP YOUR MOVIE

You've got the urge to make a movie. You might not know what it's about yet, but you've got something to say and you want people to hear it. This section has 11 chapters designed to guide you through the essentials of planning and preparing your movie as neatly as possible and with minimum hassle.

Chapter 1: **Ideas.** This one helps you figure out where your thoughts lie, what sort of movie would suit you and how to develop it into a more solid form.

Chapter 2: **Buying a Camera.** Need to know what cam to get or even whether to get one at all? Use this checklist to make sure you know what to ask for from your store.

Chapter 3: **Scriptwriting.** Now that you've got the idea looking strong, try it out as a script. Here's how to avoid clichés and try a few different methods to find what suits you.

Chapter 4: **Budgets.** How to make sure you don't get sunk by your movie, and how to get stuff for free.

Chapter 5: **Designing Your Movie.** Give your film your own particular style, and create the image and feel you want.

Chapter 6: **Cast and Crew Online.** Next up, you'll need to find people to work with. How to create the right email postings to attract crew and cast and make sure you keep them.

Chapter 7: **Previz.** That's the part where you plan how it's going to look, scene by scene. Find out how to create detailed images of your movie – even if you can't draw.

Chapter 8: **Script Breakdown and Shot List.** This can be dull, so it's short and painless here. Make it so everyone knows where to be and when.

Chapter 9: **Law and the Movies.** They always win, so avoid getting stung by The Man by making sure your movie is legit from music to story to extras.

Chapter 10: **Working with Locations.** Working anywhere but your home turf can be stressful. Use this guide to make sure you choose the right place and get the most out of it.

Chapter 11: **Brief Directory of All the Paperwork You Need.** Finally, a checklist of everything you might need to prep your movie.

Chapter | One

Ideas

OVERVIEW

You can make great movies if you find out what makes you different. Be your-self and put your own fingerprint on your movies. Forget about finding a unique new story or blend of other stories. The trick to being original is simply to give people your own unique way of seeing things. It's not what you say; it's the way that you say it.

FIGURE 1.1 Setting up a shot for the sci-fi movie *The Day I Tried to Live*, by Richard Chance and John Chance.

HOW DO YOU FIND OUT WHAT SORT OF MOVIEMAKER YOU ARE?

1. Follow your instincts.

This means relying on your instinctive, snap decisions. Trust and learn to follow your first impressions and your instincts. If an idea grabs you, chase it.

2. Avoid emulating other people.

The problem with having a big movie collection on your shelf is that it is hard not to be influenced by what you see. If you want more original ideas that are uniquely yours, focus on anything in any art form other than movies. Look at short stories, radio, songs, comics – anything except movies.

3. Focus on your own experiences.

You don't need to make your movies autobiographical – most people don't feel that comfortable with having their real lives splashed up on the screen. But use locations and people familiar to you, giving a made-up story a realistic edge. Or you can use a single moment you experienced and reinvent it somewhere else. Luke Skywalker stuck in a nowhere town on Tatooine and yearning to travel fast and far is arguably his creator George Lucas returning to his own small-town youth and love of fast cars. This grain of truth makes it something we can all relate to.

4. Don't think about the outcome.

One sure way to stay true to yourself is to focus on the day-to-day process of making your movie, rather than how it's all going to look when it's done. Keep your thoughts on the here and now, looking at how to deal with each small hurdle each day.

5. Mix and sample.

Take a look at what is in the news, or ask other people what they are hung up about, what scares them right now. A good way to take your ideas further while still being yourself is to use small parts of your own experiences and mix them with bigger, wider ones – those which make up the zeitgeist. Can you merge these ideas with what you have gone through? Or mix them with genre movies? The results could be interesting – as in George Romero's *Dawn of the Dead,* which mixes zombies with Romero's own feelings about consumerism. Or apply your own experiences to a completely different setting – such as *Blue Velvet*, where a coming-of-age movie gets transplanted into a surreal nightmare setting.

6. Next up, look at the techniques you use to make movies.

Technique means the way you shoot, edit, light, and all the rest and it's where most filmmakers tend to fall over in their desire to copy other filmmakers. The techniques you use should only arise from your main theme. Everything can come from that first germ of an idea. Play around with every different way of doing things until you know you find the one that's right for you.

7. Next, pitch it to a few people and get reactions.

You might find that on each telling the story gets refined and sharpened. The bits that are not important to you get left out and you focus on the essentials.

8. It's fine to get feedback about your movie.

It won't be so weak that any contact with the outside world destroys it. If it feels too vulnerable to people's comments then it needs to return to paper and get mapped out some more. Listen to what people say about your movie, write down their comments, and then later settle on which ones you like and don't like.

9. Next, work with actors to improvise the script and add more ideas as you work with it.

Experts' Tips

Gary Teperman, writer/director, New York

"I think that most originality comes with life experiences; writing about who you are, what you see, what you know and what you imagine. I think that traveling a lot helps, learning about different cultures, reading different kinds of material. It's hard to be original these days because of all the competition in the market and being original doesn't always sell, but it can be done. People shouldn't try too hard to be original; just learn and write."

Ben Rutkowski, filmmaker, USA

"Ask yourself what would happen if the exact opposite thing happened at that moment."

TRY IT OUT

Write down your responses to these questions. But don't think more than a few seconds about each one, just write the first things to come into your mind.

1. What was the worst day you ever had?
2. Who is the most memorable person you ever met and why?
3. What place has stuck in your mind the most and why?
4. Have you ever let someone down, double-crossed someone, had your actions uncovered, given something precious away, been in real trouble?
5. What's your worst nightmare?
6. Who would you most like to meet and why?

AND THEN ...

If you want to make a movie about these experiences you could try remaking them in a new way.

- **To start, write down the locations, the individual characters, and the events in your own experience** (say, arriving at a new town to live in).

- Next to it, **write down a new version where line-for-line you create new archetypes for each one** – usually going slightly more over the top than in reality. The new town becomes a dark Gotham city, the characters become alter-egos of the real people, and the events themselves become hyped up and exaggerated.

CREATE MOVIES OUT OF A SMALL IMAGE OR IDEA:
For example, you might come up with a core idea of **a face in a mirror.**

- You think about this some more and **focus on the spookiness of it** and the stillness, darkness and color of it.
- You ask yourself **what the face is, and who is looking at it.** Don't think about the answers long – just go with your instincts to get the answers.
- You expand further to **get a location or setting,** using an old house you pass on the way home each day.
- Then you start to **think about the characters** more – who they are and what their stories are.
- After following this track for a while you can then start to **link up some of these things** and a narrative starts to emerge, based on motives: who is doing what and why?

This can all sound too easy but it should be; it's come from you after all, and you know the idea inside out.

DIG DEEPER
Add in something more by **digging down into the idea you have and adding extra ideas underneath the main events.** It's called subtext, just like it's "under the text" or between the lines. So wherever you have an event, try to add in the subtext to it. Why bother? Because all the motivations, feelings and desires of the characters in the movie don't sound right if they are shouted out loud – instead they need to be hinted at, suggested and just kind of understood by the viewers. It just sounds too cheesy when people announce the subtext out loud.

So **how do you get subtext on screen?** Literally, as you write down what happens in the movie, leave a space on the page (set it to double-spaced as you type) and write what is underlying this moment. Write down what people's feelings are, often contradicting what they say on screen. Tell the actors what they need to say but also what their underlying feelings are.

Chapter Two

Buying a Camera

OVERVIEW

No matter what they tell you in the video store, you don't need half of what they sell. Find out what essentials you need in your next camcorder.

Table 2.1 What do you need in your next camera?

Camcorder Feature	What it Does	What to Ask Your Store For:
Manual controls	Allows you to override the auto settings.	Complete manual override on aperture, shutter, focus and white balance.
Auto controls	Allows you to shoot and have the camera sort out the image for you. It lets the right amount of light in, focuses and more.	Every camera has auto settings. Auto is OK for shooting on-the-run but you need manual settings when you really want to control the image.
Optical zoom	Optical is "real" zoom. It works like a telescope and gives you a neat, clear image.	20× optical zoom or more. It lets you zoom in without losing picture quality.
Digital zoom	Next to useless, it just blows up the image you already have, reducing quality.	When they try to wow you with high digital zoom tell them that's only useful for faking your own UFO videos.

Continued...

Table 2.1 What do you need in your next camera? (Continued)

Camcorder Feature	What it Does	What to Ask Your Store For:
LCD screen	A flip-out color monitor to let you view what you are filming.	2.5-inch screen minimum. A large screen (above 3 inch) is useful but uses more battery power. Avoid touch screen playback.
Camera to PC ports	The cable you use to connect the camera to a PC.	You need the fastest way to get images onto your PC, but also which doesn't drop frames. It has to be a Firewire port. USB 2.0 just isn't quite as good.
Sound recording	Some camcorders use only the on board mic to record sound, while others have an external mic socket so you can plug in your own mic.	At least one external mic socket. Don't rely on the on board mic at the front of the camera.
Headphone socket	Allows you to plug in headphones to listen to what you are recording.	One 3.5 mm headphone socket.
Sensor/chip	A chip that encodes and feeds information from the lens, dividing it into color and intensity of light. The size and number of the chips (the charge-coupled device) that pick up the images is crucial. You'll notice the difference in picture quality. The choice is one chip for most cameras, or three chips for higher end and professional cams.	1 x 1 megapixel CCD. If you can afford it, go for three CCD chips but check the size of these as some cameras offer three chips but they are smaller than usual. 1/3-inch chips are ideal.
Backlight compensation	This offsets the silhouetting effect you get when you shoot against a bright background. The image is digitally altered so that the bright areas are toned down and the darker enhanced.	This is not an essential feature. Don't ask the store for it.
Battery	Portable power supply.	At least two batteries – both Lithium-ion.

Continued...

Table 2.1 What do you need in your next camera? (Continued)

Camcorder Feature	What it Does	What to Ask Your Store For:
AVCHD	Advanced Video Codec High Definition fits more HD video onto a card/tape, using MPEG-4 compression. It's a good idea, but some people don't like the fact that mostly it records "interlaced" video: it includes only every second line of the image on the TV screen, interlaced with lines from the rest of the image in the next frame. The human eye sees this as one continuous image, but it saves a lot of bandwidth this way. The problem is that LCD TVs and monitors don't work well with interlaced.	AVCHD is good for holiday video but not for movies. You need the option to record without this.
Stabilizer	A method of stabilizing a shaky image by reducing the screen area.	Not a useful feature. It is better to use a real steadying device such as the affordable Hague Pro-Steadymount.
Internal flash memory	A flash memory drive inside the camera to record video.	At least 64 GB internal, plus the ability to take SDXC cards or other large flash memory.

FIGURE 2.1 The Sony HDR-SR7E holds 60 GB on internal flash memory – enough for 15 hours of normal mode footage.

Table 2.2 How much can I get onto cards and flash memory?

	How Much Video (HD) in Fine Mode?	How Much Video (HD) in Normal Mode?	How Many Photos? (at 10 Megapixel, Fine Mode)?	SD Card	SDHC Card	SDXC Card	CF Card	Hard Disk Drive
2 GB	20 mins	30 mins	770	yes			yes	
4 GB	40 mins	60 mins	1540		yes		yes	
8 GB	80 mins	120 mins	3080		yes		yes	
16 GB	160 mins	240 mins	6160		yes		yes	yes
32 GB	320 mins	480 mins	12,320		yes	yes		yes
64 GB	640 mins	960 mins	24,640			yes		yes – up to 120 GB
1 TB (1000 GB)	220 hours	330 hours	69,000			yes		
2 TB	480 hours	660 hours	138,000			yes		

FIGURE 2.2 The 2 TB Extended Capacity card from SanDisk.

TYPES OF CAMCORDER

1. High definition
2. Standard definition

With both formats, you have a few choices to record onto:

1. Hard drive (HDD)
2. 8 cm DVD disc
3. Memory stick or card
4. Tape

Think about camcorders in two ways:

1. The clarity of image they record. Either Standard Definition (SD) or
High Definition (HD). SD has been used since the development of video,
and then became the basis for digital video, at 720 × 576 screen lines in
PAL (used in the UK) while High Definition is an enhanced format with
1920 × 1080 screen lines.
2. The format they use to record. Camcorders use tape; DVD disc; hard
drive; flash memory; or SD cards.

Flash memory/SD cards: Cards are a form of Flash memory, just like stick
drives. They cope with being recorded over again and again better than most
other storage. They are strong, tend not to malfunction, and are an efficient way
to store video, but are easy to misplace due to their small size.

DVD disc: DVD camcorders record onto 8 cm wide, 1.4 GB discs, slightly smaller than standard DVD discs. DVD discs are considered a bad option by many filmmakers because they compress the image too much. Don't use them.

Blu-ray HD: Blu-ray is the common format for high definition DVD video. Camcorders that record onto Blu-ray use a combination of disc, internal storage and flash drives, for ease of use. Blu-ray uses an hour of full HD video for every 7 GB approximately, with discs usually limited to 60 minutes capacity.

Hard drive (HDD): Many camcorders use built-in memory, similar to a hard drive on a laptop, also called "solid state" or tapeless. Common sizes range from 2–120 GB storage capacity. You just plug them into your PC and go, just like a regular external hard drive, rather than having to capture video from a camcorder.

Compact flash card: A flash card, only better, with a much higher storage capacity – up to 64 GB – making it ideal for DSLR still cameras, especially ones that record video at high definition.

Tape: The old school, DV tapes are a versatile and rugged way to record. They store data in diagonal lines of code stuck to a long reel of magnetic tape. A 60-minute tape recorded at short play holds 13 GB of data and compresses at a low rate, leading to high-quality images. The downside is that they are prone to getting crumpled, they don't like heat or cold, and can get accidentally wiped if demagnetized. Tape is pretty much dying out so make the move to SD or HDD soon.

SECOND OPINION

Stop right there – don't even buy a camcorder, try a DSLR camera.

Your regular stills camera (or DSLR, Digital Single-Lens Reflex) is no longer just for stills. Now they make great camcorders. The big problem with

FIGURE 2.3 Nikon's P90 shoots high quality still images but also delivers 24 frames-per-second video. Take a look at a digital SLR camera like this one before you buy another camcorder.

DSLRs used to be how you actually recorded video, given that they don't take tapes, instead using tiny SD cards. OK, so now SD cards hold as much data as an hour of video or more, so a DSLR seems like a good option.

Stills cameras are the best-kept secret of the video maker. You don't need to spend more than you would for a mid-priced camcorder and yet the newer generation of digital SLR cameras offers HD video recording as standard. They also have the very best features for getting quality images: the finest lenses, perfect color quality, focusing that makes for a sharp and textured image, and that extra something you can only get from glass lenses made to top specifications.

Chapter Three

Scriptwriting

OVERVIEW

Avoid the curse of George Lucas (Seek out the famous advice on typing Harrison Ford meted out to the young director during the shooting of *Star Wars IV*. Harsh, but someone had to tell him).

BEFORE YOU START: WRITE A TREATMENT

Pitch the idea to your friends. Tell them what kind of movie it is, and then describe in 60 seconds what happens. Get feedback from these people and hone the idea until it's sharp and clear.

Write your story as a single paragraph. Describe everything that happens, including the plot and characters, but limited to just twenty or so lines. Pinpoint from the start the most essential things about the film: the events, the characters, the atmosphere or mood, and the genre. You then have the "bones" of the idea, onto which you can flesh it out, to make the film credible. You can even rearrange these "bones" to create a new way of telling your story. Later you can write a longer version to add detail and description.

CLASSIC THREE ACT FILM STRUCTURE – LIKE EVERYONE ELSE MAKES MOVIES

Structure is the overall "shape" of the movie. Some movies are told in flashbacks, some in a straight line. Some have just a few main chunks or "acts," containing the individual scenes. Most short films have a very clear and simple structure.

Classic structure tends to unravel the film in a straight line, according to rules that have been tried and tested through decades of Hollywood celluloid. It runs a story like this:

Act 1: Here's somebody – the main character – and **everything is normal.** It might not be a great life, but it's their kind of normal and it will carry on like this. Except, one day…

Act 2: …**something happens** to this somebody and everything gets disrupted, so they now have to take action to get themselves out of this crisis.

Act 3: Finally, after much suffering and endurance, they **overcome these problems** and get things back to how they were. But this "new state" of things is even better than before, because the hero has learned something about life and become stronger, or richer, or more powerful, or just a better person.

This is a cliché, but think of it like a dependable chassis which you can rip the panels from and add your own souped-up bodywork. Use this model and it will drive, no matter what plot, characters and crisis you put on top; in short, it delivers.

Independence Day **jumps through this model like hopscotch:**

Act 1: The film opens as Will Smith starts another day as a put-upon suburban guy unsure of his life.

Act 2: …then the aliens invade, which qualifies as a crisis. So he now has to figure out how to get rid of the aliens.

Act 3: He finally defeats the invaders but he ends up also becoming a better family man for his efforts. So it's back to normal life but now that's a *better* normal life.

Twist this model the other way and you get fascinating combinations. Chris Nolan's *Memento* simply reverses the whole structure while Tarantino's *Reservoir Dogs* chops up the model and swaps bits around. In both films you know the end before you know the beginning, but you crave to know *why* it all happened.

(BIG) SECOND OPINION

Try something different – it's your movie.

Hold fire – **Do you have a problem with the Classic Three Act Structure?** You're not the only one, a lot of people do – it starts well and delivers action or excitement early on. But it gets **most predictable in Act 3,** when it's all too easy to see where the movie is going. That's when it has least room for maneuver: it traps itself into a corner as it tries to tie up the story threads to make a convincing plot, but at the same time create unexpected twists.

The classic structure doesn't suit everyone. It's been around a while, for sure, but can it offer what you need? If you feel it is lacking something, try some of these ideas for new ways of laying out your story.

The David Lynch-messes-with-your-mind method

If you have seen a Lynch movie it looks like the director took a look at the Three Act Structure and thought it had about as much use to him as last week's cherry pie. Lynch's films are like nightmares constructed out of bits of old movies, served up on daytime TV.

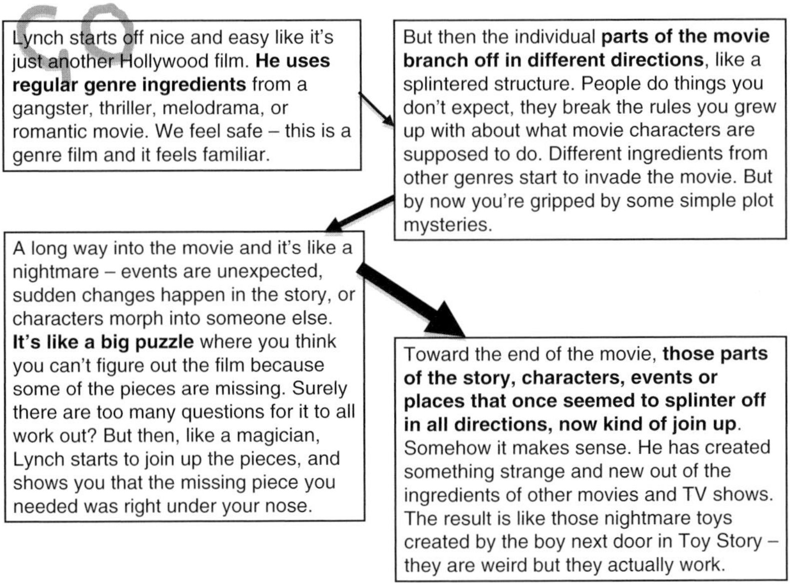

Lynch starts off nice and easy like it's just another Hollywood film. **He uses regular genre ingredients** from a gangster, thriller, melodrama, or romantic movie. We feel safe – this is a genre film and it feels familiar.

But then the individual **parts of the movie branch off in different directions**, like a splintered structure. People do things you don't expect, they break the rules you grew up with about what movie characters are supposed to do. Different ingredients from other genres start to invade the movie. But by now you're gripped by some simple plot mysteries.

A long way into the movie and it's like a nightmare – events are unexpected, sudden changes happen in the story, or characters morph into someone else. **It's like a big puzzle** where you think you can't figure out the film because some of the pieces are missing. Surely there are too many questions for it to all work out? But then, like a magician, Lynch starts to join up the pieces, and shows you that the missing piece you needed was right under your nose.

Toward the end of the movie, **those parts of the story, characters, events or places that once seemed to splinter off in all directions, now kind of join up**. Somehow it makes sense. He has created something strange and new out of the ingredients of other movies and TV shows. The result is like those nightmare toys created by the boy next door in Toy Story – they are weird but they actually work.

FIGURE 3.1

Try it: Clash a few genres together; work on several lines of story at the same time; make these plot lines collide in unexpected ways; find the absolute strangeness of the most normal suburban towns. You don't have to explain anything, in fact the more loose ends the better; but it all has to make sense in its own warped way.

THE ANY-DIRECTION-BUT-HOME METHOD

Some new indie directors think the Three-Act Structure is so far from life as we know it that it just feels plain wrong to make a movie that way. Some of the most articulate movies like this have been from the so-called "mumblecore" directors. Mumblecore movies are casual, semi-improvised, authentic and low-fi. They feel real, they let people talk over each other, stuff happens, then other stuff doesn't happen.

In movies like Joe Swanberg's *Hannah Takes the Stairs* or Zach Braff's *Garden State*, the story is so low key it's under the radar. If Three-Act Structure movies have stories that go forward in a straight line, mumblecore movies zigzag around like the path of a bumblebee (or a mumblebee). For these movies the point is in the traveling, not the arriving. It's about wonder and awe, at how life really is.

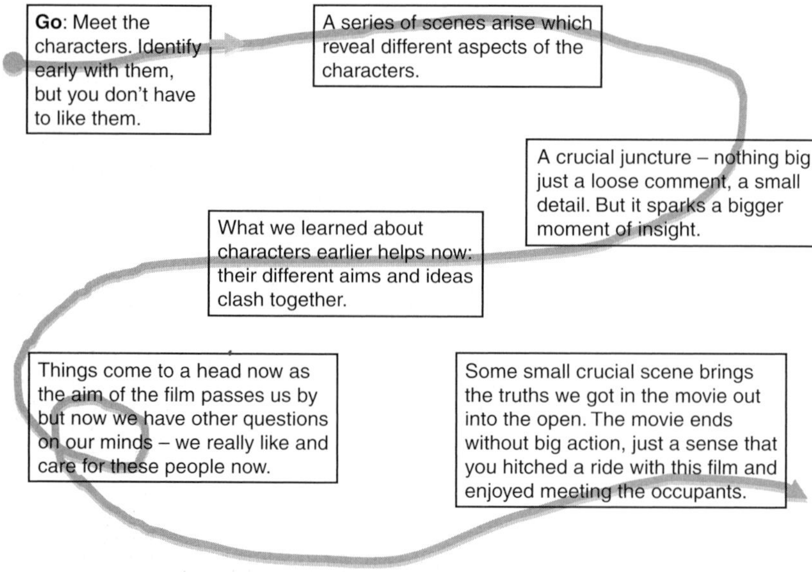

Go: Meet the characters. Identify early with them, but you don't have to like them.

A series of scenes arise which reveal different aspects of the characters.

A crucial juncture – nothing big, just a loose comment, a small detail. But it sparks a bigger moment of insight.

What we learned about characters earlier helps now: their different aims and ideas clash together.

Things come to a head now as the aim of the film passes us by but now we have other questions on our minds – we really like and care for these people now.

Some small crucial scene brings the truths we got in the movie out into the open. The movie ends without big action, just a sense that you hitched a ride with this film and enjoyed meeting the occupants.

FIGURE 3.2

Try it: Spend a long time on the characters; rehearse and improvise with your actors; thin down the plot further and further to give the characters room to explore their lives and their situations. Avoid endings.

THE LONG-PLAY-VIDEO-GAME METHOD

If you play any kind of video game you'll know that plotlines when they exist are not all wrapped up neatly at the end, and the whole point of good game-play is to stretch out the journey the game takes you on, never reaching an end. The enjoyment and thrill is in the voyage you go on, the people you meet, the obstacles you overcome. It doesn't need to give you a neat ending where the meaning of all these travels is summarized in some cheesy way – because life isn't like that anyway. It's like an action-packed version of the previous method.

And it might explain why most video games make lousy films, with scriptwriters trying to fit the long and winding route that is the video game story into the straight and narrow of the Three-Act Structure. TV shows like *Lost* work like video games, developing a multitude of stories and ideas, making it a never-ending mix of possible directions to go in. For movies this can be a great way to avoid clichés, and concentrate on characters.

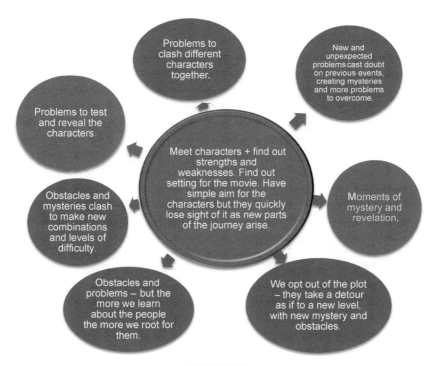

FIGURE 3.3

In this diagram, each of the circles arises out of the main central theme in the middle. They don't have to be entire episodes or parts of the movie – instead they are parts of the whole which you hop in and out of randomly. You might expect to hop onto three or four in each section or each episode of the story.

> **Try it:** Use the road movie guide in Chapter 44 as this is the closest type of movie to the video game. But also spend a lot longer developing your characters, giving them as much backstory as you can think up.

Experts' Tips

Richard Chance, director, *The Day I Tried to Live*, UK

"[A script should have] a beginning, a middle and an end, not necessarily in that order. With short films the telling of the tale has to be punctuated, there should sometimes be a twist at the end, like the telling of a good joke that will hopefully remain in the reader's mind afterwards."

Ben Rutkowski, filmmaker, USA

"Ask yourself what would happen if the exact opposite thing happened at that moment."

Jason Korsner, film director, *2 Hour Parking*, Los Angeles/London

"I always work from a script, correctly formatted, to give me a good idea as to how long it'll be. Laid out correctly, it also gives you the best chance to make sure you've shot everything and you can note shots in the margin."

WHATEVER METHOD YOU USE TO MAKE THE SCRIPT, WATCH OUT FOR THE MOST COMMON PROBLEMS IN SHORT FILMS

- **Long sentences of exposition**, like where you explain the background to the plot. Avoid this by using visual clues to show information.
- **Over-long scenes.** The audience can figure out a lot of the plot without so much help. Many of the best, for instance Robert Towne's Oscar-winning script for *Chinatown*, cuts the dialogue just when you think the punch line is coming, leaving us to fill it in.
- **Too many scenes.** Keep it simple and try to take something out of your script every time you redraft it without losing the meaning.
- **Too many characters.** Restrict your short film to three main characters, and maybe a couple more secondary characters.
- **Over-complicating.** Keep the story simple enough to enable you to add ideas while shooting. Keep dialogue simple and instead let your camera show the subtext, the real meaning below the surface.
- **Dull characters.** If you want exciting, real characters, you have to make them unreal, larger than life.
- **Cheap endings.** Avoid quick, hastily resolved endings. Let questions hang in the air rather than wrap it all up too neatly.
- **Not enough tension.** Conflict moves everything forward in a plot. Put things on a collision course: people, events, needs, desires, hopes. People argue, they miss the boat/plane/bus, they want different things out of life, they compete, they win and lose – in short, if it can go wrong, let it go wrong. Everything can be cathartic, so it doesn't have to be a depressing movie.
- **Important things in the plot don't get said or seen – they are instead hinted at or happen off-camera.** Make sure the audience is there for every important event. Let us see everything.
- **Events are toned down.** Whether your characters suffer or whether they are happy, it has to be big time, with no half measures. They'll be on cloud nine or in hell.

FIGURE 3.4 Celtx software enables you to create a script and navigate between it and the visuals.

CHARACTERS

Build your characters' backstory

1. **Real characters.** Base them on real people you have known. Think of people you have met; what they did; how they spoke; what they were like when drunk, laughing, eating, driving, and so on.

2. **Use details to bring them to life.** Include quirks of speech, like words that betray their background in a small town; or small things they do such as practicing an imaginary guitar when bored; or clothes they wear, such as a scarf with sentimental value.

3. **Give them weak spots or hang-ups.** These can be brought out in a crucial scene to raise the tension level higher. For instance, a phobia about the color blue, or a memory of a previous date that went wrong, or a nightmare that haunts them.

4. **Have opposite elements in a character.** Make your character three-dimensional by allowing them to have completely opposing forces in their personality. Try to balance a positive trait, for instance courage, with an opposing one, like a messed-up home life. How much the positive outweighs the negative is up to you.

5. **Build character dialogue.** Everyone has a rhythm in the way they talk, a bit like music. It comes from the place they grew up, from how confident

they are, what age they are and more. They have a particular accent; they use words that show what education they had; they might use professional or leisure jargon (like surfing words, or words connected to their job as a football coach). The number of words they use is due to all these things. To create fully rounded, real characters, work with your actors or with some friends and get people to talk and rehearse in character. If you have trouble writing good dialogue, just get a rehearsal going and record the conversations you have. If you record real speech it's easier then to get the rhythm right.

SOFTWARE

Software can speed up your work a lot. Free, integrated software like Celtx (www.celtx.com) can help you move easily between script and storyboard, and work on logistical stuff like budget too. You can write lines of dialogue and then switch to another page and fill in character development. You can then scan the script later to figure out who is needed for the production schedule, all in one package.

Scriptwriting software is available such as the market leader Final Draft (www.finaldraft.com) or online software such as Scripped Writer (www.scripped.com).

Experts' Tips

Kerry David, producer, *My Date with Drew*, *Agent Cody Banks*, *College Sucks*, Los Angeles

"Story is EVERYTHING! Giving us special effects or some funny lines, beautiful faces, or stylish clothes never makes up for disappointing us in story. I think that the emergence of independent cinema as a more accepted choice for mainstream audiences stems from these filmmakers having unique and distinct voices with genuine stories to tell. We go to the movies to escape and be transported to new and complete worlds, so when they fall short, we are disappointed. The studios try to capture a huge audience with each film. Understandably they have investors to please and they are trying to make money more than they are trying to make art, but we as independent filmmakers can decide to tell captivating stories and hope an audience will find us."

Chapter | Four

Budgets

OVERVIEW

Stop your movie milking you of cash – get a tight rein on your budget before you start shooting and keep your film on track.

The budget means the total that the film costs you – or would have cost you – from prep to editing. Every film has a budget, even when you get everything for free. It's good to get into the habit of doing budgets so that you think in terms of cost on every film you make.

Films divide up costs into two sections. The first (called above-the-line) is to pay those people involved artistically: director, producer, writer, and actors. The second section (called below-the-line) covers everything else, such as set construction, costumes, makeup, equipment, travel, food and so on.

In most low-budget short films the first section is usually zero, since everyone works for free, for the love of the movie. It's the second section that takes up your cash – the costs of SD (Secure Digital) cards or tapes, travel, food, lights and so on.

THE MOVIE FREEBIE EXCHANGE RATE

Filmmakers are notorious for getting stuff for free. They don't break any rules; they just know how to ask. In low-budget filmmaking, it is expected that **you get what you can for free, but also that you give something back in return.** For example, you might get a free use of a camera for a weekend, but agree to help the owner in their own shooting the following weekend.

The problem is, **it's hard to figure out exactly what you should offer to someone if you need their help.** How much is a day worth as sound recordist, runner, or caterer? Every country, state or county has its own "exchange rate" so expect certain tasks to go up or down in value. As a starting guide, try these for size:

Table 4.1

You Want	You Need to Offer
Loan of an HD camcorder for one weekend, plus spare batteries and cables.	Work for one whole weekend on a movie the owner of the camera is making.
Use of a set of lights (one key lamp, two smaller lamps) for two days.	A day's work for the owner, or assisting with preproduction duties such as preparing schedules.
Camera operator for three days.	Suggest a collaborative credit, such as co-producer, plus copies of the film. Or offer simply returning the favor by doing the same on their film.
Advice or guidance about an issue affecting your movie, several occasions or on call as a phone-in mentor.	A day as runner or driver for this mentor's production. They don't make films? Then bake a cake or buy a create of beer.
Actor for two days free of charge.	A copy of the DVD plus publicity stills on a CD, and an executive producer credit.
Use of an edit suite for two days at a public arts center.	Cleaning of this or other edit rooms, or to assist with publicity or secretarial duties, for a couple of days.
Runner or general assistant for three days.	Credit on the film, plus a copy of the DVD, plus food and travel expenses (fix a limit, however).

FIGURE 4.1 Exchange your skills and time for cameras or other equipment. If you borrow a camcorder for a weekend, offer to work another weekend for the owner on their own movie. (Photo courtesy of iStockphoto, ©bjones27 Image# 8326566.)

Table 4.2 Budget example columns for self-funded 5 min. short film

Item	Description	Page of Budget	Total
1	Props		
2	Set dressing		
3	Costume		
4	Makeup		
5	Camera operation		
6	Sound operation		
7	Travel		
8	Electrical sundries		
9	Editing sundries		
10	Insurance		
11	Catering		
12	Tapes		
13	Overheads		
14	Contingency		
15	Publicity		

> Add extra pages for each category when you have a detailed breakdown for each part.

MORE FREEBIES

- Ask TV news gathering companies if they have **old tapes they can give you for free.** They use them a limited number of times and then have to discard them, but the quality is still fine for many more uses.
- Ask friends, family and supporters to **sponsor your film at £1/$1 per second**. They buy a second of the movie and get a credit in return.
- Get discarded **paint and set design materials** from decorating companies – they partly use tins of paint and then store them.
- **Ask your former school or college** to loan you space to use as a studio, giving them a big "thanks" message in the end credits. Tell them it's good for your career.

WRITE THESE TIPS ON THE BACK OF YOUR BUDGET SHEET

1. Be realistic and make a budget you can live with and can actually pay for.
2. Add ten per cent on every predicted cost.

3. Resist mission creep: this means changes and additions you add in impulsively, which end up costing you a lot more.
4. A firm shooting schedule means a tight budget.
5. Shoot only what's on the shooting script, and only then should you change and add new scenes, or extras.
6. Watch out for shared loans, shared costs, in fact sharing anything with anyone – it ends badly.
7. Get reductions, get free stuff: the main currency of movies at zero budget is goodwill.
8. Total and exhaustive prep work makes for few surprises and fewer extra costs.
9. Cash flow is everything – keep an eye on how much you need in daily cash.
10. Never, ever use credit cards to finance your movie. Pay for all costs up front. Remember how bad it feels to pay off last year's holiday when it was a washout?

ESSENTIAL KIT OR RESOURCES

A **spreadsheet program** will help to keep costs in the right column, and will reassure people you work with that you are in control. Specialist movie software is not necessary; instead rely on tried and tested ways of having an amount to spend in one column and a second column with costs – then make sure the first stays bigger than the second.

Experts' Tips

Armen Antranikian, film director/writer, London

"I think it is important to not only see filmmaking as an artistic matter, but as a business. It is important to understand early on that as a creative filmmaker, unlike a painter or musician, expressing your vision without many compromises might cost a fortune. In order to get a film financed and distributed it is essential to understand how the industry works. It has helped me to attend industry events, including film festivals and markets, and read the Trades, such as *Variety*, *The Hollywood Reporter* and *Screen International*, to understand what is happening behind the scenes. It has influenced my creative approach and inspired my future ambitions. Even though it is essential to know about these things as a filmmaker, most film schools will never deal with it."

Chapter Five

Designing Your Movie

WHY YOU NEED THIS CHAPTER

It's your movie. Put your fingerprint on it and give it your style.

Every film needs to have a main theme, or a central idea, which guides all aspects of it. This gives the movie a mood and helps us understand what it's about.

Style is the way this main theme in the movie visibly appears on screen.

To get to know what your theme is, ask yourself, **"What's my movie really all about?"** Forget the plot or the details and look instead at the overall idea behind it – such as a journey of discovery; or revenge; or facing your past. It may also have a certain "tone" to it, from dark to light, giving the story a feeling of being perhaps menacing, or upbeat, or mysterious, or whatever.

Experts' Tips

Armen Antranikian, film director, London

"A visual style can unfold naturally as the screenplay is being developed. Personally I often work on mood-boards whilst developing the script. When thinking about the look, which includes everything from the color palette to choice of lenses, it is important to see the visual treatment as a storytelling tool. In good films the look is a direct expression of story and never a visual gimmick. It is the filmmaker's key task to interpret a screenplay visually."

What's the difference between story, theme and style?

The **story** covers the entire events within the movie. The **theme** is the overall idea that is behind this story, often talked about in just a simple word, like loss, or alienation, or hope. **Style** is the way you put this theme on screen.

Table 5.1

Take an example:

Story: An out-of-work actor returns to his small hometown for his school reunion. He gets mixed up in old rivalries and fights that happened back at school, and later that night events spiral out of control.	**Theme:** A dark, nasty journey of discovery into the actor's past. For the actor, it's like everything's closing in, like he can't escape the past.	**Style:** Dark, moody, claustrophobic, no color, not much light.

These three parts of the movie have to work together and we expect them to support each other. This film has to look dark and tense, just like the story. We want the camera, the music and the colors to match this.

It doesn't mean everything has to look clichéd though: With the menacing movie described here it might sound weird if it had a Beach Boys soundtrack, but on the other hand, that might be so unusual it could add to the menace – look at Tarantino's torture sequence in *Reservoir Dogs* and the mismatched music to accompany it. So, try using opposites (story vs. music, for instance) to get a unique style to your movie.

Experts' Tips

Stacey Harrison, film director, Seattle, USA

"For me, the look of the film does tell so much of the story. Obviously film is a visual medium and a filmmaker can do so much more to develop a character just by showing with detail where that person lives *or* how they wear clothes, for example, than pages of text ever could. The script only tells a part of the story and the visuals add the texture and feeling for each scene. As a filmmaker I wonder why shoot someone speaking in front of a blank white wall when you can show them somewhere interesting and memorable? The look of every shot is crucial for me. I'm obsessed with the details!"

DESIGNING YOUR MOVIE

Table 5.2

What You Need to Do	How to Do It
Decide whether your movie needs designing at all	**Some movies are best left raw** – like road movies, documentaries and freecording shorts.
Create an overall color palette	**Choose no more than three colors** which you feel should dominate the frame, connected to the underlying theme you have chosen. So, if your movie is a revenge thriller, it could seem right to have black, ice-blue and blood red. These mean that even when you don't have dialogue, the underlying theme is on screen all the time. Include these in almost every shot.

Continued...

Table 5.2 (Continued)

What You Need to Do	How to Do it
Evoke the atmosphere of the script	**Choose a few words that describe the theme of the movie** and stick with these throughout the design process.
Look at the budget	**A limited budget doesn't have to cramp your style.** If anything, filmmakers often say that having less cash made them more creative and resourceful. Style comes from the way you deal with what you've got.
Produce image designs before storyboards	This crosses over into previz (see Chapter 7, Previz), and means doing several sketches (or photos) of how you imagine the movie to look. **Take the three most essential moments in your film.** Sketch some of these images to show how you think it should look. Use a thick marker pen. Draw with bold, sweeping strokes so you describe the light and shadow as much as the objects and people in the image.
Play with camera settings to get the right look for the movie	**Check out your locations before you start shooting** and find out how it looks best – try different aperture settings, shutter speed and how much of the frame is in focus.
Design lighting	**Sketch out how you'd like each scene to look,** based on those few words you chose to sum up the theme. If you can, take time the day before shooting to experiment with different lighting set-ups so you are prepared before you turn up on day one.
Design details: props, clothing, decor	**Sketch or photograph crucial details** like clothing, locations and what these rooms or places look like.

Finally…

Produce a mood board	When you have the overall design of the film clear and it looks coherent, spend a short while putting all these steps from the list above onto a few large sheets which sum up the entire design for the movie. Use this to show crew and cast what your vision for the movie is.

Now you have designed the movie, push on for better ideas.

Before jumping straight into the middle of storyboarding the movie, take some time to develop the images further, pushing your ideas into more original framing.

- **Take a sheet of A3 paper, lengthways. Divide it into four vertical columns.**
- In the first column, **write a 10-word** outline of what is happening in the shot, plus a single word that adequately describes the overall atmosphere of the whole scene.

- In the next column **draw the first idea you get** as to how that part of the script could be seen.
- Next, do a better idea: **come up with another angle on this action,** maybe placing the camera above, to the side, with strong shadows across it, and so on.
- Finally, in the last column, **draw another image which is even better** – unusual but appropriate, a strong image with clarity and definition that says everything about the atmosphere you want to project.

Cast and Crew Online

GET ME A CREW

Welcome to the world of zero budget filmmaking. Unlike the movie world a few rungs further up the ladder, money isn't the only currency here – **people will work for free or in exchange for your time, just to get valuable experience.** But like any new currency you need time to adjust to the exchange rate. Take a look at Chapter 4, Budgets to see how to exchange equipment for work and vice versa. Use the same idea when it comes to getting other people to commit time on your project – ask in the right way and you'll get what you need, as long as you are willing to return the favor.

Small means fast, flexible, nimble. **Work with two or three other people and you have a real chance of scoring a film on budget,** on time and without fights.

To do this, find people you can spend time with, and who share your commitment. Look for people who really deliver, rather than people who make great claims.

You need:

- **Director:** that's probably you, or whoever had the initial idea.
- **Camera:** someone who takes good footage and can step up to being more involved artistically with you. You need to be able to bounce ideas off this person and listen to their input.

FIGURE 6.1 A small crew works well on short films, especially if people take on more than one role. (Photo courtesy of iStockphoto, ©bjones27 Image# 9215721.)

- **Sound:** someone who knows what each mic does and how to get it right each time. They'll hold the boom mic, look out for recording levels, and check footage right after each scene to identify mistakes.

Working in a team of three means that you each take on extra roles. The organizer role, **producer,** is crucial. The **director** might handle this, but even better if the other members of the team can double on it. **Sound** and **camera** are primarily roles for shooting, while producing takes place largely in preproduction.

... and if you can get more people:

- Continuity
- Runner
- Design/artist
- Lighting

RECRUITING STEP BY STEP

Ideas for crew posting:

- **Decide who you need. What job or skill area are you looking for?** Take a look at the movie genres in Section 5 and figure out how many people you need and what you need them to do. Typically, you might opt for three or four people to crew a short movie, but don't forget the secondary jobs you'd like them to be able to do, like your camera operator also being good at editing.

- Remember, **experience is not always necessary.** Instead ask for a willingness to learn and to commit.
- **What are you offering in return?** A copy of the movie on DVD, plus a recommendation on your network (such as www.linkedin.com).
- **Decide what you can afford** if respondents ask for costs towards travel, food or lodging. Can you offer people a room at your place during the shoot, or maybe just half of a return ticket to the shoot? You decide.
- **Post a note to a bulletin board, social networking site or filmmaker forum,** or if you are planning a while in advance, post a note to a regional screen/filmmakers email bulletin.

YOUR POSTING TO GET CREW

Include:

- **Who you are** (level of experience)
- **What your movie is** (no long synopsis, just the story and closest genre/ movie that describes it)
- **What skill you need** (camera, editor, sound, etc.)
- **Whether it is a short, feature or series**
- **What you are aiming for:** festivals, TV, just having a crack at it to learn something
- **What you are shooting on** (type of camera)
- **Dates you plan to shoot**
- **Level of budget** – be upfront about how small your budget is
- **Whether you are offering copies of the movie**
- **Your contact details** – email and phone

What to do next:

- Expect to have replies over the first week after your posting. Some bulletin boards have staggered mailings, where paid users receive it on day 1, while nonpaying users receive it on day 3.
- Take time to sort through replies and get back to them quickly. If you need to delay replying, send an interim email to respondents saying you'll be in touch soon.
- Once you settle on who you want to work with, email the successful respondents and send a quick thank-you to the rest.
- Arrange a meeting to get everyone together.
- Send out as much information as possible early on: script, notes, designs, schedule, previz – anything.

SHARE YOUR SKILLS

Movies gradually take shape when they get made, changing as more people work with the idea. Collaborating on movies means you get more done, get more ideas feeding into it, and ultimately get a better final movie.

It might seem like your vision of your movie gets watered down and compromised as soon as you work with other people, but it's the opposite. It strengthens it, simply by treating the crew and cast as the first audience you have. **Bounce ideas off them, watch reactions to what you are making,** and soon you see the movie through the eyes of other people. It isn't compromise, just adapting. The movie gradually evolves into a better movie more suited to the challenge of finding an audience.

SHOULD I PAY MY CREW?

Not necessarily. In the zero budget world of moviemaking no one expects to be paid. Instead you have to make it worthwhile in other ways – people want to learn, have experiences and get better at what they do. That's the pay-off, plus a copy of the DVD and a credit. Once you get in a position to be able to pay crew, look at bulletin boards such as www.shootingpeople.org to see what the going rate is (like, $100 for a day's work on camera). When you get real funding rely on union sites to give you rates that are fair. Try www.iatse-intl.org for USA film production rates, or www.bectu.org.uk for UK rates. Also click on http://www.bls.gov/OCO/CG/CGS038. HTM for average hourly payment rates.

EXPENSES

You need to put some part of the budget aside to allow for the costs of the crew in traveling to your set and perhaps items they needed to buy to do their job. Make it clear if you can't afford to pay costs – some people are still OK about working for you just to get the experience.

FOOD

Allow a lunch and evening meal allowance for crew and cast plus coffee and other refreshments.

GROUND RULES

Come up with your own ground rules for your production. Try these for starters.

1. **Collaboration means results.**
2. **Listen and be calm.**
3. Movie crews fall out with each other often … don't be one of them, **try to resolve conflicts** (get tips on how to sort out fights in Chapter 15, Manage Your Production).
4. **Commitment is crucial.**
5. **Everyone has an input,** but there's only one outcome.
6. **Integrity of the idea is king.**
7. **Technical perfection is a shared responsibility.**
8. Watch out for interpretation: **everyone hears things differently,** so be clear what you want.
9. **Everyone just wants to learn.**
10. **Exchange skills next time;** work on other peoples' movies.

Experts' Tips

Ben Winter, film student, USA

"Understand that nobody has the same vision as you, especially your actors. More importantly, understand that your film will not turn out exactly like your vision. You must be willing to adapt to changes and turn them into something that does your vision justice. However, don't compromise. Don't be satisfied if you find yourself thinking, 'I guess that will do.' Unless you walk away from a take thinking, 'Yes! That is what I wanted,' you won't be content when you're editing. Compromises are made of bits of what everyone wants, and the final product is therefore something that nobody wants."

FIGURE 6.2 www.shootingpeople.org puts you in touch with actors, film crew, students, professionals and more, and gives news and advice.

GET ME SOME ACTORS

Actors are in it for the experience just as much as you are. But the exchange rate is a little different: since most actors don't make movies, your actors are committing more than they are getting in return. Make sure you give them a DVD of the movie and links and background info on your website or social networking pages.

So who replies to your casting call? Mostly it's going to be graduates, or student actors, building up their portfolio of jobs. More experienced actors who are out of work might reply to an unpaid casting rather than have no work at all. Whoever replies, be aware that your unpaid gig will be dropped without warning if the actor gets a paid job that clashes with yours.

YOUR POSTING TO GET ACTORS
Include:

- **Who you are** (level of experience)
- **What your movie is**
- **Who you need:** complete description of the character you are casting

For instance: "Reggie: early 30s, white. Charming, big friendly guy. Well-educated and literate, but with little self-confidence. Makes pocket-money dealing drugs. East-coast accent. Has a son with Janey, but she won't let him spend much time with him until he gets a job and a home."

Or: "**Conrad:** mid/late 20s, black, gay. Camp, but earthy. Musician and social worker. Loves nightlife. Never angry, everyone's best friend, needs to be liked."

- **Dates you plan to shoot**
- **Whether you are offering copies of the movie**
- **What costs you can meet** (travel, lodging, etc.); it is expected that you provide food and refreshments
- **Your contact details** – email and phone

FIGURE 6.3 Actors prepare for a scene in a film by director Armen Antranikian.

What to do next:

- When you get enough replies to your posting, **set up a casting session if you feel you need to meet or have a screen test** from your respondents. Arrange a time and contact all respondents. Let them know whether they need to arrive dressed for the part, whether they need to learn a few lines first, and whether they need to bring a portfolio of previous work. But most short movies don't do casting sessions if the actors aren't getting paid.
- On the day of the casting, be methodical and fair about what you ask the respondents to do: give everyone equal time with you, and a few chances to get the lines right if you are doing a test.
- Take photos of everyone, while they hold a card with their name written on it.
- Decide on who has the job and inform everyone as soon as you can.
- If you don't do a casting, go straight ahead and set up a meeting for the cast a week or so before the shoot. Email them everything you have – script, photos, designs, whatever.

Experts' Tips

Kevin Powis, director, *Expresso*, London

"Best moments? Easy! When the legend Sir Norman Wisdom walked on set. I'd need a whole book to explain that. His performance was great and his presence bought attention to a short movie that I know people making feature films with 10 times the budget would kill for. I never lose sight that that was down to Norman. When I went home that night I was star struck. I just kept replaying the day in my mind – directing Sir Norman. A real honor."

Chapter Seven

Previz

OVERVIEW

You know what you want but no one else quite sees it your way. Previsualizing helps get your vision of your movie across. Take a look at how storyboards or previz software can help make your movie real.

Some people do storyboards, some don't. It's your call. In practice, storyboards are great for a big movie when you have a lot of people depending on you, time is short and every second costs money. You need to know what shot you want, and be able to show someone a piece of paper with that shot drawn out.

But on short films it's just as fine to turn up on the day you shoot and figure out what shot you want as you work. You can set up the action, play around with camera shots that look good, and then go ahead and shoot. It's enough to trust your eyes and what you see in the camera without having to think it all up days before.

On the other hand, **storyboards can help for figuring out complicated scenes,** perhaps where you have a lot of action that needs to be seen in a certain order.

Whatever you do, a lot of people prefer computer-generated image (CGI) previz, using software that creates a virtual movie location and lets you set up shots. **Previz software has now become a standard way of sharing your vision for a movie.** It also helps you test lighting ideas and work out how you're going to get a shot you want.

PREVIZ USING 3D MODELING SOFTWARE

FrameForge or StoryBoard Quick are intuitive programs that help you create a complete world from your script before you shoot, enabling you to build sets, characters, use props, costume and set up lighting. It's kind of like directing

The Sims, but with a lot of helpful print-friendly data to go with it – such as how high the camera would be from the ground in each shot, the aspect ratio, aperture, and which pieces of the script you need for each storyboard sheet. It helps save time by figuring out whether a certain shot you want is technically possible. It's also a great instructor, letting you experiment to find the right shot.

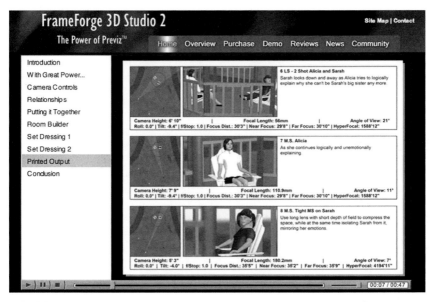

FIGURE 7.1 FrameForge software helps you produce virtual locations and figure out camera moves.

PREFER STORYBOARDS? HERE'S HOW

Storyboards tend to be drawn in small boxes about the size of a DV tape case, with three or four to a page down the side of a sheet of A4, or across a page, comic-book style. You don't have to produce storyboards for the whole movie, just the parts where you'd feel more comfortable knowing how they look.

1. **First, figure out which parts of the script you need to draw. If you have a script, go through it with a colored pencil, inserting a line break where you think you would cut on screen to a new shot,** or where there is particular movement, to break up the script in manageable chunks. You can then add more frames as you need them while you draw. If there's no script, write a list of images you need to have in the movie, in the order you think they should be seen.

2. **Start drawing with soft outlines, trying to sketch out how you imagine this scene on screen.** You don't need to restrict yourself to small boxes. Instead, try working on larger sheets of paper, and then use a cut-out viewfinder to find the exact right part of the drawing you want as the shot.

3. **Go over the sketch with darker lines.** Avoid pencil – it's too pale. Instead use a darker tool like charcoal or black marker pens. Don't worry about how accurate the drawings are yet.
4. **Include in each frame some basic information:**
   a. **Possible camera movements** such as tracking or panning. Draw arrows to show movement of camera or objects/people.
   b. The **intensity and direction of lighting.** Indicate in the sketch what direction the light is coming from.
   c. The **dominant colors** in the scene. Limit yourself to just two or three.
5. **Next to the images include the dialogue, sounds and any other notes** that you need to help direct that scene.

FIGURE 7.2 Celtx software is a favorite with student filmmakers, allowing the user to integrate storyboards with other documents.

HOW ABOUT MOVIES WITH NO STORY?

Many films you might want to make really don't benefit from the linear method of drawing each shot from a script. Music promos and any movie where there's no story might be better off with another approach where you can look at the film as a whole, and not in any particular order. You might want to work more organically, and improvise your way through.

● **Cut out some rectangles to draw individual images on.** Each image is a key point in the film.

- **Draw a single image on each card frame** so you have a pack of cards with each image on separate frames. Write on the back of each one any information you need such as dialogue, music, movement.
- **Arrange the cards in a circle.**
- **Choose the most crucial shot** – the one which would be great as a movie poster or publicity still. Place this one at the centre of the circle.
- **Choose the next most crucial frames** and place them as an inner circle.
- You will then have a **central image** which sets the tone for the entire movie, an **inner circle of images surrounding it**, and an **outer circle of images at the edges**. This outer circle is almost dispensable – if a certain image from here can't be shot, then it may not alter the overall tone of the movie.

Now you have a strong sense of what images you want and which are most important. You don't need to figure out the order in which these images will be seen until you edit.

Experts' Tips

Neville Steenson, filmmaker, UK

"I think storyboards are an incredibly valuable process to go through in preproduction. As a director it allows you to establish the visual 'grammar' of your film and by putting it down on paper you distance yourself slightly and can take a more objective view. As long as you understand what your scribbles represent it's just a personal process for you to go through so you can get the film clear in your mind. From a more pragmatic production point of view too it allows you to see how many shots you are planning on doing and this is crucial in producing a realistic shooting schedule and shot list – there's no point showing up on set wanting to do twenty different set-ups in a day when your crew is realistically only going to get through ten."

SECOND OPINION

Richard and John Chance, writers/producers, *The Day I Tried to Live*, UK

Richard Chance: "We rarely use storyboards to convey ideas as they are time-consuming to produce; however, in the past we have drawn scenes and used diagrams to explain camera angles and position of the actors within the location, et cetera, within the shot, when words aren't enough."

John Chance: "Occasionally, the storyboard is better for a larger scale cast and crew to work with. We normally take a basic shot list to film with us on the day. We explain what we're after previously and go through [the storyboard] with them."

Chapter Eight

Script Breakdown and Shot List

OVERVIEW

You've got a script, the crew are booked, and you're ready to shoot. Hold fire – take a moment to figure out all the shots you really need and you'll save time and money.

WHY YOU NEED A SCRIPT BREAKDOWN

One way to make a movie is to **turn up, shoot like crazy and figure out the mess later in the edit,** but that's way more stressful than it needs to be. Instead, think of the movie as one big shopping list – composed of clips one after the other. You go and shoot these clips in any order you like, and as long as you know exactly the separate pieces that make up the jigsaw of your movie, you'll be able to piece them together just as you intended. And then you know how much it will cost and whether your plans are workable.

To do this, you need a "script breakdown," **a list of everything you need, to shoot the whole movie, by who, when and how long it will take you.**

Here's what you do, step by step.

1. **Look at the script and go through it carefully,** noting each time a new scene appears. Draw a line under that section to show where each scene starts and ends.
2. **Copy each scene onto new separate sheets.** Then make a list of what you need for that scene – everything from props to makeup to lighting, to cast and crew.
3. **Now you've got mini breakdown sheets for each separate scene.** Go into more detail in each one to make sure everything you need is listed.
4. Next, **take a look at all your scenes** – maybe stick them all on a wall so you can quickly cross-reference between them.

5. **Then group them together** so you have the most economical and logical way to shoot them. So if two scenes are shot in the same location but are meant to be at different times in the film, shoot them both on the same day.

6. **Now you have a complete list** for every scene of everything you need to buy, everything you need to shoot, when everyone is due on set, and for how long.

7. To finish, **divide everything on your individual scene breakdown sheets into responsibilities.** Just write down a name next to each item so you know who is in charge of that job and use colored highlighters to make it stand out. It's a good way to see how much work each person has to do.

8. **You are now seriously organized.**

If you don't use scripts, take some time to write a list of events that happen in the movie, in the order in which they occur. This works well if you are the kind of filmmaker who prefers to get your actors together, let them improvise and then build the movie from there. If that's your style, create a shooting script of events when you have the whole movie mapped out. You will end up with a long list of shots you need.

FIGURE 8.1 A script supervisor keeps check on the schedule and what has been achieved each day during shooting. (Photo courtesy of iStockphoto, ©bjones27, Image# 8367158)

SHOT LIST

Next, you can go ahead and make a shot list. A shot list is a detailed list of all the shots you need for each scene. It doesn't look like a script breakdown; it only lists what we are going to see on screen, like a written storyboard.

Table 8.1 Example shot list

Shot	Scene	Type of Shot	Description
1	6	Close-up, hand held	Wide shot of house at night, seen from across the street. Two men in the foreground. Music accompanies. Men start to move toward the house.
2	6	Close-up, hand held	A close-up of the feet of one of them, from behind, as he approaches the house. Pan up to see a gun in his left hand.
3	6	Medium shot, tripod	The door bell is rung.
4	6	Wide shot, tripod	A detective at her office, viewing files, night.
5	6	Medium shot	Detective picks up phone.
6	6	Medium shot	Cut back to the house, a silhouette of the two men at the door, as they press the bell again.

If you were shooting this, you would arrange to shoot together all the parts with the detective at the police station. Then shoot the parts at the house another evening. So you could shoot numbers 1, 2, 3 and 6 together, giving you a logical way to shoot.

SECOND OPINION

A lot of people don't do shot lists – they are a big hassle to produce anyway. And do you really want to know weeks ahead what each shot is going to look like when your ideas are evolving all the time? Trust your instincts, get your camera and go shoot, relying on your inner vision of how the movie needs to look.

Experts' Tips

Kevin Powis, director, London

"During production stick to your shooting schedule and shot list. You will find no shortage of suggestions flying around sometimes from crew, sometimes from actors about an extra take or a different setup. I like to be open to all that but don't lose track of the fact that you've spent months working that shot list out to perfection to ensure it gives you the footage you need. So if you are going to change anything, do it after you've got what you came for and only if there is enough time and money for it – but not before."

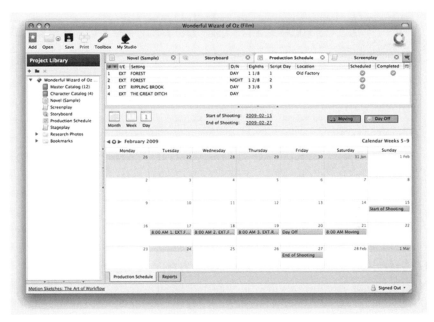

FIGURE 8.2 Celtx software integrates your schedule into other aspects of preproduction.

Chapter Nine

Law and the Movies

OVERVIEW

There's nothing lawyers like more than skewering the little guy – but they won't stand a chance with you.

10 THINGS YOU NEED TO KNOW ABOUT COPYRIGHT

When you use samples of video in your movie, or use a story you saw in the newspaper, or quote a lengthy piece from a book, you might run up against the law, by breaking copyright. **Copyright is a way of protecting you, not just the stuff you want to sample or use.**

- **Copyright is about limited ownership.** That means the law tries to be sensible about what you can use – it doesn't want to get in the way of new culture, so you can use stuff in certain ways and certain terms.
- **Acceptable/fair usage:** you don't need to tell the copyright holder if what you take is a fair amount. This is called *fair use*. Look online for The Berne Convention to tell you more – that's the body that sorts out global copyright agreements. If in doubt about how much you can use, check it out.
- **How much is OK to use?** If you sample a clip, or music or written work, you can use enough to make your point and no more. It must be credited. If in doubt, ask the copyright holder.
- If you are **a student or nonprofit group** like a charity, the same rules apply to you.
- **Well-known music is hugely expensive to use in movies.** Don't even try. Better to make a deal with local bands where it might help the band to get exposure in your movie.
- **Who owns someone's story?** Be careful when using a real-life story you read about, like a family who met aliens, or an accountant who became

a wrestler. They still own that story, and if they don't then it most likely belongs to the journalist who wrote about it.

- **The web is affecting copyright.** Lawyers will still freak out if you use music or clips without asking, but there's no doubt it is shifting. Due to Bit Torrent, the idea of ownership is evolving into the idea that copyright is about "managing exposure." Hollywood writers saw this coming when they got rights over downloaded clips of their TV work online.
- **Anything in its original form that was produced before 1922 is OK to use** free of charge.
- **Copyright of your own work.** You get copyright automatically once you put your name on it. But you need to prove it was made *when* you said it was – before someone else's idea who ripped you off. To do this, simply email the script to yourself and store the email. Or use script registration services – but they cost.
- **Watch out if you make a movie in film school,** on any sort of program. In many schools you have given up copyright and they actually own your movie. Specifically demand that the copyright stays with you, but that you grant the school certain limited rights to use it in promotional material, for a specific length of time, after which the agreement lapses and it reverts wholly to you – try it and they'll think you're the next Harvey Weinstein.

FREE STUFF: WHAT'S IN THE PUBLIC DOMAIN – SO I DON'T HAVE TO PAY FOR IT?

Public domain means works that were made so long ago that the copyright has expired. Some things were never copyrighted, and (strangely) many government documents or films are not covered.

FIND STORIES OR BOOKS TO USE FREE OF CHARGE
Total list (USA):

- **Published before December 31, 1922.** You're OK, it's now in public domain.
- **Published between 1923 and 1963.** Copyright expires 28 years after publication but can then be renewed (and usually is) for an additional 47 years, now extended by an additional 67 years (thanks to Sonny Bono). Check with the publisher or the estate of the author if you are not sure if there are renewals.
- **Published between 1964 and 1977.** It again has 28 years copyright after publication but then is automatically renewed for an additional 67 years as a second term.
- **Published since 1978.** The work is protected only from when the work was fixed in what is called a "tangible means of expression," such as when filmed or put into print. Total copyright is the life of the author plus 70 years.

All other countries:

The Berne Convention makes it a general rule throughout countries who signed up to it that copyright covers the lifetime of the author plus 50 years.

With anonymous works, it's 50 years since the work was first made available to the public.

RIGHTS: WHO OWNS PARTS OF YOUR MOVIE?

YOU'VE GOT TO GET LEGAL

There's this thing called "**the rights chain**" and it covers everything in the movie that could be a problem. Wherever you send your movie they'll want to know that the rights chain is clear.

Table 9.1

Part of the Rights Chain	What It Is	What to Do About It
Funders	Has anyone given you cash to help make the movie, and do they own a piece of it (it's called "having partial rights")?	Not really a problem unless it's big bucks we're talking about. But if you want to get the movie out into the real world of movie festivals, get a signature which says they agree to hand over control of the movie to the person who has a majority stake in it.
Music clearance	Every track used in the movie must come with permission from the copyright holder – often the music publisher and/or record company. Snippets of music heard on a radio in a scene are OK as long as it's just a short segment.	Use music from local bands – they may not be signed yet and will be glad of the publicity in your movie.
Video clips/ segments	All pieces of video or film must be cleared with the owner for you to use.	**The "fair use" code of practice** helps you use someone else's video clips to create new works and limits how you do that. The code says that if you transform the original clip into a new work of art for a new purpose then it's OK. But if you use it for the same purpose and value as the original then it's not OK. Also, the length and content has to be appropriate, so don't use excessive amounts. So a 60-second clip of a TV show with new subtitles or voices should be OK, but a 3-minute clip presented as it was will be illegal. If you are doing club visuals you should be fine.

Continued...

Table 9.1 (Continued)

Part of the Rights Chain	What It Is	What to Do About It
People, actors and interviewees	Everyone in the movie needs to agree to appear in it. People need to give their permission to you in writing.	**Use a "release form" for each person.** You need different ones for minors, for actors, or interviewees. Use templates found online (try www.docstoc.com/search/video-permission-release-forms/)
Story, people	You need to make sure no one – people, companies or other groups – is insulted or defamed in your movie and could sue you. It's not enough to change names and places – you may have to go further if the characters are recognizable. Unless, of course, what your movie says is correct and the guy in your movie really is a proven low-life crook.	**Check the movie** and look for anything that could reasonably lead to legal action. If in doubt, change it. Alter names, products (e.g., a car with faulty brakes was a certain manufacturer), and company logos.
Sales	Has anyone already bought your movie – like for showing on a cable TV show, or for a DVD?	If so, be open and clear about it with whoever you are trying to get the movie seen by. Most online channels have a more realistic view of rights, and assume that a movie gets seen everywhere, in lots of formats, simultaneously.

SHOOTING IN STREETS AND PUBLIC PLACES

Most large cities have a policy about filmmakers working in public streets and places. You must get permission to film, in the form of a paper permit, or risk getting trouble from the police. In some places you don't need a permit if your team is less than 10 crew members. But this is often ignored by police who can move you on if they think you are causing congestion, or are near sensitive buildings like government offices, or they just don't like you. Even with a permit, be on your best behavior and avoid getting in the way of the public or traffic.

Check with the city hall whether you need a permit.

If you do, download the relevant documents and get them returned weeks before you plan to shoot. Some places will say it's fine to shoot unless you use a tripod, which can get in the way of passers-by.

Remember, many public places are in fact private – such as shopping malls, churches and schools. You'll need specific permission from the right person – principal, mall security chief, and so on – before you start.

SHOOTING IN NON-PUBLIC PLACES

Private places such as offices, hospitals and car parks are under no obligation to be nice to filmmakers. You are unlikely to get permission to film if your story reflects badly on the place. For instance, a movie about drug dealing in a school will probably not get you through the door, nor would a movie shot in a real bank in which a heist is helped by a crooked employee.

Chapter | Ten

Working with Locations

OVERVIEW

Find locations and get the info you need to use them well.

FIGURE 10.1 Crew members working on location for a scene from a film by Armen Antranikian.

WHY USE LOCATIONS?

- A few locations in your short movie make it look more authentic, and give it a bigger "feel," a more cinematic sweep, than one which is set in just one place.
- Even though some things are going to be harder when on location (using power, travel, weather) it is all offset by the realism you get and the added professionalism it brings your movie.
- Many movies don't have the choice – documentary, event movies such as sports, and music promos, all require you to leave the garage or studio and work in a busy, real setting.

HOW DO YOU LOOK FOR LOCATIONS?

If you are doing a drama movie the location might have been in your mind from the start, basing the theme around a certain place that you knew would be ideal for your movie. Movies that are based solely around locations, like road trips, are going to need you to think a lot about where to shoot – as if the location is the additional actor in the script.

Some movies need great locations more than others. Movies inspired by westerns and film noir, for example, rely on the landscape or city more than any other movie. In these movies the location setting is like a chorus line in a musical – it helps get the main theme of the movie across, by echoing or repeating or reinforcing what the actors feel or what is going on. Like, it rains on a dark derelict street in a scene when the main hero is in turmoil; or the sun beats down on a parched yellow plain as the hero stands alone and isolated. Whatever the scene, your location can emphasize it and make it more real so we feel it more fully.

WHAT MAKES A GOOD LOCATION?

When you find a possible place, think about:

- **Travel distance** (costs). How far is the location from your home and how far from all the other locations?
- **Risks and problems** (go to Chapter 18, Health and Safety). Is it safe to get your crew and cast out there?
- **Power availability.** Does it have access to electricity? Outdoor locations probably won't, so does that affect your filming?
- **Ownership and permission** (go to Chapter 9, Law and the Movies). Who owns the land and will they let you film there?
- **What else can affect you at particular times** like tides, or rush-hour traffic?

WHEN YOU FIND A GOOD LOCATION

- Use your camcorder to look through the lens and **get a feel for how a place looks** in a rectangular screen.
- Shoot a few moments to **check the lighting** – is it going to be bright enough?

- **Take photos.** Shoot as many as you need from any angle to show what the location has all around it. If you have a geotag or a smart phone, set it to record the map reference.
- Take some photos of actual shots as you imagine them, **as if they were shots from the movie** with people or actors missing.
- **Take measurements.** Make a note of each part of the location such as how wide the doors to a house are, how long a field is, how wide a street is and how many floors the buildings have.

FIGURE 10.2 Check that you have access to power in your chosen location if you need extra lighting. Or improvise with other sources of light. (Photo courtesy of iStockphoto, © Image# 911398.)

WHEN YOU GET BACK HOME

- **Look at your photos** and sketch in the people or objects that will appear in that scene.
- Maybe try creating the location in FrameForge or other 3D simulation software. You can **create a virtual environment** and play around with how to shoot the scene. This would be really useful in sports events where you get only one chance to shoot it right (see Chapter 7, Previz).

Experts' Tips

Derek Flagge, filmmaker, Coral Springs, Florida

"Keep the set positive; whether it's two people or ten people in a movie, always make everyone happy. Make sure you have everyone laughing even if it's a horror movie. If the cast is laughing the movie will turn out better because everyone is in a good mood."

Chapter Eleven

Brief Directory of All the Paperwork You Need

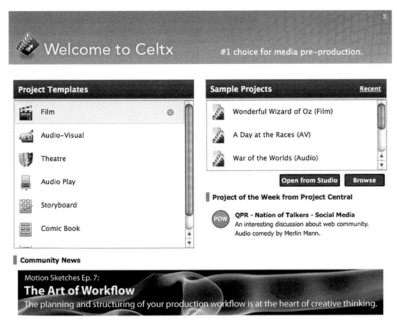

FIGURE 11.1 Using software like Celtx is an ideal way to connect all the essential documents you need for your movie.

Table 11.1

Document	What It's For	Movies It's Useful For	Get Help from Chapter:
Treatment	An outline of your movie in a few pages, like a short story with description and dialogue.	Any work of fiction, where there's a story.	Ch 3 Scriptwriting
Budget	A list of what everything is scheduled to cost.	Any movie where the costs extend to more than tapes/SD cards and your own travel.	Ch 4 Budgets
Script	The whole movie told in a specific format with dialogue, screen direction and description.	Any work of fiction.	Ch 3 Scriptwriting
Storyboards	A visual story of the movie, like a comic strip.	Action sequences, music promos, any part of a film where you need to coordinate a lot of people or props.	Ch 7 Previz
Previz	A mostly computer-based process of creating 3D virtual worlds of your locations to figure out the best camera moves and lighting.	Action movies, works of fiction, genre movies.	Ch 7 Previz
Contracts	A legal document for cast or crew, to safeguard and protect rights.	Any movie where you have a crew or cast.	Ch 9 Law and the Movies
Location photos	Still images taken at a location to help you plan how to work there.	Any movie where you use locations.	Ch 10 Working with Locations
Designs	Ideas showing key scenes from the movie to help decide what overall colors and mood or atmosphere you want.	Music promos, fiction and some documentaries.	Ch 5 Designing Your movie

	Description	When to use	Chapter
Costume designs	Designs showing what characters in the movie will wear.	Any work of fiction.	Ch 5 Designing Your movie
Lighting designs	Drawings of key scenes showing how you want the lighting to look. They show the intensity of light, the color of it and where lights will be placed.	Any movie where you use additional lights.	Ch 16 Lighting
Health and safety sheets	Documents showing the results of a risk assessment for a particular location where you want to shoot. They show hazards and how to deal with them.	Just about any movie.	Ch 18 Health and Safety
Shooting schedule	A complete breakdown of all the shots you need in the movie and where and when they will be shot, plus all the people and kit you need.	Any movie except documentaries, freecording, news and sports.	Sect 6 Make It Happen (Schedules)
Shot list	A list of all the shots you need to shoot to complete the movie.	Any movie where you can plan in advance what you want – as opposed to movies such as sports, news, freecording, road trips and so on.	Ch 8 Script Breakdown and Shot List
Edit decision list	A list of all the shots you want to use, based on the edit log, to help you do a complete edit.	All movies.	Ch 20 Pre-edit Footage Viewing
Edit log	A complete list with timecode of all the takes you shot and whether they are useable.	All movies.	Ch 20 Pre-edit Footage Viewing

SECOND OPINION

Why bother doing any of this stuff? Does it really matter whether or not you know exactly how the camera will frame something in advance? The many great films that come out of those 48-hour film challenge competitions show that weeks of planning aren't necessary.

Many directors feel that excessive paperwork drains the life out of a movie, as it gets planned to within an inch of its life. On the other hand, being disorganized drains the people out of the movie too, as they quit the set because no one knows what's happening. It's your call, but tread carefully – whether you use it all or use none of it.

Section Two: Shoot

SHOOT YOUR MOVIE
HOW DO I KNOW I NEED THIS SECTION?

Now the movie's planned out, and you are ready to go for it. What matters most right now is that the footage you end up with looks something like the movie that played in your mind when you first thought of it. Use this next section of the book to get each part of the movie looking good, sounding right, in a safe set, and all with a happy crew. Cherry-pick the chapters you want as you need them, or roll through each one from 12 to 18 to cover all bases.

Chapter 12: Using a Camcorder. If you are new to camcorders, or just want to check you are doing the right thing, check out this brief list.

Chapter 13: Shooting. Pared-down advice on getting the very best out of your camera, this chapter shows how to get heart and soul in each image, rather than just describe what goes on.

Chapter 14: Continuity. Next, a nice and easy list of how to avoid big on-screen mistakes that hole your movie below the waterline.

Chapter 15: Manage Your Production: Be a Producer. Behind-the-scenes stuff next, with advice on keeping a happy production, and how to become a producer who means it.

Chapter 16: Lighting. Two chapters you can't do without next. Lighting and sound are the twin lungs of your film. Lighting brings your movie emotional life.

Chapter 17: Sound Recording. It's not just about hearing what goes on – this chapter shows you that you can make more emotional oomph with creative sound.

Chapter 18: Health and Safety. Take a break from the artistic stuff and get the real advice on how to avoid your production being memorable for all the wrong reasons.

Chapter Twelve

Using a Camcorder

OVERVIEW

Knowing how the camcorder works is not just for technical geeks. Every part of the camera can become a new tool for your imagination, helping to put what you see in your mind onto the screen.

Table 12.1 The 20-second guide to how a DV camcorder works.

Light goes through a hole in front of the camera

passes through a first set of lenses which zoom in or out

gets focused with a second set of lenses

gets picked up by a small chip and...

. . . is divided into binary code for colors and light intensity, and compressed slightly

and is finally stored on tape or drive.

Table 12.2

Camera Part	What It Does
Iris	The front of the camera has a small opening called the **iris**, which gets larger or smaller according to how much light the camera needs. It works just like the human eye: smaller when it's bright and sunny, wider when it's in low light conditions. You can manually alter the iris to create effects, making a location seem like it's at night by reducing the light coming in.
Shutter	Next, the **shutter** also reacts to the light – opening and closing according to how much light there is. Don't get shutter speed mixed up with frame rate. Frame rate stays the same wherever you are, dependent on which system your camera uses: 25 frames per second for UK and others using PAL system; 29.9 per second, rounded up to 30 fps, for the USA and others on the NTSC system. **Tip:** **You can alter the shutter speed for better clarity.** If you imagine the shutter opening and closing 30 times a second (on NTSC, or 25 on PAL), each of those can be relatively quick or slow, depending on the setting. Opening in 1/50 of a second is the standard for a camcorder. Increase this to 1/1000 and you get better images of fast-moving objects. The reason for this is that the fast-moving object – a fast car, for instance – doesn't move enough in just 1/1000 of a second to make an image blurred. But at 1/50 of a second it moves enough distance to blur the image a lot. But be careful: making the shutter open for such a short time means less light gets in – which darkens the image slightly. Check it out on the LCD monitor to see you don't go too far.
Lens	The **lens** area at the front of the camcorder is actually several pieces of precision-made glass (or plastic in lower-end models) in two groups: one set at the front of the camcorder to zoom in or out, and the other a little behind to focus. **Tip:** **You can manually use the focus, iris, and shutter speed together to get the right shot,** unlocking a whole lot more from your camcorder. If you set the camcorder to "auto" each feature will pull in different ways, but when you work in "manual" mode you can make them work together. For example, if you shoot in low-light conditions, the iris will open up a little, but then you might notice that some parts of the frame are now blurred. This is because a wider iris will shorten how much of your image is in focus. Instead, try increasing the shutter speed to reduce light, allowing the iris to open a little wider – all operated manually. Just look at the LCD monitor until the image you see looks sharp (without graininess) and with good contrast, with more of your subject in focus.

Continued...

Table 12.2 (Continued)

Camera Part	What It Does
CCD chip	After the light has been focused through the second set of lenses it falls onto an area with a charge-coupled device (CCD), a small chip that assesses the light according to intensity and color. How well made these lenses are, and how big that chip is, will all affect the eventual quality of the image.
White balancing	White balance is a feature that helps correct color of light. Every light situation renders color slightly differently. The auto white balance feature automatically figures out the best color rendition, based on the color white. But it is unreliable and can change easily within a scene leading to odd continuity errors – one minute the screen looks fine, the next it has a blue cast. **Tip:** **Set white balance manually:** Set the white balance to auto. Point the camera at a white sheet of paper, nonreflective, so it fills the frame. Focus and let the iris settle on auto so it's not too dark or too light. Select white balance on the menu and wait a few seconds to find its correct setting. Leave the setting as it is and avoid changing it while you are shooting that particular location or scene. You might want to change the white balance to create a particular effect, or avoid a true white balance setting. For instance, if you are recording an outdoor wedding or graduation ceremony, you want to portray it as a happy event, but the weather conditions may be creating a blue color cast to the proceedings. You'll then need to manually alter the setting to offset some of the blue.
Sound recording	Meanwhile, the sounds accompanying your images get recorded. The open-board mic picks up sound all around it, so it's not great for filmmaking. You should have an external mic socket on your camcorder, a small 3.5 mm pin. **Tip:** **Record two sources at once.** Buy a small mic splitter that lets you connect two mics to it, feeding into the single one mic socket on your camera.
In-camera features	At this point the camera can alter the images a lot to compensate for camera shake, or for night conditions, or alter color or tone.

Continued...

Table 12.2 (Continued)

Camera Part	What It Does
Compression	Before all this information is sent to be stored on your tape or flash drive or SD card, it needs to be reduced in size, or "compressed." This compression takes place on almost all camcorders except high-end professional models, and is essential to make it viable to store the massive data video images create.
Timecode	Each frame gets given a unique 8-digit number, known as timecode, so it can be retrieved easily when editing.
Storage	The now reduced data gets stored on your camcorder or direct to its internal flash drive memory. **Tip:** **Make sure your SD cards are fast enough for video.** It's crucial that your camcorder send data to flash or SD card fast enough. Speeds on Standard cards tend to be around 6 MB per second, which sounds fast but this can limit how many frames per second you can record. Even fast cards such as Panasonic's Gold SD run at 10–20 MB per second, but this looks like the slow lane when compared to the massive SDXC card with speeds of up to 300 MBps, capable of holding 2 TB of video data.

Experts' Tips

Walter Murch, filmmaker, editor, *Apocalypse Now!*, *The Godfather*, *Cold Mountain*.

"You need:

1. Familiarity with your equipment, knowing a few of the buttons and what they do.
2. Planning out what you're going to do.
3. Being open to chance and spontaneity and how you can make that work in a story. You'll see something that wasn't planned but can use it a creative way, like you find a stray dog on top of a hill.
4. Be professional and steady, like using a tripod.
5. Teamwork and spontaneity. Some people are open to new ideas coming in and you have to adopt those."

FIGURE 12.1 Hand-held shooting is great for documentary and news but also for creating a more dramatic effect in other movies. (Photo courtesy of iStockphoto, ©WilliamSherman, Image# 8254976)

FIGURE 12.2 Fast-moving objects blur when shutter speed is low (around 1/50) and become sharper at higher settings (1/1000 and above), but the image becomes darker the higher the speed. (Photo courtesy of iStockphoto, ©Nikada, Image# 8387135)

Chapter | Thirteen

Shooting

OVERVIEW

It's not your actors, it's not your story, it's not the price tag on your camera – what really affects your film is the way you use the camera.

IF YOU ONLY READ ONE PIECE OF THIS CHAPTER, GO FOR THIS ONE
What you shoot and the way you show it.

The way you point the camera is crucial – and it's not about just describing the action so we keep up with the plot. You need to do two things at once: you've got to show what is happening in the scene, but also give it some feeling or mood.

The difference between just showing the action and actually giving it some mood is huge. It's like the difference between a statistics chart of a football game (who scored and when) and a high-octane commentary of the same game, with all the emotional highs and lows that the chart can't show. One describes what happened but the other actually puts you in the game. So, show what you have to show, but do it with feeling.

DIAGNOSE YOUR FRAMING

Take a look at what your movies are like so far. Discover your good traits and figure out which ones you have to lose. Get a bunch of your previous movies or footage, lock the door, get a pen and paper, and start:

1. **Do you have a color palette?** Speed-play your last movie and as the images go streaming before you try to notice what overall colors you see. A limited color range of three or four colors that complement each other means you're doing OK with design; if all you see is a murky mess then you need to rein in your color range.

2. **Freeze on random frames and take a long hard look at the image.** Divide up the screen into nine equal rectangles and see whether each of

them has a purpose. Each of these has to either make a contribution to what the shot is for – either by having something we need to see, or by staying empty and clear, to direct our eyes to the important stuff.

3. **Fast-forward play and check whether you have a variety of camera angles.** Is all the action roughly the same distance from the camera, or do you have a range of close-ups, mid-shots and so on?

4. **Finally, freeze on random frames and figure out how much is broadly shadow and how much light.** Many cinematographers suggest that if you push about two-thirds of the screen into darker tones it creates a better look. Are you overlighting your frame?

WHAT TO DO WHEN SETTING UP A SHOT

Good camerawork is about bringing together the tools you have developed so far. It means juggling these different things in your mind to give us story and mood.

Use these tools:

- Lighting
- Where you place objects and people in the frame
- Color, and white balance
- Shapes
- Symbols
- How much is in focus
- Aperture – or how much light the camera lets in through the iris

These starting points apply just as much to still photography, but in film-making, we can add in two more:

- The **movement of the camera** in and around the action
- The **movement of the objects or people** in the frame

When you put all these things together it can feel like a huge 3D puzzle where all the elements interact. It can be pretty daunting to have to juggle these in your head while trying to handle the realities of shooting like bad weather, late nights or unhappy actors. But it all gets easier if you focus on just two questions for every scene you set up:

1. **What's happening for the story in this scene?**
2. **What is the atmosphere? What's it supposed to feel like?**

You can go a little deeper into these questions – the first is about what is explicitly seen, is obvious, and is a fact. But the second is where it gets interesting, because that's the bit that is implicit, or under the surface, hinted at.

Try an example:

1. A man picks up a gun and walks into a store: that's the story, the facts. That's the **explicit** bit.

2. But the atmosphere is suggested, it's **implicit:** shown by the lighting, the way the camera is used, sound and so on.

You need a balance between the explicit (the plot) and implicit (the mood). If you go too far one way or the other, too often it all goes wrong. If you go too far away from the plot you get into a big weird, experimental mess of a movie. No one knows what is going on so people switch off. But if you stick too much with just showing the plot, with no mood, you end up with a dead movie that looks like a corporate how-to video.

Table 13.1 How images use hidden meanings

This is what's in the script:	
Explicit	A man picks up a gun and walks into a store
Implied	Menace

If we pick apart this image, this is how it works:	
Tool	**How It's Used**
Lighting	Shadows in the room suggest menace, by casting a lot of the man's face and body in shadow, perhaps lit partly from behind so he throws a long shadow across the room.
Camera angle	Camera tilt suggests that the heist is about to go wrong, or he's nervous.
Framing	A wide shot from low down, zoomed out with the man in the center to show that he is alone, and dangerous.
Movement of camera	Erratic, shifting, nervous, hand-held camera.
Cutaways	Quick shots of the man's hand on the gun; the faces of the customers; the clock ticking on the wall.
Color	No strong colors, instead mostly muted and dark tones including blue and black. Icy blue colors where there's strong light. White balance settings remove warm tones and add more blue to the image.
Aperture	The iris is closed down a little to add to the gloom, and increase the darkness of the shadows.
Depth	Lots of depth so we see people all around, the doors at the back of the store, and the goods he wants to take. This increases the impact and drama of the shot.

In this scene, we have to be able to see that the man has a gun, and we have to be able to see where he is going, to see that it is a store. But we need to have the mood spelled out for us too, using lighting, color and the angle of the camera.

Next, go a little further by creating a second and more subtle meaning in the shot. In the one above, the guy robbing the store, perhaps we could add in that he is nervous, reckless or unsure. That could increase the sense that bad stuff could happen at any moment. It makes him less like a comic-book robber and more real.

Try some movie stills:

FIGURE 13.1 Scene: A beach party at sunset. Mood: Warmth, harmony. But also with an added layer of meaning: mystery. (Photo courtesy of iStockphoto, ©ranplett, Image# 9308322)

Table 13.2 Beach party at sunset (Figure 13.1): how this image works

Tool	How It's Used
Lighting	No artificial light. The camera is placed so that the setting sun is behind the silhouetted actors. **Implies: mystery**.
Camera angle	Level, at head height, to give us a point of view as one of the group. You can't see much detail, each person looks similar. **Implies: harmony**.
Framing	Balanced composition. **Implies: harmony** and **warmth**.
Movement of camera	Moving slightly in and around the group. **Implies:** a point of view as if we are part of the group. The viewer is in **harmony** with the group.
Cutaways	Show close-ups of faces, feet dancing, waves. **Implies:** good party.
Color	White balance is set to enhance warm tones, allowing yellow/orange to dominate. **Implies: warmth**.
Aperture	Closed slightly to increase silhouetting of figures and reduce detail of the figures. **Implies: mystery** and **harmony**.
Depth	The group is close to the camera. There's no depth, except for the distant sun, or glimpses of the beach. **Implies: closeness** and **harmony**.

FIGURE 13.2 Scene: Man descends staircase in horror film. Mood: Tense, anticipating something bad. Second layer of meaning: The man is powerful. (Photo courtesy of iStockphoto, ©sandocir, Image# 54695)

Table 13.3 Man descends staircase in horror film (Figure 13.2): how this image works

Tool	How It's Used
Lighting	Dark, with a few strong pools of light, while the reflections help to make it more interesting. The light also keeps us looking at the man. **Implies:** the silhouette creates a **tense** mood.
Camera angle	Man in center shows he is important, but also alone. Looking up at him **implies** he is **powerful**.
Framing	All the elements in the frame point toward the man. The wide angle means that the sides of the frame show a lot of detail, and the windows look more elongated. Also, he's in the center of the frame, making him look perhaps less warm, less human. **Implies:** all eyes are on him, he's **powerful**.
Movement of camera	Backs away slowly as he descends. **Implies:** we should move away from him, he's **powerful**.

Continued...

Table 13.3 Man descends staircase in horror film (Figure 13.2): how this image works (Continued)

Tool	How It's Used
Cutaways	Looking at his feet as he descends, he's powerful so we need to create a sense of mystery about him, like we don't know what he is capable of. **Implies: power, tension**
Color	Black, blue, brown. **Implies: gloom, horror.**
Aperture	The light areas are over-bright while the shadows stay dark, creating a high-contrast image. **Implies: tension.**
Depth	The extreme depth makes the picture unnerving and strange, like a dream or nightmare. **Implies: horror**

FIGURE 13.3 Scene: Girl in room looks forward to a better life away from her city apartment. Mood: She is hopeful and determined, but also trapped right now. (Photo courtesy of iStockphoto, ©DOConnell, Image# 8458845)

Table 13.4 Girl in city apartment (Figure 13.3): how this image works

Tool	How It's Used
Lighting	Just a small pool of light shines on the girl, from above. **Implies:** the thing she **hopes** for is positive, and is almost within reach. She'll get there.
Camera angle	Slightly below the girl. **Implies:** that she is going to succeed, she has some **determination** to help herself. Placing the camera close to the girl increases the emotion in the shot.
Framing	Close to the girl with dark areas surrounding her. **Implies:** she is **trapped** and hemmed in on all sides.
Movement of camera	The camera is mostly still, but gradually and slowly moves down and angled up so she is higher in the frame and we almost see what she sees above her. **Implies:** she is moving closer to the thing she **hopes** for.
Cutaways	None, we don't want to detract from the drama or diffuse it.
Color	Cold colors in the room, but the warmer tones on her face from the source of her hope tell us she is **hopeful**.
Aperture	Darker, with a slightly closed iris, to increase the darkness surrounding the girl. **Implies:** she is **trapped**.
Depth	Very little depth, so the girl's hand and the background is out of focus, leaving us to look at just her face. It makes her look even more **trapped**.

SETTING UP A SHOT STEP BY STEP

- If you use a script, look at it the night before you shoot. From it you need **a single word that sums up the atmosphere** for that scene. Get this word and write it on a sticky note on the camera. Tell everyone that word is the aim of this scene.
- **Take time to set up the shot,** but don't use a tripod as you move freely around trying to see which shot will look best. When you have found it, then use a tripod or stabilizer.
- **Set up lighting.** Again ask yourself what the script needs in terms of mood, plus how to make sure we see what's essential. Simplify the lighting so there are fewer but larger shadows, making larger shapes in the frame.
- **Don't over light.** Many films have too much light, especially given the enhanced ability of video to see in low-light conditions. Even worse, avoid an even spread of mid-level light. Instead, use strong lamps (300 W) to create strong shadows. Use these shadows to create big, simple compositions.

- Walk around with the camera **checking out various ways you could shoot it,** thinking all the time about how to get across your key word for that scene. Go with your instincts on this.
- Do a **brief run-through.** When the action starts move around with the camera, checking how it looks from the different angles you have planned.
- When you shoot, make editing easier by starting to roll the camera at least **five seconds before the action,** and cut five seconds after it ends.
- **Get extra footage,** also known as "pick-up shots." Although you might have set up the perfect shot your film might look a little "over-cooked" if every shot is too planned out. Allow rougher, off-the-cuff shots to get included now and then. In Michael Mann's *Collateral*, there are a lot of rough, almost documentary-style shots sitting next to the glossy, neat ones. It gives the film more vigor and life.
- **Watch it through,** checking sound on your headphones.

FIGURE 13.4 Close-up shots increase the emotional impact in a scene, as in this film by Armen Antranikian.

Experts' Tips

Ben Winter, film student, USA

"Don't be afraid to get in close with the camera. People are excellent observers. We're trained to interpret the most elusive facial and body movements. But it does no good for an actor to emote at that level of subtlety if you can't see it properly on screen. And when you do, don't back the camera away and zoom in just to get that shallow depth of field so many filmmakers crave, because your talent will just overact for a camera that's on the other side of the room. Invade their space."

Ashvin Kumar, Best Live Action Short Oscar nominee, *The Little Terrorist*, Delhi, India

"I compensated for the lack of lighting with costumes and sets knowing that the lighting would be quite even, and trying to obtain as much contrast as was possible with reflectors and scrims; and shooting the beauty shots at hours that give us contrast naturally (early morning or just before sundown). The dramatic scenes were therefore shot during the harsh time of the day in the semi-interiors and when the film calls for mid-shots and close-ups. We tried to avoid shooting the sky in those scenes which was not too much of a problem since the scenes were dramatic."

SECOND OPINION

Just skip these rules and follow your heart. Why shoot like this and end up with a film that looks just like everyone else's? Sure, it's a useful shortcut and your movie will look like you mean business, but where's the unique **you** in all of this? Where's your totally unique view of the world? Don't they just think up these rules to keep movies like a select club? – you can't join because you didn't go to film school and learn all this stuff. Wasn't it like that once with music – you had to know what key you were in and had to have the right gear? That's why garage bands and hip hop started.

If you want to try a different method, try **Dogme 95**, a bunch of Danish directors who overturned just about every rule in the book to get back to raw, emotional storytelling. They didn't mind about how it looked as long as it had heart and soul, and could move you to laughter, tears, hell and cloud 9. No effects, no tripod, no music, no lamps, just real, authentic, here and now.

Experts' Tips

Ben Winter, film student, USA

"Dogme 95 is a standard of filmmaking that Lars von Trier created – mostly as a joke – that dispenses with the formalities of filmmaking and strips the medium down to its bare minimum. You'd think they would be trivial films with little pomp and circumstance. But they're absolutely brilliant, and riddled with nuance. These films, like *The Celebration*, influenced me strongly because they changed my perception of what was important about filmmaking. They taught me that you don't need big lights or a big camera to tell a convincing, compelling story. The effectiveness of the film astonished me at the time. I was completely blown away."

Chapter Fourteen

Continuity

OVERVIEW

Continuity is the catch-all term for most of those blips and mistakes that make up your blooper reel. Here's how to ensure continuity is perfect each time.

Continuity is a way of making sure that a scene makes visual and verbal sense when we watch it.

Movies don't get shot in sequence, and some parts of the same scene might be shot days apart but edited so they **look like everything happened in one continuous flow** of events.

On a movie, continuity is the job of the **Script Supervisor**, who has to note every detail of a shot to make sure that continuity errors like the following don't creep in:

- In *Spider-Man*, Mary Jane gets mugged but Spidey fights off the four muggers and throws two of them through nearby windows. When Mary Jane picks herself up, we see the windows now intact behind her.
- **In the first Harry Potter movie**, we see Harry sit down for a feast on the right side of the table next to Ron, but when we cut back after the meal appears, he is on the other side next to Hermione. (Thanks to the guys at www.moviemistakes.com.)

Table 14.1

Part of Production	What to Do
Technical and camera continuity:	Use the same aspect ratio throughout – choose 16:9 if you're not sure which. Record on **short play** throughout. **Shutter speed** needs to be kept the same throughout a scene, and only altered slightly within the entire movie. **Aperture:** Use one setting for each scene. Use **action-line rules and 30-degree rules**, eye matching and shot-reverse shot (see later in this chapter to find out about them). **White balance:** use the same manual setting throughout each scene, and for all scenes in that location. **Camera style:** use the same approach throughout a scene, such as how much the camera moves and whether you use hand-held or steady. **Check that all details match** between takes. Make notes, take photos and mark the position of your actors. Play back the last section of the scene to check the next flows on from it: objects need to be exactly where they were; hair, clothes and makeup needs to be consistent. **Check the frame is clear** of boom mic, crew or other things that will disrupt our perception of the scene.
Lighting	**Light quality and intensity** is the same throughout a scene unless the script says otherwise. **Visual space:** make sure we can see elements of the room or location in each shot so we always know where we are. **Daylight:** beware of fading light toward the end of the day – it can be hard to notice changes over an hour or more.
Color	**Use the same color palette throughout a scene**, and limit how far you alter it across the whole movie. Choose three dominant colors as your overall design. Some scenes will focus on one color more than another.
Sound	**Record a wild track** or ambient track to smooth over possible inconsistent sound later. While recording, **make sure levels (of loudness) are equal** throughout the movie Use the same mic method for all similar scenes – for instance, all interior dialogue scenes could be with a boom mic, or all exteriors with boom and tie mics.

Continued...

Table 14.1 (Continued)

Part of Production	What to Do
Editing:	Edit between completely separate scenes by using **simple visual clues** such as: A noise that occurs at the end of one scene and the start of the next, like a police siren. An image that looks or sounds similar at the end of one scene and the start of the next, like a drill at the end of scene 1 that merges into a scream in the start of scene 2. **Keep time constant:** Show that events are happening simultaneously by using "parallel montage" (see Ch 22 Editing Methods: Montage). Or show passage of time by fading to and from black.

FIGURE 14.1 Location filming means keeping a close check on continuity. A production image from *Like Dandelion Dust* (2009). Image: Kerry David.

FIGURE 14.2 Makeup needs to be carefully noted and applied in the same way for each part of a scene to avoid continuity problems. (Photo courtesy of iStockphoto, ©bjones27, Image# 8321924)

Getting the perfect shot is a whole lot easier if you have some agreed upon ideas to begin with that prevent simple mistakes. Some things look good on film, some things don't, but luckily other filmmakers have trodden this ground before you and figured out the difference between the two.

THREE RULES THAT HELP – REALLY

- **The rule of thirds:**

Sometime in the fifteenth century, painters figured out that their compositions looked better if **the main objects were not placed in the middle but slightly to the sides.** Known in art as The Golden Mean, it meant that a tree is placed about one third of the way from the side of the frame, while a horizon would be the same from either the top or bottom of the frame. It makes your frame look balanced and increases a sense of depth. It also avoids symmetrical compositions, which can look dull and lifeless. To use it well, divide your camera viewfinder up into nine equal rectangles – so you have three equal columns and three equal rows – and place all the elements in the frame along these lines.

- **The 30-degree rule:**

When you set up a frame, **never shoot another frame less than 30 degrees away from the last one.** Think of a semicircle with the main action in the center of the straight line. Then imagine angles coming from this main subject at 30 degrees, like bicycle spokes. You shouldn't be able to get more than five camera angles within this complete 180-degree area plus two more directly from either side. If you cut between two shots that are quite close in angle, then the edit seems to jump, or worse makes the action appear to move. Two shots that are more than 30 degrees apart edit together more softly than those that are less.

- **The action line, or axis:**

This can turn out to be one of the most useful rules if you want to make sure you keep the audience up with the plot. The action line means **an imaginary line that cuts through the action from left to right along the screen.** So a scene showing two people arguing in a car park would have the camera placed directly in front of them to start with, and the action line running through them both from one side of the screen to the other. So Actor A is on the left of the screen and Actor B on the right. However, if you cross the line, and go around the actors to the back and carry on shooting, then Actor A now appears to be on the right of the screen and B switches over to the left. The effect is total disorientation, looking as if we have skipped a reel somewhere.

SECOND OPINION

Don't do it! Your movie really won't suffer if you ignore each and every one of these rules. This just wraps the viewer up in cotton wool, like they can't handle any disruption of the movie experience, or suspension of disbelief. Throw everything at 'em, including the rule book. Check out *Run Lola Run* (1998) or the wacko *Un Chien Andalou* (1929) or anything by the Dogme 95 directors. Did they care? No, that's why they won all those awards.

Chapter Fifteen

Manage Your Production:
Be a Producer

OVERVIEW

Prevent fights on set, make friends with the people you work with, gain respect for being cool under pressure – that's producing.

Experts' Tips

Walter Murch, filmmaker, editor, *Apocalypse Now!*, *The Godfather*, *Cold Mountain.*

"You need a tremendous amount of teamwork which everyone is fulfilled by and where everyone feels appreciated. No one sits there idly. Everyone has input. Everyone has a viewpoint and you can see that viewpoint."

QUALITIES YOU NEED AS PRODUCER

Business sense. You need to be able to juggle various ideas and issues at the same time. Can you think of a project in a long-term way, and how all the various elements of it come together? You need to be able to think quickly about costs, and about how to keep them down, being tough enough to resist the calls to spend more from your crew.

Leadership. If you like being in charge, and tend to be good with people and teams, then you could make a good producer. Leadership means putting yourself right at the front of the production and not waiting to be told what to do. This really suits some people – the sort of person who sees what needs to be done before anyone else, and who isn't afraid of getting it wrong from time to time.

People skills. You will also be able to listen and talk to people well, avoiding being aggressive even when you get tough about what they need to do. A quiet, forceful manner is ideal – think Yoda mixed with Kindergarten Cop.

Logistics. You will be able to organize the production well. You are able to set up a whole host of things that need to work together, like transport, food, booking cameras to borrow, buying props and making sure everyone knows what they need to do. It's like a military campaign without the bad food.

What the producer does:

1. Believes in the vision of the script.
2. Coordinates the planning stage, holding meetings, and so on.
3. Gets funding.
4. Manages the day-to-day production while shooting.
5. Deals with publicity and getting the movie seen.

It's OK to produce and direct your own movie, especially if control freakery comes easy to you.

COPING WITH PEOPLE

FLASHPOINTS

There are many ways – too many – to get into fights while you make your movie. Even simple problems can lead to major upsets if not handled well. The most common flashpoints that cause problems include:

Table 15.1 What can go wrong and how to deal with it

Flashpoint	What Goes Wrong	Solution
Poor admin	People can't communicate properly with each other and don't know what they are supposed to be doing.	Spend time on the script breakdown, the production schedules and the daily organization sheets such as call sheets and other ways to organize the work.
Poor chain of command	Mild-mannered director doesn't want to assert what everyone needs to do, and is too polite to deal with problems. This leads to anxiety that no one is in charge and the crew don't know who to turn to with problems.	**Assign roles and ask everyone at the first meeting to tell everyone else who they are, what their role is and what they are specifically in charge of.** Talk about possible problems and agree who is responsible if things go wrong. As producer make yourself available to deal with problems and don't shy away from laying down the law about what needs to happen.

Continued...

Table 15.1 What can go wrong and how to deal with it (Continued)

Flashpoint	What Goes Wrong	Solution
Not enough resources for the job	Not enough money means people can't do their jobs properly, which in turn leads to stress and poor work.	**Work solidly within your means.** Be aware of what your budget is, what you can afford, and what you can't. Work in an extra 10% of costs to everything, making a more realistic budget.
Cost overruns	The production spirals out of control as the director adds in more scenes, or makes radical changes.	**Obvious, but stay within the budget and the script.** Everyone deviates by about a quarter with what they originally intended to shoot, making changes to the movie as they see better opportunities. But there has to be a limit. Avoid mission creep – it's every army general's worst nightmare, and is the path to ruin for a filmmaker.
Bad schedule	The schedule is too optimistic or just plain wrong. One day's shooting becomes two, pushing back other jobs, or forcing crew or cast to drop out.	**Always add in a large margin of error to allow for extra time needed.** You always need to reshoot, usually need extra time to set up shots and almost always get something you didn't expect which interrupts the scene.

Experts' Tips

Kerry David, producer, *My Date with Drew, Agent Cody Banks, College Sucks*, Los Angeles

"I'm a creative producer, not a physical producer, and by that I mean that I love to put all the creative elements of a film together, but I don't relish haggling over the price of a camera package. At the beginning of any project I will write treatments and adaptations if appropriate or just work with a screenwriter to develop the story until it's ready to film. I bring the key creative teams on board (the department heads that shape a film) meaning I cherry pick the director, director of photography, composer, editor, costumer, makeup artist, casting director, sound editor, and on and on, as every one of these artists shapes the film to be made. I scout locations and come up with actor suggestions with our director and casting director. I strategize about the project as a whole, where it should be submitted (at the studio level, or certain financiers) and then I set up meetings with financiers, distributors and studio executives to pitch the project as these are the people who will make my film a reality if they respond well. When I'm on set, if I have done my job well I'm there to put out any fires that might erupt but for the most part as a support to my director and be ready with answers to any department that runs into challenges while filming. I'm also the person that the actors turn to with issues they may have while filming so I can be a therapist or friend when necessary."

FIGURE 15.1 A good working atmosphere helps smooth a low-budget production along. Cast and crew of Jason Korsner's Hollywood-set comedy *2 Hour Parking* (2007).

HOW TO MANAGE YOUR SHOW

1. **Be around, be contactable.** You need to be a visible and open presence. Your phone is always on, you turn up early to meetings, you are the last to leave. You are ready to listen and never too busy to stop and talk about the production. And you're calm.

2. **Preparation is all; you can't do too much of it.** Spend time on storyboards, script, rehearsing actors, meeting with each member of the crew, reading through the schedules and plans. Look at every step of your plans in 360° to look for possible problems.

3. Always assume that **no one will ever do anything unless you ask them to.** They are not being lazy, they are just being respectful and waiting for you to tell them to do it. After a while they'll start to take the initiative and do things before you ask.

4. **Your most important pieces of paper** are the script breakdown and scheduling plans. Spend time getting these as detailed as possible (see Chapter 11, All the Paperwork You Need).
5. **Budgets are king.** Never go over budget, but be realistic about what you can afford and what you need. Your budget becomes the big reason why you can't do everything everyone asks you to do. Whatever the request, just point at the budget and say "sorry, budget says no."
6. **Schedule and shot list will determine budget** and length of shoot.
7. **Hold meetings where you write down what was agreed.** Get everyone together regularly and agree that one person will write down what was said and what each person agreed to do.
8. **Establish ground rules for involvement in the movie.** Agree what happens if someone doesn't show up frequently, or if they fail to keep up what they agreed to do. Make it fair and easy for everyone to see why someone has been asked to leave the production.

HOW TO SORT OUT FIGHTS

You have a great team with a lot of skills and diversity, but that diversity means sometimes trouble can break out when people disagree. People have different goals and ways of doing things and this causes conflicts. But conflict is not necessarily destructive if you manage it properly.

1. **Openness of communication.** Use Twitter, blogs or any method that lets other people into your thought processes. Be open about the ups and the downs, and keep people close to what is going on.
2. **Direct raising of issues.** Meet a problem head-on and bring it right into the open quickly. Bring everyone in and you should get a sense of resolution if everyone has their say. Many problems get smaller once you talk about them, often finding out that underneath it all everyone is just tired or needs a break.
3. **Bargaining:** if you really can't find common ground then come to a compromise, but this tends to mean everyone is dissatisfied. Avoid putting your own position on the line – instead ask the two sides to come up with a solution with your help.
4. **Prevent issues from arising in the first place** by agreeing before anything starts what your shared values are.
5. **...and then remind people about these agreed ground rules and shared ideas,** if someone is not taking part or handling their responsibilities.
6. **Work around the problem.** Use this if everything else fails. Simply walk away and find a common starting point, like, "We all want to do our best on this film." Play down the problem and walk away.

Experts' Tips

Kerry David, producer, *My Date with Drew, Agent Cody Banks, College Sucks*, Los Angeles

"Whatever part of the filmmaking process you decide is your path, only attach yourself to projects you are truly passionate about. If you are a writer, write something that captivates you, as a director take on projects that you know need your imprint. I believe that it is passion and tenacity that gets a project to the big screen and the person who has the most passion and tenacity pushes their project past the finish line. It's also too difficult an industry not to be! Work with people you love to be around. There's a reason that filmmakers like Steven Spielberg and Clint Eastwood work with the same people over and over again."

"Filmmaking is so rewarding but it's also a difficult process and you will be asking a lot of your team constantly. You need to know that they have your back and that you have theirs, so work with people you trust and admire. I always try to work with people much more experienced than I am so I can learn from them."

"It's not always possible but sometimes you have that luxury and I say always accept it as both you and your project will benefit from it. Enjoy the process. Relish the journey. Don't take yourself too seriously and appreciate the people around you and what they bring to the project – no film gets made alone and take it from me, it feels much better to accept awards for your films with your friends from the project right there with you."

Chapter Sixteen

Lighting

OVERVIEW

How to make the most of your movie on screen – using any available light you can get your hands on.

Your movie needs light like oxygen. Give it enough and it comes alive; too much and it's overcooked. Without good lighting it's just a series of events, with no meaning, no purpose and no feeling. Whatever you put into the film – whether it's a gripping script or a unique subject – it only becomes vibrant and living once you feed it with the right lighting.

Lighting is to movies what descriptive words are to novels. In a movie, lighting is *describing* everything rather than just labeling. With good lighting, a "man at a desk" becomes a *menacing* man at a desk, "a room" becomes an *inviting* room, "a staircase" becomes a *spooky* staircase. So take a look at the initial ideas you had before you think up ways to get the lighting right; everything you need is right there in your script or your ideas.

BEFORE YOU START

Almost everything you need to know about lighting you know already. You hear a lot in film school, books or online about the various ways you should light a movie and the rules you have to follow – like three-point lighting, contrast ratio and the rest. Ignore it. There are no rules, just a lot of very useful safety tips (you need those) and some shopping hints.

Almost every shot needs some help with lighting. House lamps or proper film lights, big wattage or small, it's rare to get through a scene without using some additional artificial lights. Even scenes shot in good daylight need some help with reflectors, helping to enhance available light.

FIGURE 16.1 Make use of reflectors when shooting in studio, to maximize available light. (Photo courtesy of iStockphoto, ©jay_b Image# 1123566.)

Trust your eyes: ignore technical limitations. Look at the movie you first saw in your mind when you first dreamt it up. Stick with that and search for the light – any light, anywhere, from any source – that will reproduce it. Some film-makers just won't settle for anything less. Stanley Kubrick avoided electric light for a lot of *Barry Lyndon*, shooting a lot by candlelight. He knew the look he wanted and didn't settle for a predictable "period costume" movie.

Terrence Malick wanted certain kinds of daylight only found in "the magic hour," like dusk or dawn. You can't recreate that artificially or buy it with CGI – it has to be real, shooting when the low sun makes the ground purple and blue, the sky pink and the clouds ochre.

NEXT: PLAY AROUND

Teach yourself how the camera deals with light, and how lights affect what you shoot. It's easy. Play around with lights, move them up, down, sideways, swing them back and forth (like that great scene in the end of *Psycho* in the basement). Cover them in wraps, colored gels, cloth – all flameproof. Put stuff in front of lights, make shadows. Bounce light around the walls. Reflect light upwards, downwards, anywhere you want it. Shine lights through glass panes covered in dripping water. Bounce light against water trays to make ripples on the walls. Throw smoke or dust into the air to make light appear as shafts. Just don't light it like you see it in every other movie.

You know what you want and how it should look. So play until you see what you like.

NEXT: GET TECHNICAL

There's no short way round – **it helps to know what each of your lights do and how to make the most of them.** You could buy some lights from a home hardware store, like garage and yard lights, or portable car repair lights.

Anything that makes light is a potential lamp for your movie. Proper movie lamps can make your movie look less interesting, just like everyone else's. Use desk lamps, candles, torches, fires, car headlamps – anything. You don't need real movie lamps. Experiment to find just how much light your camera needs before it makes "noise" (those snowy white dots all over the screen when the camera doesn't have enough light). But it is surprising how little you need. Watch *Collateral* (2004) to see how great video can look at night in the city.

Use the camera as a member of your lighting team. Remember it does half the job of lighting as you open or close the iris, or change shutter speed, or alter white balance.

FIGURE 16.2 Use shadows and reflections to create innovative ways to depict action. (Photo courtesy of iStockphoto, ©ulamonge Image# 167997.)

BUY YOUR KIT

Zero budget kit: Look for table lamps, desk lamps or garage lights – anything which can be maneuvered and pointed. Look around in your basement or attic or try yard sales for old slide projectors: these are good for throwing strong, nondiffused light at the action, so you get sharp, deep shadows and bright white areas. Also get a reflector (white card or stiff plastic sheet) and extension cables.

Budget kit: Try a complete set of three lamps from specialist film and video lighting companies, or through high street photographic suppliers. This will contain a key, fill and smaller back light, often with tripods and reflectors, in a sturdy aluminum case. Your biggest lamp needs to be at least 300–400 W.

FIGURE 16.3 Reflectors are great for making use of what little light you have. Improvise with any firm, portable white surface. (Photo courtesy of iStockphoto, ©bjones27, Image# 9397028)

Bigger kit: If you want to get hold of a bigger kit try getting:

- At least two large versatile key lamps, from 400 W to 800 W, such as a Redhead. Make sure these have "barn doors" with them, to direct the light to the subject.
- At least two small, directional lamps, such as Mizars (small and powerful) or Dedos (small, portable, low voltage, with sharper light).
- A wide fill lamp with a diffuse beam.
- Extension cables.
- Distribution boards or multisockets.
- A large, flat, reflective surface such as white card or flexible polystyrene.
- Fireproof colored gels, for placing on the lamps and altering the light color.
- Some greaseproof paper to diffuse strong light.
- Bull-clips or pegs to attach cookies or gobos – opaque patterns cut out of board to create particular shadows.
- Spare bulbs.
- Gaffer/duct tape.

FIGURE 16.4 A studio Fresnel lamp. Fresnel (pronounced fre-nel) makes a softer light, and can be focused into spots or cast a wider beam. (Photo courtesy of iStockphoto, ©Soundsnaps, Image# 837558)

Table 16.1 Use these starting points to decide how to get your lighting right. Then experiment from there to get the right look for you.

Choose What You Want for Your Movie: Start Here
Naturalistic lighting This is lighting that you don't notice is there. It's enough light just to help out the camera, to make sure it can pick up the action. To get it, use light from large sources, spread out for big areas. Rely on natural daylight where you can. Back it up with soft lights if you need to. Your first question before you shoot is, "Can I avoid lighting this scene?" It's subtle, avoids flashy effects, and is low-key. It's a very cheap way to work.

No, thanks, I want something more like the movies, a little more punchy.

Realistic lighting This is a kind of natural effect, but amps it up to exaggerate things a little. Faces get more expressive, and places get more atmospheric and moody. It's a good middle route between naturalistic and expressionistic but can risk looking like every other manufactured movie. Set the aperture so you get darker shadows, with fewer grays so they become black, and the lighter areas are the most defined.

Continued...

Table 16.1 Use these starting points to decide how to get your lighting right. Then experiment from there to get the right look for you. (Continued)

Choose What You Want for Your Movie: Start Here

No, still not enough – I want a more
emotional effect, all high drama and high emotion.

Expressionistic lighting

Expressionistic lighting is for emotional impact only. It doesn't look anything like reality, and isn't supposed to. It's great for music promos, looks cheesy in dramas, and is a no-no for most movies. But you can try sampling a bit of it to add a twist to your more sedate lighting set-ups.

FIGURE 16.5 Reflectors are used to bounce light in this production by filmmaker Preston Randolph.

LIGHTING IDEAS

Take a look at these ideas as starting points for you to light a scene. Then build on the idea and twist it your way, by adding or taking away lights, or combining it with other ideas on the list.

Table 16.2 Light ideas to set a scene

What I Need	Where to Start
Standard light, no specific atmosphere	One strong lamp 300 W to illuminate subject. Avoid daylight through windows, watch for blue color cast outside against the orange cast indoors. Useful to have smaller desk lamps too.
Softer atmosphere	One 300 W at side/front of face/subject, softened with a softer side light to show up the background too. Reduce shadows.
Harder atmosphere	Create shadows, remove other lights except for 300 W.
Upbeat mood	Open aperture slightly. White balance set to enhance orange. Use stronger light, no higher than head height.
Colder light	Raise the lamp so it points downwards, and use sharp shadows. White balance set to filter out orange.
Warmer light	Use softer, smaller lights, lower down, below head height.
Two people talking	One light pointing at one side of the couple. Use reflector to bounce light upwards to neck and chin. Soften background if needed.
Brighter light	Move lamps closer (half the distance between light and subject and light gets increased × 4)
More expression	Hard light, strong shadows, raise tripod to have lights above pointing down to faces. Then increase contrast by altering aperture/iris.
Denser atmosphere	Add smoke or dust to reveal light. Or try swinging lights to create moving shadows.
More exotic, dreamlike effect	Try adding water reflections on ceiling. Project light through colored cloth or paper (flameproof – they get hot. Open the aperture/iris.
Light at outdoor location	Bounce light – use white card, reflectors. Avoid in-camera lights. If power source available use 300–800 W lamp, far enough away from subject to reduce artificial look.
Fast action	Try 1/1000 shutter speed, with strong lighting. If image is too dark increase aperture to compensate.
Night during day	Close aperture down. Use smaller pools of light to pick out subject.

FIGURE 16.6 Harsh light from above, creating a tense, dramatic effect. It also makes the figure seem more threatening. (Photo courtesy of iStockphoto, ©AVTG, Image# 8413209)

FIGURE 16.7 Create a warmer look by softening shadows. (Photo courtesy of iStockphoto, ©suricoma, Image# 7923934)

FIGURE 16.8 Use a white umbrella (available for less than $10) to diffuse light from a strong lamp. (Photo courtesy of iStockphoto, ©dorusana, Image# 5050281)

Experts' Tips

Ryan Bilsborrow-Koo, maker of *The West Side*, Webby Award-winning web series, Los Angeles

"We had no funding whatsoever and our lighting kit consisted of a few shop lights purchased from Home Depot."

FIGURE 16.9 Ryan Bilsborrow-Koo, setting up a scene for *The West Side*, using a reflector to bounce light at the action.

Chapter | Seventeen

Sound Recording

OVERVIEW

This is the big one that can really undermine your movie. Everyone notices if you get sound wrong, but yours is going to be right. Here's how.

Quick start recording:

1. **Pack your video and audio kit** (see essential shopping list later).
2. **Set up the scene** you want to record.
3. **Check out the list below of the hierarchy of recording techniques** to find the best way to record.
4. **Plug in headphones and listen** to the clarity of what is being recorded.

Watch out for sound interference from cell phones and other electrical stuff. You'll know it – it sounds awful.

When you have the scene recorded just fine, send the crew off for a coffee and spend a few minutes gathering extras for the rest of your soundtrack:

1. **First get "room tone," or "ambient presence."** That's the totally unnoticed background sound behind the talking – like traffic, crowds, birdsong and so on. Check out the box later on recording it.
2. **Then get your sound effects**. You can't reproduce these in a studio as Foley because your budget is too small. Use a lavalier mic or uni-mic.

Then play back what you have got on headphones to find out whether the sound is useable.

FIGURE 17.1 A boom mic makes a very natural recording, and allows you to move the mic closer to whoever is talking. (Photo courtesy of iStockphoto, ©bjones27 Image# 6452283.)

MICROPHONES

A mic is basically a device for turning one kind of energy into another – sound energy gets turned into electrical energy. A loudspeaker simply reverses this process at the other end.

You need external mics. The on board mic on your camcorder is not great for real movie recording. Use it for freecording, travel and improvised movies but avoid it for any place where you need to control the sound on your movie – which is nearly all the time.

There are two types of mic, dynamic and **condenser**, with dynamic the most common for camcorders since they don't need any power to run. These are based on the idea that a magnet placed near a coil creates an electrical current. At the front of the mic a thin diaphragm vibrates as sound waves hit it, which in turn moves the coil against a magnet. The pulses which this creates are then recorded to match the images. Condenser mics work differently, needing their own power source, but can produce stronger sound, and are better suited to studio work. They have two diaphragms at the front of the mic separated by a small voltage. When sound waves hit the mic, the distance between these two diaphragms alters as the front one vibrates, discharging a current to create a signal, which again gets recorded to match your images.

Think of mics in the same way we talk about vision – some work near, some far away, some wide and some narrow, just like our eyes.

- **Unidirectional** or **cardioid** mic picks up sounds in front of the mic, with least sensitivity to the sides. Where you point the mic is what you get. The most common ones are hand-held versions or fixed at the end of a pole, or a "boom."
- **Omnidirectional** mic picks up sound equally all around it, making it ideal for general ambience recording.
- **Lavalier** mic is a short range omnidirectional mic, small enough to clip to a person's clothing. It's ideal for clear, close-up, voice recording.

YOU'VE GOT THREE AIMS WHEN RECORDING AUDIO

1. **Record clean sound.**
   - Use mics that pick just what you want and nothing else. Make sure you use a mic with the right range and use headphones to tell if the sound is too loud or quiet.
   - Always record at the maximum level, without it tipping into distortion. Look at the LCD monitor on the camcorder; find the "audio levels" or *gain*. Usually, there is a sliding scale with red on the right side of the scale, green on the left. Avoid slipping into the red too often; instead your sound should just skip into it now and then, hovering around the ideal point just before red.
2. **Control the sound environment** (see later for more on that).
   - To make a good movie soundtrack, you need to be able to control what's in your sound environment, and you can then add a few extras to make the movie more atmospheric. To do this, record each part of the sound environment separately – either at the same time or after you finish shooting a scene.
3. **Match what we see to what we hear.**

Your next challenge is to make sure that the sounds match what we see on screen. This means looking carefully at what is on the screen and making sure these sounds are present. For example, if a bus rolls past as the actors are talking, then we expect to hear it in the background. The easiest way to make sure you have everything is to record a separate ambient background track at the same time as you record the main action.

- **Use a mic socket splitter** which means you can plug two mics into one mic socket on your camcorder. A headphone splitter (two people can listen in) for your MP3 player might do the job.
- **Use the boom** to record the actors' voices, or whatever is the most important piece of sound we need to hear.

- At the same time, **record general background sound** with an omnidirectional mic, or if there's too much background noise going on, use a handheld uni mic.

Finally, check whether there are one-off sounds you missed but which appear in shot – such as a plane overhead. Get these sound effects from the web or record them if you can.

FIGURE 17.2 Preston Randolph and crew working on location with a boom mic.

GET IT RIGHT IN ANY SITUATION

This is a quick and easy way to set up every shot so you record good sound every time.

It goes like this. The first method (overhead boom mic) is the best and will work most times in most situations, so use it. If you can't then switch to the second method (boom mic from below). If that is not possible, then move to the third and so on (see Table 17.1).

Table 17.1

Mic Setup	How to Do It	You Need	Movies It's Good For
Method 1: **Overhead boom mic**	Hold an extended boom mic over the action. Works every time for natural and authentic sound. Keep it out of camera frame.	Unidirectional boom mic	Most narrative movies; documentary
Method 2: **Boom from below**	Maybe the camera is looking up at the actors so you can't avoid getting the mic in shot. Try switching it to below the actors. You might even prefer this rather than use the first method – the sound can be quite resonant.	Unidirectional boom mic	Most narrative movies, news, documentary
Method 3: **Boom mic planted**	This means having the boom mic fixed somewhere close to the actors. You might have a big wide shot and can't avoid getting the sound crew in shot. Place the boom discretely so it can pick up what you want.	Unidirectional boom mic	Most narrative movies, particularly good for location work
Method 4: **Lavalier mic on actor**	You might not be able to record clearly because there's too much noise around you – in a football game, or in a crowded bar, in which case you need a lavalier or tie-clip mic. It's got a small range, less than the length of your arm. Clip it to an actor, near the heart, fixed to clothing. Watch out for manmade fabrics as these can create a static sound. Lavalier mics sound like you are in a studio – clear but maybe too clear and sterile, so make sure you pile on layers of ambient sound in the background later. You can plug in two Lavalier mics for dialogue. Again, use a splitter to connect them to the cam.	Lavalier mic	News, documentary, and most other movies if you don't mind the clear but boring sound
Method 5: **Planted lavalier mic**	You can plant any mic on set to pick up one particular sound. You don't even need to connect it to the camcorder. It could be a one-off sound or piece of dialogue and could be recorded straight to any digital recorder.	Lavalier mic	Ideal for any movie where you need to conceal a mic from the camera, but a regular mic is too big
Method 6: **Radio mic**	If cables are a problem and you need to hear what actors are saying on the move, you might need radio mics. It can be tough getting clear sound free from interference but the benefits are huge.	Radio mic	Distant scenes, big wide shots, location work

FIGURE 17.3 Radio mics allow your actors to move about more freely.

ON LOCATION

- **Each place you shoot in sounds different, because of the surfaces and size of the location.** Sound waves are like balls that bounce around a room – the harder the surface, the more they keep bouncing; the softer, the more they get absorbed and die down. The hard tiles of a bathroom will let sounds bounce around, while the soft fabrics of a bedroom will absorb them. The larger a space is with hard edges, the more you create an echo.

- **Get practiced in listening to the acoustics of your location** – use good headphones to hear the quality of the sound and judge whether the acoustics of the place are a problem or not.

- You need a natural, realistic effect to your sound so **don't remove all traces of the acoustics in your location,** but on the other hand you need to keep them in check so that main sounds – actors talking, for example – are clear and up front.

FIGURE 17.4 Using headphones while you shoot means you know the quality of the sound, and whether there is any interference affecting the mics. (Photo courtesy of iStockphoto, ©helenecanada, Image# 6234702)

EVEN BETTER AUDIO RECORDING

If you want to go one stage further, opt for an XLR mixer. This is a neat box that fits under the camcorder and into which you can plug two mics or more. It's small, tucked out of the way and ideal for documentary makers who don't want to mess around with loads of cables and don't want the extra crew that a much larger separate mixer would need. Try BeachTek for good mixers.

The XLR mixer is a small box that plugs into your camera and allows you to **blend the sounds from each mic as you record** and boost the gain (the volume) on any. If your camera doesn't have the right input for an external mixer, try the Beach Box (about $200), using a simple line-in plug to connect it to the camcorder.

If you use a mixer, you can try a tip for getting even more professional sound by **recording with two mics at the same time:** use channel 1 to record ambient sounds or "presence" using an omnidirectional mic; and use a regular unidirectional or lavalier or whatever you need to record the crucial sounds like voices or action. The total sound will feel more believable when edited.

If you can't get a mixer, check whether you have two audio inputs on your camera. Or, an even cheaper option, record the main action on the camcorder and the simultaneous background ambience on an MP3 player/recorder.

THE SOUND ENVIRONMENT

Your brain sorts out the sounds around you to help figure out what to pay attention to; you home in on the voice in front of you and ignore the sound of nearby traffic. This jumble of noises is the "sound environment." **You can create your own sound environment made up of sounds which are not actually present on location.** It's a great way to add atmosphere to your movie, and you can make the movie feel bigger – having bigger production values than you can afford. Many movies add layers of sound to add denser texture to a scene. Try it out – record some extra sounds from other places and store these ready for when you edit later. Why not add some city street sounds to make your small town scene seem like it's in a gritty, urban setting?

RECORD LAYERS OF SOUND

1. **Use directional or cardioid mics.**
2. **Focus in on just the single sound effect** you need.
3. If you are gathering **background sounds, use an omnidirectional mic,** or the on board one on your camcorder.
4. Use a **lavalier mic for clear sound effects** where you need a hyper-real feel to it.
5. Where possible, **create the sound effect in the actual place you shot.** The acoustics will fit perfectly, especially if you use a boom mic to record it.

Record onto any digital device, but it's nice and easy to record straight to the camcorder. Write a description of the sound you are recording on a piece of paper and point the camcorder at it as it records the sound – this will help when you come to look for these sounds when you edit.

ESSENTIAL KIT OR RESOURCES

Low budget kit:

- Lavalier mic. Stretch your budget to two of these if you can, preferably Sennheisers.
- You'll also need a mic splitter to plug two into one socket on your cam.
- Boom mic. To improvise try using a unidirectional mic fixed to a boom pole.
- Ear-covered headphones. Try AKG or Sony for 'phones.
- An XLR mixer if you can.

Zero budget kit:

- A hand-held unidirectional mic; improvise with a pole to create a boom.

TRY IT OUT

Make an audio mash-up.

A mash-up is where you grab images and freely stitch them together in a way that just looks good and feels good. It's half-coordinated and half thrown together intuitively. It makes sense listened to later, but probably not when you make it.

You need:

Unidirectional mic

Lavalier mic

MP3/4 recorder/player or a camcorder

Step-by-step:

Go out and look for sounds that are diverse enough to stand out from each other: voices, cars, birds, sirens, crowds.

Try to get a range of sounds in your recording, from high-pitched sounds at the top to bass sounds below. Record 15 seconds of each one.

Next gather some found sounds. Use TV news, or phrases you have found elsewhere, on TV shows or films.

Next, find a sound that can go under everything, like a conversation, or a busy street, or a video game.

Go home. Load everything onto your PC. Arrange it all just as you would as a movie edit, with each sound placed ready to use. Edit them together – using layers of audio tracks. Make it two minutes long.

Experts' Tips

Ben Winter, film student, USA

"Don't spend any money on extra audio equipment. Audio hit its technological peak long ago; microphones made twenty years ago sound as good as microphones made today, so if you buy nice equipment now, chances are you'll be using it well into your filmmaking career. The quality of your picture is nugatory compared to the sound. If the audio is ruined during a take, redo it, no matter how good the take was otherwise. It will be difficult and more cumbersome than you'd like, but this is a sacrifice a filmmaker must make."

Chapter Eighteen

Health and Safety

OVERVIEW

Don't get sued. In the UK alone there are over 150 serious injuries on movie sets each year. The buck stops with you so make a safe and happy set.

ONE-STOP PLAN TO MAKE A SAFE SET

- Choose **one person who is in charge** of worrying about health and safety. Most often the producer is in charge of it.
- You, or the person whose job it is, must **figure out all the potential risks** to crew and cast, and passers-by, on your production.
- **Communication is the key** to good risk avoidance. Talk to people, send emails, provide lists – all helping to avoid risks.
- When you have figured out what risks there are on set, **rate them** according to how bad they could be, and then what you can do to lower this risk.
- Use all equipment and props according to the **manufacturers' instructions.**
- The overall key to being good at health and safety is **knowing how to spot hazards.** What seems like just a small problem for one person might be a huge hazard for another person.

FIGURE 18.1 Make sure one person on your movie is in charge of safety. Cables need to be wrapped and made safe to avoid tripping up the crew. (Photo courtesy of iStockphoto, ©bjones27, Image# 6092023)

DRAW UP A RISK ASSESSMENT SHEET FOR EACH LOCATION OR STUDIO

Include in this sheet:
- Risks from your equipment
- Risks from the place where you are filming
- Risks from people or animals
- Risks after production (editing, etc.)

How to do a risk assessment:
1. Look for hazards.
2. Decide who this might harm.
3. Figure out how bad this would be if it happened.
4. Write down what you have found, and tell those people it affects.
5. Take action to avoid this hazard.

Table 18.1 Example risk assessment sheet

Hazard Source	Who it Affects	What Could Happen	Chance of Injury	Severity of Injury	Risk	Action Taken
Loose cables	Floor crew, cast	Tripping, leading to injury	High	Moderate: bruises, cuts	Moderate	Use duct tape to restrain cables.
Lamps	Cast	Lamps unsteady on tripods, falling onto cast	Moderate	High: burns	High	Use lamps only at recommended tripod height. Restrain tripods with fire resistant cord if necessary.

FIGURE 18.2 In any location filming, hazards need to be identified, as in this production shot from *The West Side* web series. Working on the roof of a building is just one of several potential hazards in this action scene.

MOST COMMON RISKS

- **Lamps** falling over due to unsteady tripods; lamp cables overloading the electrical supply, lamp bulbs exploding.
- **Cables** as tripping hazards.

- Working **long hours** leads to accidents not normally seen as hazards. Legally, keep to no more than a 12-hour day at maximum.
- **Noise:** If there is continuous noise over 85 dB, you must have ear defenders.
- **Lifting** and moving: crew moving heavy items without bending properly, causing back injury.
- **Editing:** fatigue and stress – you need a five-minute break every half hour. Try placing screens at different distances so that your eyes need to refocus. Stretch and move around.
- **Poor weather:** watch out for rainwater or dust affecting equipment and people.

LIGHTING SAFETY

- **Don't overload your home supply.** A couple of 300 W lamps may cause problems, if you add in the other stuff you have got in the house already.
- **Wait for lamps to cool** for a few minutes before packing away or moving.
- Cables trip people up – use duct tape at all times to keep the cables out of the way.
- **Lamps on tall tripods topple easily** – make sure no one knocks into them.
- **Lamps are hot up close** – don't burn your actors or crew.

Section Three: Cut

CUT AND SHARE YOUR MOVIE

This section guides you through the final stage of making your movie as you cut it into shape. Start by setting up your home studio, then playing around with different ways to edit, and then move on to perfect your soundtrack.

Chapter 19: **Your Home Editing Studio.** This chapter takes you through the basics you need to start editing at home, from RAM to capturing the audio playback.

Chapter 20: **Pre-edit Footage Viewing.** If you've just shot your movie, this chapter tells you what to do next – sit down, take your time and plan the edit.

Chapter 21: **Editing Methods: Narrative Continuity.** Next, two chapters to help cut the movie in the way that suits you. This chapter shows you how to cut a narrative movie, for action, drama or documentary.

Chapter 22: **Editing Methods: Montage.** This chapter guides you through editing movies without stories, like music promos, or when you just need something a little different in your movie.

Chapter 23: **Audio Editing.** This chapter takes you through the ways to get the audio mix right. Find out how to layer sounds to create a bigger world than the one you actually shot, and why color is just like sound.

Chapter 24: **Foley.** If you made a narrative movie, stop here and pick up some tips on amping up your soundtrack with added real sounds.

Chapter 25: **Screening for Feedback.** OK, it's in the bag – isn't it? Sort of. Find out how to roll out a Beta version of your movie for people to take a look at before you unveil it for real to the world.

Chapter Nineteen

Your Home Editing Studio

OVERVIEW

For less than the cost of a secondhand car, you could build an industry-standard edit studio.

Your home edit setup is like a painter's studio – it's where the real work takes place. After everyone else has gone home, you are left to come to grips with the real art and craft of editing your movie.

Your ideal edit suite is in a small, airy room, with a large desk to hold two monitors, a large stack PC or Mac tower below, and good-quality speakers to allow for excellent audio playback. You'll have a soft chair, designed for long sessions of late-night editing. An angle-poise lamp will illuminate your keyboard, and a softer one lights the wall behind the monitors to offset eye strain from looking at a bright monitor against a dark wall.

It's organized, with drawers for scripts and old tapes and racks for CDs and DVDs. The room has good acoustics, which means that the sounds from your movie don't echo and bounce around the room, distorting what you hear. You achieved that through carpeting the floor and using drapes on the windows.

WHICH SOFTWARE?

Oscar-winning editor Walter Murch (*Apocalypse Now*) is a big fan of Apple's Final Cut Pro and has helped make Hollywood feel safe with it. In the indie sector many feature films are now edited on FCP. UK director Robin King, of Standalone Films, wouldn't use anything else. "I love it – it feels really intuitive and it's easy to work in a way that allows for backtracking, should you change your mind. For me it's fun too. Final Cut Pro is a professional tool and one could quite easily edit a feature film with it."

Table 19.1

What You Need	The Lowdown
Computer	When it comes to your PC, a tower is essential rather than a laptop. But if you have just invested in a new laptop and want to stick with it, simply add on external hard drives. Macs are the preferred system for many video makers. An Intel dual-core tower will give you an advantage over other systems, and Final Cut Pro is itself reason enough to invest in a Mac. System stability tends to be excellent and since there are so few viruses for Macs you certainly sleep better at night knowing that you are unlikely to lose everything suddenly through outside attack. Even the basic MacBook provides a solid and reliable way to edit video, if used with an external hard drive.
RAM	In either external or internal drives, aim for ones with at least 7200 revs. Aim for the biggest your expansion slots will allow, at least 2 GB.
Monitors	Beyond needing extra space to park all that HDV footage, you'll need a pair of monitors that let you see the quality. Flat-panel monitors with native high resolution that don't simply scale up the images are not cheap, but are worth the cash. Why two monitors? It frees up a lot of space by placing editing windows on separate screens. You get a larger playback screen, and can expand the timeline a lot more to see more detail. You can also have a bigger range of tools on view, such as effects, transitions and color.
Audio playback	Speakers in your computer are not up to the job when it comes to editing sound. The easiest solution is to plug in a small, cheap 3.5 mm converter which lets you connect phono cables between it and the input sockets on a separate amp, the one you use to play your CDs. You can then hear your PC on your main amp speakers. Place these a few yards apart, on either side of your monitors.

Figure 19.1 Final Cut Pro is a hugely popular edit program from Apple. Many editors believe it offers the best solution for video editing.

Chapter Twenty

Pre-edit Footage Viewing

> **OVERVIEW**
>
> You thought of it, you shot it, now it's time to find out what your footage really looks like.

Right now you will have:

- A few tapes with your movie on them, all scenes probably in the wrong order, or
- A number of flash drives (external), or
- SD cards or a large external drive with everything on it, or
- DVD discs containing footage

So you need to:

- Figure out where in all this footage is the really good stuff you want in your movie
- Whether each good clip you choose has any problems like bad sound
- How to find these good clips easily

You will likely have **up to 20 times the footage you need,** so a five-minute short might generate a couple of SD cards or tapes. You might have shot scenes lots of times, trying to get the right take. Or someone messed up so you had to do it again, or a car went past and messed the sound.

SECOND OPINION

What if you just start editing and skip this job?

That's fine, it won't affect your movie, but editing will probably take three or four times as long, and be a lot more frustrating.

STEP 1

QUICK VIEW TAPES/CARDS

Sit down and scan through the footage to see how it looks overall. You need an overview to check whether a big problem has come up – like your continuity is thrown because a whole scene has been shot in the wrong color temperature (see "white balance" tips in Chapter 12, Using a Camcorder).

HAVE YOU GOT TIMECODE?

If you don't know what timecode is, that's fine – it won't affect your movie, it just makes this whole step much easier. Timecode is that 8-digit number that whizzes by on the LCD monitor as you record – like 01:28:53:12. The first two digits are hours, followed by minutes, seconds and frames, which is why these last two only go up to 24 or 29, depending on the system you use: PAL or NTSC (note that your LCD camera display actually says it's one less than the total frames per second, because it includes the zero).

If you do have timecode on your footage, use it to note the start and end of each good clip you want to use.

STEP 2: LOG FOOTAGE

You can do this step either of two ways: either **write down and log every single clip** in the order they occur on your tapes/cards/drives, so you have a long list of every moment of the tape, good bits and bad. Or you can **just note the good parts only**. Best to do the first option if you think you might need to go back and get extra clips later. Either way, you need to use timecode to note where to find the clips.

STEP 3

Now you have a working list of the useable clips, you can **reorder them so they are in the order you want them to be in the movie.** You now have an edit decision list (EDL). An EDL is useful because you can just go ahead and grab all the clips listed on it, and place them on the timeline and that's your movie edited. Of course, it always changes a lot as you edit, so expect to mess around with this edit long after it's on the timeline.

ADDING CLIPS TO YOUR PC

You next need to **transfer the clips you want to your PC**, so you can edit them. Use an external hard drive if you have one to store the footage separately, connecting it to your PC. If you are capturing from tape, connect your camcorder and only take what you need to use, leaving the leftovers on tape to get later if you really need extras. Arrange them in the order you decided on in the EDL.

STEP 4: SAVING AND STORING

It helps to be tidy and organized with all your clips. Create a folder with all the clips in, and subfolders with different scenes in each.

Experts' Tips

Benjamin Rutkowski, film student, USA

"If your first dailies don't look so hot, do not give up. Learn from your mistakes and *a lot* can be done in the editing process."

Chapter | Twenty-One

Editing Methods: Narrative Continuity

Use this style for: Any narrative movie.

OVERVIEW

It's the silent and invisible form of editing – the way we edit to create a flowing story. It's not arty or tricksy, just gets the story going fast.

This chapter goes well with Chapter 14, Continuity – use it to help get more ideas for making a smooth narrative.

This style is called **continuity editing** and is pretty much the only way Hollywood and mainstream movies like to edit. It is designed purely to help the story move along, but also to get the audience quickly rooting for the characters and feeling what they feel, but without doing anything too weird. There are a lot of rules that have built up over the decades, and while it doesn't fit everyone, it is the most acceptable way to edit stories.

Table 21.1 What does continuity editing do?

Clarity	Everyone can see easily what's supposed to be happening. Don't confuse us. Give us the action, let us hear the talking, show us where we are, what time it is, whether it's the past or the future and so on.
Moves the action along	That doesn't just mean high action like car chases, but any part of the story at all. It has to keep moving forward, with few detours or diversions.

Continued...

Table 21.1 What does continuity editing do? (Continued)

Doesn't let viewers see the editing and 'suspends disbelief'	Editing in this style is like a magic show – we get swept along and no one wants to see behind the scenes or get reminded it's just all make-believe. So don't do strange, gimmicky editing where you show off all your box of tricks. We don't even want to know an editor got near the movie – in fact we don't even want to be reminded it's just a movie.
Helps you identify with the characters	We need to see what they see, hear what they hear, feel what they feel – and that means using neat editing to keep us pegged next to the characters all the time so the story is from their point of view all the time.
Creates intensity	Now and then you have to stray from this straight-down-the-line editing and know when to bring in the cavalry – to create real excitement and suspense. You'll need a few other ways to edit, stealing a few ideas from montage editing (see Ch 22, Editing Methods: Montage) but knowing when to rein it in too.
. . .And this is what you do to get it:	
Rhythm	In editing, rhythm is about how fast each shot occurs. For instance, in an action scene you might have shot lengths of two seconds or less, making a quick, intense, and exciting sequence. But then you need to slow things down later, so you have longer shots of six or seven seconds each. It's just like music, where you have quiet verses and louder choruses. If you are aware of rhythm you can use it to crank up the excitement and then calm it down again. To do this, check out the timeline on your edit program. You can see how small the clips get when there's big action, and how long they get when it's calm again. Use this as a guide to help you see a rhythm evolve in the movie
Pace	Pace keeps a check on the overall rhythm of the movie. You can pace the movie so that it gets steadily more exciting, or tense, or happy or whatever it needs to build to a finale. Often the first parts of the film are slower than the last, you get a middle where we take a breather, and then you can plot where the fastest or most intense part of the film is. Or try more unusual structures – see Ch 3, Scriptwriting.
Same style all the time	However you came up with the style of the movie – it could have been through doing designs or you might have just stumbled across it while shooting – you need to stick to it. It needs to look like the work of one person, not as if it was passed around for different people to make different bits. To keep it consistent, use one way to edit throughout, keeping shot lengths similar depending on what the script needs. And don't pull new surprises halfway through the movie, like trying a new experimental way to edit.

Continued...

Table 21.1 What does continuity editing do? (Continued)

Control of time	You need to be able to show how much time is passing, either during a scene or between scenes. For a long passage of time, use slow dissolve transitions to black, dissolving from black again at the start of a new scene. Within a scene, several lengthy and wide camera shots will suggest that time is stretching a little, and you can use quick dissolves to push it further, for instance during an interrogation scene in a police cell, where you might want to suggest it is taking place over a few hours.
Eyeline match	This puts us in the point of view of a character. For instance, we see a person stop in a street and they notice something in a window. We then need to cut to a shot of what they see, as if the camera were their eyes.
Shot reverse shot	Usually used when two people are talking, you'll show each face in the frame, but with part of the back of the head and shoulder of the other person also in shot, so we know who exactly they are talking to. When you get to edit you just need to cut these two together – called "shot and reverse shots". You could also use cutaways to break up the monotony of this, like cutting to the person's hands as they talk, or to a clock on the wall.
Establishing shot	You can open a scene with a big wide shot showing the whole room, or location. This gives the audience all the information they need – who's there, where they are and whether it is day or night. It sets the scene, or "establishes" it.
Cut in and cut away	In a short sequence, you can open with an establishing wide shot, then move in with a few close-ups of the action, then back out again with a similar wide shot, this time showing the action moving on, such as the car driving away, and fading to black again. This can create a rhythmic kind of sequence.
Common space	You took the time to shoot an establishing shot, so now you need to remind us now and then that we are still in the same place. To do this, include cuts where you showed the same objects repeatedly, or the same background.
Object matching/ graphic match	This is a neat way to cut between two scenes – simply use shots that look visually similar, like cutting from a shot showing an eye in close-up to a shot of a round plug hole as water washes down it – as in Hitchcock's *Psycho*.
Cut on action	Try to start and end shots with movement. If there's action, start the shot a split second into the action so it is already happening.

Continued...

Table 21.1 What does continuity editing do? (Continued)

Sounds to amplify action	Use sound layers to increase the sensation of what is happening. Don't rely on the sounds you got while shooting – they just won't seem real enough. In continuity editing you need sounds to be hyper-real. A car door goes clunk loud and clear, a fist makes a big thump and a footstep is a solid crunch. Go to Ch 23, Audio Editing, or Ch 24, Foley.
Use of camera angles	Continuity editing uses camera angles in quite a predictable way – and that's the way we like it as an audience. You need to work this into the way you shoot the movie, but providing you have the right shots, make sure you know how to use them. A wide shot opens the action, a medium shot brings us in a little, and a close-up is for emotional, high drama moments. You know a lot about these shots because this vocabulary of movie language is something you've absorbed over years of viewing.
30-degree rule	Check out Ch 14, Continuity to find out about this and other rules. Make sure you don't edit together two shots that are closer than 30 degrees to each other against the center of action.
Transitions/wipes	Use them to help move the action on, or to slow it down. Apart from the straight cut between shots, use cross dissolves. Use other transitions only if you have a really good reason to do otherwise. Fade to black is OK, but reserve fade to white for flashbacks or dream sequences.
Cross cutting/ parallel editing	This is where you cut between two areas of action to show simultaneous events. It's a good device to speed up the plot and build up a sense of drama or excitement. Don't use dissolves or we'll think there is a period of time separating the two scenes; instead use straight cuts to get between the two.

CLOSE-UPS, WIDE SHOTS AND HOW LONG THEY NEED TO BE

Each genre has its own approach to how long shots should be and what sort of camera shots they use. There's always a link between the two – **the more tense and dramatic the movie, the more close-ups and the fewer wide shots there will be.**

Take a look at how long shots in the movies tend to be, and how the length of the cut is connected to whether it's a close-up or a wide shot.

Silence of the Lambs (horror/thriller/action) has 330 close-ups or extreme close-ups (ECUs), and only 43 wide shots, while the average shot length is 6.4 seconds.

Martin Scorcese's *Raging Bull* has an average shot length of 6.9 seconds, hyping up to a fast-paced 3.2 seconds for one of the big fight sequences.

In Michael Mann's tense *The Insider*, with Russell Crowe as a paranoid tobacco industry whistleblower, each shot lasts just 5.4 seconds with 301 close-ups against just 32 wide shots – barely enough wide shots to open each new scene with.

TV dramas and soap operas are the same. An episode of the Australian soap *Neighbours* had 363 close-ups against just 15 wide shots, with an average shot length of 5.7 seconds – just right for a dramatic and emotional show.

More stylized movies get even faster shots, as in Alex Proyas' gothic thriller *Dark City* (1999) where the average shot length is just 2 seconds.

Meanwhile, comedy or dialogue-heavy movies need longer shots, such as Oscar-winning comedy *Annie Hall* at an average length of 14 seconds, and the talkative *Chinatown* (which won an Oscar for its script) of 16 seconds.

Thanks to the hard work of Barry Salt, David Bordwell and others for compiling this data. Get more information from www.cinemetrics.lv/database.php.

SERGIO LEONE AND HOW TO CUT FOR ACTION AND SUSPENSE

Take a few tips from the master of the steady build-up, Sergio Leone. In his finale to *The Good, the Bad and the Ugly*, a three-way shoot-out takes over nine minutes for the shooters to set up, pace around and fire. Dissecting the scene reveals how Leone gradually draws us in to the ensuing fight.

- **First, we see the three characters:** Clint Eastwood, Lee Van Cleef and Eli Wallach. Eastwood's Blondie strides into the middle of the frame where he remains commanding the screen.
- The three **slowly take up their positions** equidistant from each other in the empty yard. The camera lingers as they move, resisting the urge to cut.
- We then **cut slowly between the three enemies,** first in medium shots, then wide shots of the whole scene with all three at the edges of the frame.
- Leone revs the engine next as we start the **steady build-up to the shoot-out.** With steady timing, he takes seven seconds for each character, then six seconds each, then four. He ups the odds against Eli Wallach by focusing more on the two faster gunslingers, drawing out for a medium shot of a nervous Wallach.
- Then we **draw out for a long, wide shot lasting over 30 seconds** while we hold our breath. The stage is set and then the editor gets to work.
- We close in for **a series of fixed, five-second shots of each man**, the rhythm building with the soundtrack. Then comes the extreme close-ups, with added sweat, one after the other. The sound of the musical watch offers a brief respite.

- With the faces filling the frame, now we move **from two-second shots of each, to one-second, then – like a countdown – to 12 frames,** before the shooting starts. Van Cleef falls, and Eastwood shoots the dead man's hat and gun into the ready-made grave after the body.

DON'T KNOW WHERE TO START? TIPS TO KICK OFF

- Try editing a big, **important sequence first.** You don't have to start at the beginning.
- **Listen to music that matches the mood** of the film while you edit. It can set the rhythm and pace for you.
- **Edit standing up,** to speed up the process. It's also better for your back.
- **Edit from the middle outwards.** Start from the center of the movie and then do the start, then the bits either side of the center, then the end. It doesn't work for everyone but can make you move faster and make better decisions.
- On the timeline, **work on several sequences at the same time,** separated onto different video tracks. You can move between them and edit across all of them, encouraging you to keep the same style throughout.
- Try working in a highly organic way if you are making a travel movie, freecording or any other kind of nonstory movie. That means **grabbing clips onto the timeline in a free and loose way,** just seeing how they look together. Don't plan on paper at all, just work on your gut instinct as you get shots and arrange them on the timeline.
- Aim to edit in two hours to create a five-minute rough cut.

Chapter | Twenty-Two

Editing Methods: Montage

Use this style for: Any movie without a regular story.

OVERVIEW

Call in the cavalry. Sometimes regular editing just won't cut it, especially when your movie is a little unusual or if it's a sports movie, music promo, or travel movie. When you need to go that extra mile to create a sequence that really affects people, you need montage.

As soon as you start editing a movie such as a music promo or a road trip, you soon realize that you don't want a story and you don't need one. The movie is enough by itself – the images, the way the visuals unfold. It's a whole different animal. So another method is needed, one where you hook up to a very different way of doing things. Montage editing is kind of "Zen and the Art of Editing," a slightly mystical experience. One of the masters of montage, Nic Roeg (of spooky horror film *Don't Look Now* with the famous opening montage) once said that to edit you have to tap into "unseen forces." This is like editing with the brakes off, the gloves off, and definitely no prisoners taken. It's a full-on head-rush, aimed at drawing the viewer right into the world you are creating. They no longer just watch the movie, they go through it.

Montage editing is different from continuity editing in that it doesn't matter if we see the editing at work. In continuity editing, the aim is to hide the fact that it's been edited at all – don't remind people it's just a movie. But montage doesn't care about that. It's too busy messing with your mind, and you are too busy trying to keep up with the pace to care.

Montage gets you right under the skin of the movie. It speaks to a different part of your mind than regular editing, just like **reading a sentence** and **looking at a picture** seem to need different parts of your mind.

ONE AND ONE MAKES THREE

One of the most basic ideas in montage editing is that you put one image side by side with another image and create a third idea out of them both. How does it work? It uses the human brain to do the hard work, because when we see two unexplained things we immediately try to imagine what happened in between or what happened next. We join the dots to make an idea.

In the following sequence of three images, the first two are on screen, but the last one is what we have figured out in our minds. If we get a picture of a **house on fire,** then we cut to a picture of a **man walking down a railroad track,** we can't help it, we just rush in and imagine he has something to do with that fire. Nothing in the clip links them in any way; we just make the connection for ourselves.

Figure 22.1 (Photo courtesy of iStockphoto, ©sunara, Image# 4677386)

+

Figure 22.2 (Photo courtesy of iStockphoto, ©ilmwa555, Image# 8894785)

Added together, what do these make you think of?

Figure 22.3 (Photo courtesy of iStockphoto, ©Tpopova, Image# 5986374)

Or try a more sophisticated one:

Figure 22.4 (Photo courtesy of iStockphoto, ©sebastian-julian, Image# 9833396)

Figure 22.5 (Photo courtesy of iStockphoto, ©W1zzard, Image# 4057917)

Added together, what do these make you think of?

Figure 22.6 (Photo courtesy of iStockphoto, ©Claudiad, Image# 6569069)

In this sequence we see a few seconds of a **rollercoaster at full speed,** then cut to a woman **sitting on the edge of a building, looking like she's going to jump**. There's no connection between the two but your brain joins them up and we think she feels like she is on an **emotional rollercoaster**, maybe life has been rough for her, or getting out of control. Cut back and forth between these two even faster and the effect is made even stronger.

Montage works by giving us lots of these disjointed images and firing them at us too quickly for us to process. All the images fall over each other, creating new ideas all the time. Try it out – put a few clips together that seem totally random and watch them back. Add some music to really lose yourself in the process.

STEP BY STEP: USING MONTAGE

The way you tell it is the message. Montage is so interesting because **it's the editing style itself that is telling a lot of the meaning of the movie**, as much as the actual stuff you shot. It's what music has been doing for decades, since sampling and hip-hop kicked off. In old-school sampled hip-hop

(Grandmaster Flash, et al.) it was the way you assembled sounds together, **the way they collide and join up,** that makes it fun. The lyrics weren't always too important.

And another thing that makes hip-hop so similar to montage is **the way it uses these collisions.** You get completely unlikely sounds and put them together – like a clip from a 1950s air raid information film, over the theme from *Sesame Street*, followed by a line from a Malcolm X speech. That's sampling – playfully roaming freely across the world of culture and history, and always unexpected. With this kind of music and this style of movie editing **it's the way you say it that is important, not always what you say.**

ADDING, NOT TAKING AWAY

A lot of people say that continuity editing is about taking shots away, while montage is about adding shots in. There's some truth in this simple idea – we sometimes call montage **additive** editing, while continuity editing might be called **reductive** editing. When creating montage, always go for adding shots in rather than taking them out. You might need to make each shot shorter and faster, but that helps to disorientate the viewer.

DISORIENTATE

The aim of montage editing is the opposite of continuity. Now you need to try everything you can to **throw us off balance, to disorientate us and unsettle us.** We get confused and disturbed. Weirdly, this doesn't mean we disconnect from the movie; instead we get more involved, like a puzzle you can't figure out, like Alice following the rabbit down the hole. You keep watching and following the movie because you need to make it add up somehow. The more opposite the images that clash against each other, the more disorientated we'll be.

DREAMS

In dreams we tend to see a **mix of our authentic, real lives with small but crucial bits of weirdness.** It gives this weirdness a context and makes it stand out. If your dreams were movies, they'd seem to have no rhythm (see Chapter 14, Continuity), and they change suddenly without warning. People change places, change shape, outfits, expressions. The weather alters like you flicked a switch; time speeds up and slows down. In fact, just about everything that we do in continuity editing is turned on its head.

USE SYMBOLS

Symbols are a neat way to get across ideas without having to shout them out. Lay the clips on the timeline on your editing app and scan through them to **look for connections or threads, such as objects, colors or shapes,** anything that can link together two shots. Look for any shot that reminds you of another shot, and start pairing them up. Try Nic Roeg's opening montage from *Don't Look Now* for an example of this – two places become linked by the connections in what happens in the countdown to a girl's death.

LOSE CONTROL

Editing in the Hollywood continuity style means being totally in control all the time. Nothing should creep in that could derail the straight path of the freight train that is the plot. Not so in montage. **Montage asks that you lose control and trust your instincts;** you don't need to know why you like a certain shot and you don't need to explain it. You like it and it feels right, so move on.

MIX CLOSE-UPS AND DEEP SHOTS

Montage works by keeping you guessing, by throwing you off-balance because you just don't know what is coming next. But you don't always need to place two totally random clips side by side. Terry Gilliam creates a similar effect in the viewer's mind by **putting shots that constantly alter depth on screen.** You've got a dramatic close-up and then a long, wide shot, then both together as a part of the image enters the frame close by. Surrealist painters like Dali used this to confuse height and depth and produce a kind of **horizontal vertigo.**

USE COLOR AND TONE

The only problem with montage is that it can get a little out of hand, sometimes too crazy. So **rein it in with a use of color** (or black and white) which stays the same throughout the whole sequence. If your sequence looks too diverse, give it a color that carries through every clip. Or try increasing or decreasing color saturation by a small amount (maybe 15%), or boost contrast dramatically so every clip looks similar. Try other tips from Chapter 14, Continuity.

USE MUSIC

Use music to enhance the montage. If two images can collide with each other to create other ideas, then music can add to the battle even further. Music that seems out of place, or contradicts what we see, can be really effective. Even regular continuity editing benefits from this now and then.

FINALLY, TWO OTHER TYPES OF MONTAGE USEFUL FOR MOVIES WHICH USE CONTINUITY EDITING:
Parallel montage is when you cut quickly between two separate locations, to show simultaneous events going on. They can be related or unrelated – either way we'll make connections and get some interesting ideas out of it.

Accelerated montage is where you use faster and faster cuts to create a turbulent stream of images that the viewer just can't process fast enough to keep up. The result is a big disorientating overload, but if the images relate somehow it should add up to an overwhelming theme or feeling. Cuts should be shorter than two frames, preferably ten frames long.

Chapter | Twenty-Three

Audio Editing

OVERVIEW

More than half of what we get from a movie is from the soundtrack. Make it work harder for you.

If you've got:

Footage with voices, sound effects, background sounds, music, or any other sounds.

Then you need to:

Organize these sounds into a coherent shape on the edit timeline. It'll sound huge.

DESIGN YOUR SOUNDTRACK

Walter Murch is the guy who invented sound design, and he talks about sound like it's light and color. You get hot colors and cold colors, so you get hot and cold sounds.

Murch divided sounds up like a **color spectrum,** from violet to red, placing warmer sounds (like a feline purr, or wind in the trees) in the red zone, and cooler sounds (like speech or machines) in the violet. We react to these sounds just like we do with colors – we like warm ones and dislike cold.

And it's not just the sounds themselves that feel "warm," but they actually hit us immediately and emotionally, like music. On the other hand, sounds that are cooler need to be understood with your head rather than your heart, like language so they don't have such an immediate impact on us.

Within this spectrum there are subtle shades of each, with Arnie's *Terminator* talking with an ice-cold rattle against Sean Connery's warmer tones.

While working on films such as *Apocalypse Now!* and *The Godfather II*, Murch thought up this way of designing the soundtrack for a movie, and got the first of three Oscars for sound design. He found that **if you spread out different sounds across this spectrum, the human ear could tolerate more** than it could when they were piled in one corner of it, which means you create a more dense and exciting soundtrack, and yet it is still crystal clear to the ear. (Find out more at www.filmsound.org/murch.)

How much sound can you put in one area of this spectrum? As a starting point, **use two to three layers if they are grouped in just one area of the spectrum**. If spread across the whole spectrum, use up to five. Murch puts the brakes on more than five as there is a limit to what we can actually understand over this amount. Using this spectrum, you can create a sound environment that uses a spread of sounds from warm to cold.

WHAT'S YOUR SOUNDSCAPE?

Using the ideas above by Murch, **take a moment to think about the overall soundscape of the movie.** Think beyond what is actually on screen – instead try to imagine the total landscape surrounding the scene. Write down the ideas you have and then start to arrange these in a 3D order. What is close by, what is further away, what sounds pass by from loud to quiet? Imagine the scene as a vast IMAX arena with a soundscape that envelopes the viewer.

AUDIO POST-PRODUCTION: STEP BY STEP

To get to this point you will have edited the movie but it has not been mixed yet. That means the sounds are just as you left them, attached to each video clip on the timeline.

1. First, **make sure you have "spotted" the film** thoroughly, going through it up close and noting where you need effects, music, or Foley. You then work through this list, recording extra effects if you missed any. But ideally you got everything you needed while shooting.

2. Next, **start working on scenes,** but don't necessarily start at the opening credits. Sometimes it is better to identify the most central scene in terms of importance to the film, so work on this one first and let the results determine how every scene before and after it is created. Think of it like laying out the furniture in a room; you start by placing in the set-piece items and work outwards from these.

3. Once you have earmarked a scene, **start to block in the layers of sound** on the edit timeline according to two factors: how clear the sound needs to be for the necessary information in the scene – such as actors talking or critical sound effects – and how important the sound is in terms of

creating atmosphere. It's useful to figure out **the difference between a layer and a one-off effect.** A layer is usually a linked series of sounds, similar in tone and volume, which run more or less continuously. A background street sound, of traffic and crowds, is a layer, but an individual police siren would be a sound effect. You could keep one audio track on the timeline just for one-off effects.

4. **But look out for logjam,** where the sheer number of layers you are having to juggle threatens to overwhelm you. Keep in mind the order in which sounds need to appear on the timeline.

FIGURE 23.1 Most editing programs enable sound mixing using intuitive on-screen mixers, as in this one from inexpensive software Magix's Movie Edit Pro.

LAY OUT YOUR TIMELINE LIKE THIS

1. **Create six additional audio tracks** in addition to the main tracks – sometimes called the A/B tracks.
2. **Leave the linked audio from the main visuals in the A/B tracks.**
3. If you have **recorded dialogue** separately, place it on the next track down.
4. Next, **include lower-level background sounds.** Use this one for individual, one-off sounds like gunshots or doors closing. Most of this track on

the timeline will look pretty empty, but that's a good sign – it shows that you are prioritizing your soundtrack and laying these further back in the soundscape.

5. Further down, **add music,** if used. This could be a continuous track which runs throughout a scene or it could be a sudden moment used for dramatic effect. If it's the latter, you usually keep other sounds quiet, with little or no dialogue.

6. Finally, use the last track for other **ambient sound, or "presence."** This is the continuous track of sound which you would have recorded in each location after each scene. It consists of an uninterrupted clip of sound containing a more or less constant level of background sound, more like a kind of hum or murmur which is pretty much impossible to recreate but easy to get as long as you take it from real life. Simply ask your actors to take five after a scene while you record an ambient track.

To mix: Next you'll want to make some tracks louder and some quieter. To get it right without getting distortion, simply leave the volume (or gain) of the top layer untouched and decrease the ones below. Never actually raise any gain above the level it started with.

A tool that helps you create three-dimensionality in the mix is to use multichannel audio, usually at 5.1 surround sound. You can spread your separate sound layers across these speakers to reflect to the image on screen.

Straightforward stereo has its drawbacks, as it tends to work only if the viewer is placed exactly between the two speakers. Any further to one side or another and the brain hears the sounds closest to it as only coming from one speaker, distorting the sonic space – a problem known as the Haas Effect. The way to avoid this is to use foreground sounds such as speech across both left and right tracks, even though this will flatten the sonic space slightly. But if you have a center speaker then bleed both tracks into the center as a mono feed.

FREE SOFTWARE FOR AUDIO MIXING

Audacity, available from http://audacity.sourceforge.net, is a broad program that encompasses capture, editing, export and clean-up. It doesn't replace that high-end audio suite but it is quick to master and frequent updates keep you in touch with its rolling development.

Download from http://audacity.sourceforge.net.

It works on Mac, Linux and PC, and since it's open source other developers can add plug-ins and push its scope further. For now, though, it gets any discerning filmmaker off the starting blocks with mic capture of up to 16 simultaneous tracks, as well as line-in capture.

ESSENTIAL KIT OR RESOURCES

1. You need an edit software program which lets you use multiple sound layers.

2. Or you can use a dedicated sound mixing program such as Audacity.

3. It really helps if you have some quality loudspeakers hitched up to your computer. Try connecting the computer directly into your amp on your music system. Sit between the two speakers.

4. Alternatively, get hold of good-quality headphones – a better option if you need to keep your work noise to a minimum.

Health and safety tip: You may be used to louder sounds at a live concert but headphone sounds can seriously affect your hearing if you work for years in making movies. As a guide, 110 decibels (dB) is about how loud a nightclub is, and yet in filmmaking a worker is allowed to endure only 30 minutes of that level. A full working day should have a level of only 90 dB, roughly the volume of a food blender close by.

SECOND OPINION

Why so complicated? Who needs all this hassle and technical sleight-of-hand? As soon as you start messing with the audio tracks you get an artificial movie, totally different from real life. When is real life like listening through a pair of Bose earphones? No, skip this and check those at Dogme again. For them sound is served up plain and simple, without garnish or fries to go.

There's no effects, no ambient track, just whatever made it to the mic on the day they shot. If your movie has enough heart and soul, it'll sing its way to its audience whatever the levels on your timeline…

Chapter | Twenty-Four

Foley

OVERVIEW

Sound effects – or Foley – are a great way to make your movie more real, and to make up for a lack of budget.

Foley is the process of getting additional sound effects to add extra quality to images – anything from footsteps to dismembered heads.

These real-life sound effects have a huge impact on your movie. They bring it to life, just like the focus on a camera lens throws sharpness and clarity into the frame. Although most filmmakers want things to look natural in their films, to achieve this natural effect you have to use artificial means. Recording sounds as they were on location isn't quite enough to enable them to conjure up that location. They need a little help, just like a coat of varnish brings out the grain in wood.

Often you need Foley because certain sounds were not picked up well enough on location. When an actor opens a door to leave a room, for instance, it is almost impossible to get a wide shot of the actor and also pick up a close sound of the door handle being turned. And yet when we watch the movie we need to get a sound of the door up-close, to make us feel that the scene is real.

To record good Foley, the quality of your studio is crucial. You'll need a large space, big enough to make a mess with trays of gravel to walk on, for instance. Typically, Foley is best recorded at a distance of three to eight feet from the subject. Experts suggest covering the walls of a small studio with sound-absorbent material to deaden the acoustics.

RECORDING FOLEY

WHAT DO YOU RECORD ONTO?

It is easier to record straight onto video; when you view the tape later, you can visually see the Foley being created on screen so it's easy to maneuver around the footage to find the right section. Or you could record onto a digital audio recorder, a hard drive unit that records high quality audio.

MOVES TRACKS

The problem with recording sound on video is that it seems too perfect and not authentic enough to be real. Usually this is because it's the little background noises that are missing, the ones we don't really hear but which we notice if they are not there. Your first job, then, is to record the sound of clothing moving as people walk or move. Sit near your mic (use a unidirectional external mic) and simply rustle the cloth that your actors wore, while watching the playback of the movie.

WALKING TRACKS

You might often need a walking track to add some realism to a scene. Again, it's very hard to get realistic walking on set, but you might prefer to record your walking Foley just after you finish shooting the main scene, while you are still on location, as then you get a realistic sound of what that particular floor sounds like.

If you do it in a small studio, get the right floor covering and pace it three feet away or more to get the right atmosphere. Walk on the spot.

AMBIENCE

To get an authentic feel of the sound effect, double record the sound. Use a mic splitter that plugs into your camcorder, letting you then plug two mics into it. The first mic is the one close by your sound effect. The second is a boom mic placed much further away, picking up general room ambience or "presence." The combination of these two tracks recorded together is much more full and rounded than a simple sound effect.

SPOT EFFECTS

Bats flying: quickly open and close an umbrella, recording from about four feet. For birds, use a leather glove flapping.

Crunching bones: stuff a cooked chicken with thin wooden rods, then beat with hammer. Vegetarians can use frozen whole carrots or celery.

Punches: hit rolled-up newspaper with a stick. Or try punching the palm of your hand, then adding some extra treble and distortion on your audio software.

Elevator door: close a filing cabinet while a single bell rings.

Heartbeat: stretch a piece of fabric and pull in a sudden, double pounding sound.

Human mutilation: stab into watermelon. For serious beatings, use a broom stick hitting a mattress.

Robots, moving: photocopiers replicate that convincing whining, almost hydraulic, sound. Increase bass for larger, scarier robots.

Weapons: many Foley artists suggest using standard gunshot noise, from an air rifle or existing gunshot effect, but adding in the details, such as clinking metal and a sudden hydraulic burst of air. Mix to the middle of the range, rather than treble or bass. For gun loading sounds, use a metal staple gun or stapler, and open and close the fixings.

Walking: on snow, lay a piece of carpet on some gravel and walk gingerly. For moving through a swamp or mud, use your hands to imitate footsteps in a small tank of mud and water.

For other sounds of crunching snow, fill a small leather bag with flour or small seeds and push down.

Underwater explosives: record a toilet flushing and slow down to half speed with reverb.

Thanks to David Filskov at Epic Sound (www.epicsound.com/sfx/)

Experts' Tips

Paul McFadden, sound designer, *Doctor Who*, Bang Productions, London

"We set about creating the mood of the film by laying atmosphere tracks. This would be birdsong, wind, rain, et cetera along with more weird atmospheres that create a feeling of suspense. We then lay the 'spot effects' which give the series the 'Hollywood' feel. These would include explosions, gunshots, spaceships, table smashes and so on. The sound editorial team work alongside the picture guys and use sound to point out certain visuals that you the audience may not have seen. Let's take for example an episode of *Doctor Who* series 2 called 'Tooth and Claw.' This was a huge sound job for us at Bang. A totally CGI werewolf eating people. Without the sound of werewolf feet, growls, Foley effects and crowd screams and so on, the werewolf wouldn't have half the impact that it eventually had. In total I produced about 32 tracks of sound just for the werewolf alone.

"When I designed the werewolf I actually growled and acted the scene vocally. I then pitch shifted my voice to give it weight and mass. I really closely mic'd it so I could get all the glottal effect that I was producing with my voice. I then 'beefed up' the big growls with various animal noises. Lion roars, bear growls, et cetera. I then synced these with my original voice growl so that they were in time with each other. Most of the time the growls were made up of about six tracks. Then we would record the Foley feet and hair moves and anything that the werewolf touched or walked over (smashed doors, et cetera). This gave the wolf a 'real' feel."

SECOND OPINION

Foley? No way. It'll sound artificial and obvious. You want a B-movie, go right ahead. Any sounds you want can get recorded on location when the acoustics sound perfect and realistic. Just move the mic a little closer when you shoot, or redo the action just for the mic. And when exactly do you need to know how to record underwater explosives unless you make Steven Segal movies?

Chapter | Twenty-Five

Screening for Feedback

OVERVIEW

You made the film – now get some feedback on how it is. Test it out as a Beta version before you go wide with it for real.

Experts' Tips

Nick Broomfield, film director, *The Battle for Haditha*, London/LA

"Have lots of screenings afterwards. Often you get so close to the film that you don't give information, often fundamental information, because you assume everyone knows it, and they don't and you only learn that by showing it. Show it to friends, other filmmakers, but more than anything people who respond on an emotional level, rather than get intellectual about it."

Screenings are a way of showing your movie to a small number of people to find out how it looks so far.

However much you try, you can never see the movie as it really is because you are too close to it, you spent too much time on it – it's your baby. You don't even know when you have finished: you can edit and edit for days and weeks and never quite decide that you have the final cut. **You need to step outside of your own view of it and find out how it is for everyone else.** How do they see the movie? What do they like best? Do they even notice the bits you were most proud of? Do the jokes hit the mark? And do they know what it's all about? You also need to know who likes your film best: age, gender, and what other films they tend to like. Ultimately, let the screening become a way of getting more objective about the film.

There's no way of knowing except to show it to a few people and gauge their reactions. That's a screening, and it's going to be your first audience.

STEP BY STEP

1. **Set yourself a fixed time to edit and stick to it.** A three-hour session per final minute of screen time is a good starting guide for how much time you need.

2. When you know your footage is OK and you start editing, **go ahead and fix yourself a date to show it.** Don't push the date back, just go for that screening as the first draft of the movie.

3. **Get a venue.** Go for neutral ground away from your place – you'll be more objective. Ideal places are rooms in clubs and bars where you can access a projector, keep uninvited people out but also include a few drinks and snacks. Ask your local arts center if you can use a room. You might get it for free if you plead poverty or suggest you commit to work for free for the center for a few hours. Schools, universities and colleges are also likely to offer you space, and often for free if you are local.

4. **Invite people.** Ask a number of friends so you get some support but also ask them to each bring at least one other person unconnected with making movies. You need **a mix of gender, age and background,** but if you know for certain that your film is aimed at a certain kind of person, you could restrict your invitation to a particular group.

HOW TO RUN YOUR SCREENING

1. **Get to the venue early** and lay out enough chairs, checking that every seat has a good view of the screen.

2. **Run the movie on screen** so you know the projector works with your disc format. Check sound quality and play the movie while you sit furthest from the speakers to check everyone can hear dialogue.

3. When people arrive, **tell them what the movie is about briefly,** what you hope to do with it and then move briskly on to the screening.

4. After it's finished, you need to **get feedback.** You can either ask the audience to fill out cards, or you could simply have an open discussion about it, maybe as a question-and-answer session. There are pros and cons either way: some people feel more comfortable giving verbal feedback straight away rather than writing it all down, and they are more likely to give more detail. But you might get more truthful answers in anonymous cards. It's your call. Either way, be prepared to hear some hard truths.

5. **Take your notes of the discussion, or the completed cards,** away with you and make some time to go through them. Put the results into categories such as technical (like not being able to hear the dialogue); story (not being able to follow the plot); characters, and so on.

SECOND OPINION

What if everyone else is wrong, and you are right? **Resist overreacting** and making huge changes to the movie. After all, it isn't a Pepsi taste challenge; it's art not consumer testing. The reaction at the screening is just one audience, so think carefully before taking on board what people say to you about the film.

Instead, **trust your own reactions to watching the film.** When you watched it during the screening you will have seen the movie through fresh eyes, as you sit among the audience, so go with your own feelings about what works and what doesn't.

ESSENTIAL RESOURCES:

A venue to show the film with projector and screen, connected to a DVD player or PC, or camcorder.

Postcards for audience to write comments.

Section Four: Share Online

SHARE ONLINE

This section is all about how to get seen on the web. Your film deserves the biggest audience, and one that really understands your work. Find out how to create a hit on YouTube, get a workable plan to make the most of the web, and make use of networking sites, all to publicize and share your movie.

Chapter 26: **Create a YouTube Hit.** This chapter talks about how to make the most of the biggest sharing site, and to ensure your film gets seen in big numbers.

Chapter 27: **Web Your Movie.** Does your movie look bad online? This chapter helps sort out technical problems that can seriously affect how your movie looks on the web.

Chapter 28: **Your Web Plan.** Now the campaign starts. Find out how to create a strategy that uses every part of the web to work hard for your film.

Chapter 29: **Social Networking.** A brief guide to the best networking sites to find advice, news and share wisdom.

Chapter 30: **Create Your Own Web Series.** Make a series of films that create a buzz like a network show.

Chapter 31: **Your Online Publicity Kit.** A complete guide to what you need to create a professional and well-oiled publicity machine for your movie.

Chapter 32: **Online Screenings and Festivals.** Show your movie at an online festival, or on a TV slot, or on one of the many local and national screenings near you.

Chapter | Twenty-Six

Create a YouTube Hit

OVERVIEW

Your movie deserves a big audience but sometimes it's hard to shout loud enough to get people to watch it. With YouTube, Vimeo and other video sharing sites, there are a lot of ways to create a buzz around your movie that are legal, don't use spam and help bring it to the viewers.

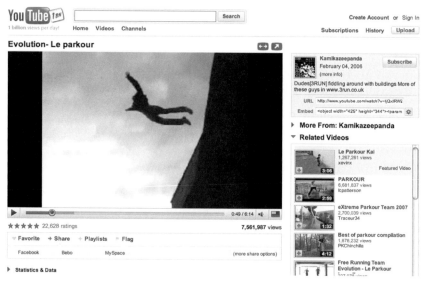

FIGURE 26.1 This parkour video scored over 7 million hits, mostly in Brazil and Eastern Europe, and its maker has over 4000 subscribers to a dedicated YouTube channel.

WHY BOTHER?

YouTube and other sites have grown massively in a short space of time. **With so many movies on line now it's harder than ever to make sure yours gets a fair viewing.** So it figures that you should take advantage of YouTube features so that the maximum number of people see your video. Only then can you be sure that it finds the right audience who really connect with your movie.

There are pros and cons to each video sharing site but whichever one you prefer, a lot of the same tips apply if you want to increase the number of people watching your movie.

Start with two big ideas: first, the quote from that great baseball movie *Field of Dreams* – "build it and they will come" – just doesn't work on the web. **People don't just stumble across your movie,** they won't seek out quality movies, and the number of hits a movie gets isn't connected to how great that movie is. Second, **you're pushing this movie of yours because it's a neat, original movie.**

If you have any doubts about whether you should try to create a buzz for your film, ignore them. This is no different from the pre-Oscar campaigns run by the big studios, but without the free Gucci bags. Just avoid spam-style methods and stay on the right side of YouTube, aiming for as big an audience as you can, legally. You deserve to get seen.

STEP-BY-STEP

1. **Start by making a unique video that's creative, imaginative or does something new.** A movie that has something new to say, or says something in a new way or with a new twist, gets a real chance of scoring a big audience. It's not enough by itself but all the steps from here onwards are no help if the basic movie is poor. Most likely you are proud of your film, if a little nervous that people are going to see your prized new work for real.

2. **Make sure the movie fits and works well on a small screen.** Check out Chapter 27, Web Your Movie to help your movie survive being compressed for the web. That's all about the technical stuff, like checking your screen text is readable on a small web screen, and that your shots and editing, colors and lighting all look OK after compression.

3. **As you shoot, use social networking sites and messaging (like Twitter) to keep people in the loop about your project.** It's easy to lose interest about a short movie that a friend is making if the last time they told you about it was a few months ago. Simply send emails each week to friends who supported you, film students, people who helped your budget, and people you may have met briefly at screenings, shows, or video industry expos.

4. Stop for a moment and **think about whether you want your movie to be a YouTube hit now or maybe later.** That's because if you want it shown in film festivals – online or on Main Street – it needs to be an exclusive for them, not something that people have already seen. The same goes for TV slots (see Chapter 32, Online Screening and Festivals).

5. **If you are ready, upload the movie to YouTube and your preferred video sites.** Some sites take longer than others to complete the process – YouTube is slower to upload at certain peak-usage times, but generally faster than most other sites. Vimeo might crash more often but gives better presentation for your video. Facebook can be a little slower to upload.

6. **Then sort out tags and other stuff on YouTube,** as described in the table below, to make the most of the site. Go through the points about how to create the right category, use thumbnails, and so on.

7. **Find the right community.** Vimeo is especially good at letting you create your own bespoke community that matches your movie. Use this as the core support for your film, with members pushing it heavily in every other site they link in to. You can also create mini-communities within groups, like having your own corner of the Experimental Film community, just for Scottish filmmakers.

8. **Keep your email and message campaign about your movie live, even now you have finished editing and are ready to upload it.** Ask people to leave feedback, rate the film, and pass it on to friends. Open your campaign with a party – like a regular film premiere – where you give out cards with details about the film and ask everyone to help create a buzz for it.

9. **Check out problems you might have with your movie.** Will anyone get offended to see themselves on YouTube in your movie? Did you ask and get written permission to use them? Check out Chapter 9, Law and the Movies to make sure you are covered. Look at YouTube's Ground Rules for videos, and for how you interact with other people online. Movies that cause offence get flagged up and removed, so check that what seems like a comedy to one person is not offending another.

10. **Now you are ready to move on to the pyramid plan in Ch 28, Your Web Plan.** It's going to help you create one big organic campaign, where every site energizes the others and all traffic moves to and from each site, all the time creating a bigger wave about your movie. **The key thing is not to rely on one site only.**

FIGURE 26.2 Aaron Yorkin, maker of *Life and Death of a Pumpkin*, directs viewers to his own site to boost hits for his series of Star Wars spoofs, *Chad Vader*. Yorkin's Blame Society Productions channel has 134,000 subscribers, creating over 7 million hits for one episode alone of *Chad Vader*.

FIGURE 26.3 Firecracker Films has built up a huge following on YouTube with its own channel of documentaries and shorts.

Table 26.1 Making the most of YouTube

Area	What to Do
Unique tags	Grab the passing viewer and get them to look in by **choosing tags that reflect your movie in a unique way,** using words that aren't used too often alongside regular descriptions that most people look for. Avoid using tags that might grab attention but have no connection to the movie.
Category	**Make the category match the video so it's relevant.** Find out what people expect to see in a category to check whether yours is in the right place. For instance, a short documentary about a fashion show might sit in Film and Animation or in Style. Fully two-thirds of all videos go into just three categories: entertainment, music and comedy, according to the University of Calgary, 2007. So consider whether your video will get more hits in those categories or whether it will get swamped by too much choice for viewers.
Title and description	**For the title, use descriptive words to grab the audience.** Don't just describe your movie as a kite-surfing clip – instead go for a "scary, awesome, unbelievable kite-surfing." Descriptive tags also help the casual viewer decide sooner whether to watch the movie. Find words that describe the movie well, in a concise way.
Movie length	Short movies get watched more often. If a movie is just 30 seconds long it doesn't need much commitment from the viewer – they'll give it a try and need less convincing. **Movies lasting 1–2 minutes do really well,** but anything above 3 minutes is out of many people's attention range. For longer movies, try Vimeo, or chop up the movie into episodes.Only 21% of movies viewed were larger than 21 MB (Calgary study).
Use words concisely	Avoid standard "stopwords," in what is called Natural Language Processing (NLP) – words like 'and,' 'on,' 'to,' 'with' and so on, which get filtered out in web searches. These are wasted words which don't help describe or flag up your movie.
Links	As well as communities or groups you might join, link the film to other sites and get the movie embedded elsewhere. Be smart about which ones to go for, choosing particular forums or sites where you know people who might like your movie tend to get together. For instance, if your film is a UFO story, start linking with UFOlogist discussion boards and conspiracy theory sites.

Continued...

Table 26.1 Making the most of YouTube (Continued)

Area	What to Do
Thumbnails	**Make full use of thumbnails used to show the film in lists on YouTube.** YouTube lets you select the thumbnail image from the quarter, halfway and three-quarter mark. Some people purposely select frames that look good or show off the best parts of the movie.
Remixes	If your movie is suitable, **allow your video to be remixed by other users,** by using simple images and visuals that don't rely on words. Comedy works best in this area.
Related videos	Related videos are those that viewers link together. Your video gets tagged from the title you give it plus any other tags you added. Then, as it gets watched a few times it gets placed next to other videos according to how other users link them together. So if people watch a high-ranking video, yours could link next to it simply by being similar. It doesn't matter whether your movie has only had a few dozen hits, nor whether it's new or old, it can still get linked to a big-hitter. It's a fair system because it all rests on how other people link videos together, and not necessarily on the numbers who watched it yet. So, **use the tags well, and find movies that you can hitch a ride with, by using similar words as tags.** Everything is fair in this area – if the movie is closely linked by other people it will get listed.
Video responses	On YouTube and other sites, videos can be linked as a response to a film. **If you watch a video that inspires you, you can post your video – or move one that's already online – so it's listed as a response.** That means it appears as a link below the video, increasing the number of hits you'll get. Some responses can be the exact opposite of the main video, like a repost to a sexist movie, or an alternative viewpoint to a news item. Others might be simply a similar movie inspired by it. But go easy on what films you respond to – it looks cheap if you hitch up next to a multimillion hit clip that has no connection to your movie. Choose movies that have some similarity to yours.

FIGURE 26.4 This YouTube hit, *The Life and Death of a Pumpkin* was made by Aaron Yorkin and scored a Best Short prize at the Chicago Horror Film Festival. It attracted 31 video responses from viewers with similar videos.

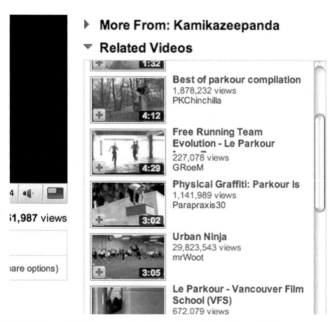

FIGURE 26.5 If you think viewers who like a clip on YouTube will like yours, upload it as a "related video." The list of related videos is not connected to how many hits you get, just on whether viewers think your film is related.

YOUR MOVIE GOES VIRAL

A viral movie is one that gets huge viewing figures and seems to break out of its own usual audience, getting passed around between friends and co-workers. Many virals are adverts, and marketing people have found lots of ways to manipulate online viewing by paying bloggers to spread the word about films that advertise products. But beyond the commercial world, films made by people who love film do get spread around widely, eventually snowballing into viral success stories. Despite what the guys in suits want us to watch, people still seem able to discover great shorts and pass them around.

There are no sure fire rules to make your film "go viral" but start with these, based on successful viral videos:

- **Your movie has to have something with impact** – whether it's something gory, something bizarre, scary, funny or whatever. It has to be so memorable that you can sum it up in just a few words.
- **It has to encourage repeated viewing,** maybe by having something totally unexpected or visually interesting.
- **A movie might go viral because it is about an issue people feel strongly about.** A 2009 public information film to warn people about texting while driving made for a small police force in South Wales, UK, attracted millions of hits around the world after gradually going viral. Director Peter Watkins-Hughes put a clip on YouTube to show a friend, and from

FIGURE 26.6 A public information video on the dangers of texting while driving became a huge online hit in 2009, reaching over 7 million viewers around the world.

there it got copied to other sites. Within two weeks it beat a Jay-Z music promo in the top 10 viral chart. The horrific and explicit images of the car crash showed in this film certainly helped push it viral but it was also the skill of the director in wringing every last drop of emotion out of a common road traffic accident.

- **Political campaigns make good virals.** A video showing factory hens got huge hits despite being shot with poor quality video and shaky images.
- **It doesn't have to be dumb.** Some of the top viral videos are long, wordy, no-action epics, like the top-viewing 9-minute one-shot of Al Franken (a US senator and author) shouting down a crowd as he explains his voting on a bill. Or there's the text-heavy 4-minute film about the growth of social networking sites, which went huge despite it looking like a college lecture. If it's interesting, people want to know.
- **Emotional is good.** People like high emotional stuff, such as the 2009 hit viral film *Free Hugs Campaign,* (60 million hits and counting).
- **A neat idea, cheaply done** and with a low-tech feel to it. Videos that avoid expensive effects and instead opt for an original idea get strong hits. Singer-songwriter Oren Lavie's *Her Morning Elegance* video transformed a little-known performer after a massive viral spread led to millions of viewings.
- **Make it recyclable,** so that it can be used and remixed by other people.
- **Create a buzz** through social networking sites, emails, friends, links to other sites, all asking people to click to the video and pass it on. Use tags on YouTube to ensure it gets linked to other fast viral videos in the "related videos" list.

HOW TO LINK TO THE RIGHT SITE AND FIND THE RIGHT COMMUNITY

You might spend valuable time creating links with certain sites, or you might link up with existing communities to share your video. **But take a moment to check out whether the site is really going to work hard for you**, or whether you are better off elsewhere.

Click on the excellent web research site **www.alexa.com.** Alexa is a vast resource of data to help you find sites on a certain theme, and then investigate all sorts of useful facts about who visits.

Take a sci-fi movie for instance. You might have made a neat short sci-fi and want to try to flag it up with sci-fi enthusiasts. Alexa brings up a long list of sci-fi sites, among them www.mania.com which also hosts various blogs, communities and groups. But is it a site that is growing or shrinking? Alexa's data says that it grew 22% in the one three-month period, and that people spend an average of six minutes looking around, which is a relatively long time. It also says that 51% of users come from the USA, so that might suit your movie.

Meanwhile, a similar site was down 2% in the same period, but on the other hand was a particularly fast site to get into, a whole 85% faster than other similar sites.

Also use www.alexa.com to investigate which social networking site is most suitable for you and your movies.

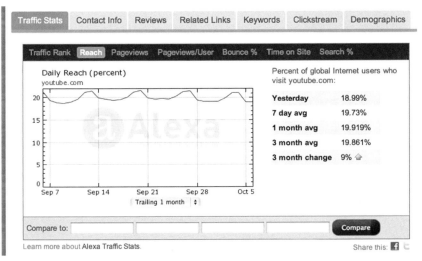

FIGURE 26.7 www.alexa.com lets you find out the traffic and spread of any website. This graph from www.alexa.com shows how YouTube performed over one month.

STUFF THAT DOESN'T WORK

- **Tags can be unreliable**. YouTube can only use the tags you give it, so choose them carefully.
- **Avoid tags that have nothing to do with your movie.**
- **Don't upload repetitive videos or clips copied from TV just so it links to your main movie.**
- **Beware of spam tools** that tell you they will "optimize" your video for you. They are irritating to viewers, and can get you removed from YouTube. A lot of videos do get removed because they become a nuisance to viewers.
- **Don't use automatic generators to automatically share videos.** These are software services that automatically send and upload your movie to over a dozen other video sharing sites. A lot of users don't like this kind of approach because it treads pretty close to spam, but the benefits may attract you, especially if you are doing commercial work. It also gives you stats, showing you which sites are watching it more. You usually have to pay, but rates vary. If you really want to do this, try www.heyspread.com/

or www.vidmetrix.com/ at the budget end of the market. Beware, though, your movie instantly becomes a product just like ads and marketing campaigns and you lose respect among filmmakers.

- **It's impossible to try to get your movie onto the YouTube "featured video" list.** It's an internal and very secretive YouTube process so don't bother trying to influence it. But you can affect the outcome of "most discussed" by encouraging your group members to talk about it on YouTube.

- **Music without copyright can't be used.** YouTube and other sites are quick to remove videos that use copyright music without permission. This can be frustrating so use music that's legal – check out Chapter 9, Law and the Movies to get more ideas.

Chapter Twenty-Seven

Web Your Movie

OVERVIEW

Tailor your movie to the web's narrow bandwidth and low resolution – and make sure it makes the most of the smallest screen.

Everything looks different on the web. What started as just another way to show movies has become the default way to see anything. It does this at a cost – what you see looks pretty bad because the data that makes up the movie is reduced massively. Colors are dull or too garish, the image jerks and details are lost.

But if you think about all this in advance then you can turn in a movie that sidesteps these problems and looks better than anyone else's online. Shoot for the web, not against it, and your movie will somehow look more professional. It will stand out and get more viewers.

Table 27.1 How to make your movie web-proof

Possible Problem	What it Means	What to Do About It
Stories and ideas	The place we usually watch web movies – on the bus, at a lecture, when we are doing something else as well – means you can't rely on a viewer's full attention.	**You need to be more clear about what is happening in the plot.** We can't see so much screen, so make it easy for us to pick up on what's happening by having events up close and obvious.

Continued...

Table 27.1 How to make your movie web-proof (Continued)

Possible Problem	What it Means	What to Do About It
Acting	Actors know that you need to be a little different for each place you act – theatre is different from the movies	Your actors need to be clear, to add a little mime as they talk, echoing old-school acting where stars like Cary Grant (a former acrobat) acted with body language as well as words, hyping up the performance as on a stage. Watch Grant's wordless wait for a bus in a deserted road in *North By Northwest*, where he gets paranoid, puzzled, amused, and then fearful of his life – all without saying a word.
Length of movie	**Online viewing is different: most people expect a quick hit, and can't commit to anything longer than five minutes.** If it's over five minutes it has to work harder to attract and keep its viewers.	**Make the movie short.** 1–2.5 minutes is an ideal limit. Most videos on YouTube average 2 minutes. It streams quickly, the viewer knows it's all over soon, and compression can be less noticeable. And actually this ultra-short limit is a kind of haiku method of filmmaking – inspiring in its limitations.
Audio	Sounds on the web get compressed much less than images, so quality will be good. But there are limitations, especially if you view on a phone or MP4 player.	**Keep it to just three audio layers on the timeline** when you edit: one for main voices or most prominent sounds, another for essential sound effects and a final one for ambient sound or music. With your sound design (check out Ch 23, Audio Editing for help) you will need to be more explicit and put important sounds up close, instead of going for subtlety. Test it out by playing the soundtrack over the telephone. It's a useful exercise to see what sounds are most crucial to your movie. In an interview, sound is crucial so you might leave it relatively high at 32 bit mono, but frame rate can be cut right down to 10 frames per second (fps) as there is very little movement. Or for a sports movie you might increase the frame rate to 15 fps but massively reduce sound quality.

Continued...

Table 27.1 How to make your movie web-proof (Continued)

Possible Problem	What it Means	What to Do About It
Using the camera	The screen on smart phones, the web or other devices is way smaller than TV so you have to change the way you think about the screen.	**Shoot as if it will be watched on the camcorder LCD monitor instead** – it's just a little smaller than the standard web movie screen so stand a couple of feet away as you shoot now and then to gauge whether an image is clear at this scale. Move the camera up close but don't zoom in. Avoid panning or tracking if you can. On the plus side, a movie that plays it cool with this sort of framing – steady images and slow movement – tends to look a little more classy than others.
Movement	The problem is the frame rate used in most video compression. Uncompressed movie on your TV is played at 29.9 frames per second (fps) or 25 in the UK. That's a lot of still images to be streamed each second, so the movie gets squeezed down to 15 fps or lower. This creates shuddering or jerky movements.	**Tell your actors to avoid too much fast movement.** Instead, try close-ups to make it clearer what is happening, with rapid cutting between steady shots of detail.
Lighting	Web and phone playback is less subtle than your TV screen, and compression can reduce the range of shades in the image.	**Go for a strong key lamp so you get your main subject lit well with strong shadows.** Avoid a cluttered background, so reduce smaller filler lights behind the subject. Use shadows on the face of your subject to reveal expressions more easily.
Aspect ratio	Most web or phone players will add black bars top and bottom of your movie rather than crop it to fit. That means your image is reduced even further.	**Work in 4:3, or 16:9, especially for YouTube.**

Continued...

Table 27.1 How to make your movie web-proof (Continued)

Possible Problem	What it Means	What to Do About It
Text	Web and phone players are small, so text is unreadable at normal movie size.	**Credits, subtitles and titles need to be large enough to be readable,** with simple colors, little movement and in high contrast. Avoid words that spin into the frame or morph into other shapes. As a starting point, take the size of your font to be at least 20% of the height of the frame. Test it by standing a couple of feet away from the camera LCD monitor to see how easy it is to read.
Colors	The range of contrast and subtle tones is reduced on small screens. Compression software on the web looks for significant changes between frames, and if colors or tones are too similar doesn't bother updating them. It can also flatten parts of the frame by grouping together pixels in a small section and summing them up with the color or tone they mostly resemble, so you lose definition.	**You'll need to amp up the lighting and make your images more clear.** You can't get away with too many mid-tones as they will just merge to form a mass of sludgy colors. Choose three colors maximum and stick to these as the main palette for your film – a good choice for your movie whatever size it gets seen at, as it tends to make a stronger style overall. Adjust the filter for colors so that blacks are deepened. Look for a section of your movie where shadows and dark areas are most obvious, play around with the color levels so that you increase the amount of richer, deeper, darker hues. Practice this in Photoshop, using a still from your movie and play around with the Curves command in the adjustments palette.
Editing	The combination of very small screen and poor frame rate means that you quickly get a strobe effect from editing in a fast MTV-style. Also, the screen size gives you less ability to see what's happening, so each shot needs to be on screen for longer.	You need to be very chilled out and slow paced in editing for the web. **Go for clips that last more than 1 second.**
Format	Some sites prefer different file formats.	For YouTube, use only H.264, MPEG-2, or MPEG-4.

Continued...

Table 27.1 How to make your movie web-proof (Continued)

Possible Problem	What it Means	What to Do About It
File size	Sites like YouTube restrict the size of your video file.	You have a 1 GB limit on file size, raised from the old 100 MB for high-res versions of your video. But 90% of videos are smaller than 21 MB (from a study by the University of Calgary).
Encoding	There are lots of ways to encode your video before uploading it to YouTube.	The best way to encode your movie for YouTube is to use the H.264 compressor. Most edit programs have easy-to-use compressors to create a small version suitable for YouTube restrictions. To do your own compression, follow these steps: If you have H.264, set it to 480×360 screen size, at 30 frames per second (fps) if using NTSC (that's the USA system of video images). Set the bit-rate (the speed the data is conveyed) to 13 Mbps. Set the sound quality to 96 Kbps in mono.
Deinterlacing	Interlaced video is a way of **making video look more smooth on your TV, but on the web it will look stuttering and jerky.** Diagonal lines look like steps and lose their clarity. It also plays havoc with text.	Make it the very last thing you do. If you use Final Cut Pro, it helps you deinterlace if you chose Export to QuickTime, or use filters to click "deinterlace." If you use another edit software, look for the same command within Export options, or use a compression program such as Cleaner.
Contrast	Video on the web tends to squeeze the life out of your images by **reducing color and light contrast.** Your images end up looking flat and dull.	Use the contrast adjustments filter and increase very slightly, by no more than around 15%. Play back a few sections of your movie to see how this affects the images.
Screen size	Compression software on the website you are uploading to may **shrink the screen size,** but if you have a choice preset it yourself.	If you know the movie is destined for mobile phones, then you can shrink it down, or "scale it," to 160×90 pixels as a very small screen, or 480×360 for average web use.

FIGURE 27.1 Make sure text is visible in the playback screen as you edit, to ensure it's readable when watched on similar-sized web screens.

FIGURE 27.2 Shoot close-ups wherever possible if your movie is aimed at phone or web viewing, as in this student project by the Brothers Cho.

FIGURE 27.3 Web and phone movies benefit from stronger light with higher contrast, as in this student noir short.

Chapter Twenty-Eight

Your Web Plan

OVERVIEW

Get a strategy that helps your movie reach the best audience and which links you up with the right people.

Most video websites offer one or more of the following:

- Share videos
- Give and get tips, advice and tutorials
- Talk with other filmmakers
- Work for other people on their movies or recruit people to work with you

Decide what you want a site to do for you, and what you can offer. **Most people making short films want all of the above** but they also want it in different ways, so they use different sites for each of these categories depending on what each site is good at. They want to show their videos to as many people as possible, but they also want to get them shown on more sophisticated sites where you get better quality feedback. They want to belong to local communities but also global ones. So it all means getting the right mix of sites and knowing how to integrate them so they work hard.

CREATING YOUR PYRAMID WEB PRESENCE

You need a plan to make use of what the web can do for your movies. The answer is to use a range of video sharing sites and social networking sites – but to use them in the right ways. Use them for their individual strengths, without relying solely on just one of them.

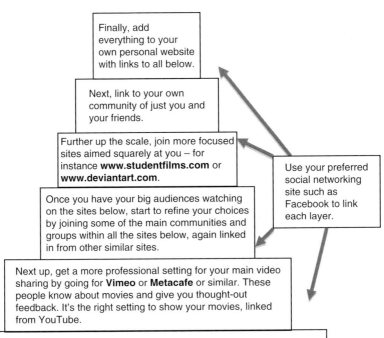

FIGURE 28.1 Create a pyramid of sites.

The trick with this model is to use every layer all the time, not just one of them. Don't start at the bottom and then gradually work your way up over time – join everything and upload everywhere all at once, on the same day. Also, make sure you have one constant networking site to act as the focus and center for your work, such as Facebook. Also add in links to people you meet with LinkedIn, and keep it live by using Twitter messages.

The first layer – YouTube: The sites at the bottom of the pyramid have the biggest hits, the biggest spread, and could get you thousands or even millions of viewings. But these viewings might not help you much – feedback is poor and your movie quickly gets lost in the mass of videos. But that's OK – the purpose here is mass coverage so upload all your movies here.

The next layer up has the niche filmmaker sites: These sites are also big, though not on the same scale as the mass-sharing sites like YouTube. Upload your movies but expect better feedback. This is the site you check into to see what people really think of your movie.

Next up, join and link in to communities and groups: in YouTube and Vimeo. Hitch up with people like yourself.

FIGURE 28.2 YouTube hosts a huge range of individual channels, like these activist ones, each of which have groups attached.

Next, getting smaller but more focused on you and your particular work: there are the smaller niche sites. Find out which ones are right for you. Check out the list in **Chapter 29, Social Networking** since most blend networking with video sharing.

Toward the top there's you and your own small community or group: This is the one you set up rather than joined. You call the shots here and invite people you like and work with to join. It has a tight and dedicated bunch of people who you respect and like. At this level of community, audiences get smaller but quality of feedback and who you link with gets better and better.

Then, right at the top there's your own personal site: showcasing your work and who you are. People don't stumble across this, instead they get directed to it from the other sites below.

WHAT'S THE DIFFERENCE?

MASS SHARING VERSUS NICHE SHARING SITES

What are the pros and cons of mass sites like YouTube and niche filmmaker sites like Vimeo?

I LIKE MASS-SHARING SITES

- **YouTube is great for being able to see everything you want any time.** It's become a kind of video encyclopedia so you can access any of the great moments of cinema history, world events and TV.

FIGURE 28.3 Set up your own website dedicated to displaying your movies just the way you want, like this one for YouTube success story Lone Bannana Productions. It links to a host of other sites on the left of the screen, including Facebook, Twitter and MySpace.

- **YouTube has a greater turnover than other sites.** Videos rise faster and dive quicker, and new "most watched" appear often.
- **YouTube and other big sites are great for how-tos and instructional videos.** Whatever you want to find out, there's a big chance someone has uploaded a film on how to do it – from putting up a tepee, to mending a broken zipper, to making a batik wall hanging.
- **YouTube is like a video library.** Use it to store your work for anyone to access anytime you need to show people what you do.
- **You can't beat the YouTube stats** – people tune in for far longer than on other sites, upload more and create more viral buzz than anywhere else.
- **YouTube has become a valuable tool for democracy in places where freedom of speech is poor.** Iranian videos about repression in 2009 spread around the world on YouTube to expose events during the spring demonstrations.
- **YouTube has far greater creative possibilities because more people tune in.** (See experts' tips on page 162).
- **Uploading is quicker on YouTube than elsewhere,** especially so if you upload at around lunchtime in Central US time or early evening in the UK.

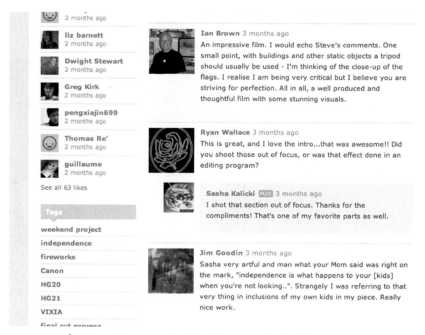

2 months ago

liz barnett
2 months ago

Dwight Stewart
2 months ago

Greg Kirk
2 months ago

pengxiajin699
2 months ago

Thomas Re'
2 months ago

guillaume
2 months ago

See all 63 likes

Tags

weekend project

independence

fireworks

Canon

HG20

HG21

VIXIA

final cut express

Ian Brown 3 months ago
An impressive film. I would echo Steve's comments. One small point, with buildings and other static objects a tripod should usually be used - I'm thinking of the close-up of the flags. I realise I am being very critical but I believe you are striving for perfection. All in all, a well produced and thoughtful film with some stunning visuals.

Ryan Wallace 3 months ago
This is great, and I love the intro...that was awesome!! Did you shoot those out of focus, or was that effect done in an editing program?

Sasha Kalicki PLUS 3 months ago
I shot that section out of focus. Thanks for the compliments! That's one of my favorite parts as well.

Jim Goodin 3 months ago
Sasha very artful and man what your Mom said was right on the mark, "independence is what happens to your [kids] when you're not looking..". Strangely I was referring to that very thing in inclusions of my own kids in my piece. Really nice work.

FIGURE 28.4   Vimeo viewers tend to leave better quality feedback than on mass sites.

See all 21 collections >

Statistics

	plays	likes	comments
Total	▸ **15.7K**	♥ **244**	💬 **40**
Oct 5th	▸ **3,159**	♥ **37**	💬 **4**
Oct 4th	▸ **6,262**	♥ **57**	💬 **8**
Oct 3rd	▸ **4,558**	♥ **71**	💬 **8**
Oct 2nd	▸ **1,070**	♥ **13**	💬 **1**
Oct 1st	▸ **16**		
Sep 30th	▸ **12**		
Sep 29th	▸ **10**		
Sep 28th	▸ **17**		
‹ Previous Week			

or motion!

Downloads

Please join Vimeo or log in to download the original file. It only takes a few seconds.

lonev

FIGURE 28.5   Vimeo's feedback stats give you instant overview of how people rate your film.

I LIKE NICHE SITES

- **Some mass video sharing sites are way too big,** so wading through to find anything worth watching is getting harder and harder.
- **YouTube and some other sites have music clearance issues for many filmmakers.** If you put a video up with music which you don't have permission to use, the soundtrack might get wiped so it runs silent when people watch it.
- **YouTube is too big and too "corporate."** MySpace peaked after a few years, especially when it was bought out by News Corporation in 2005, and although still popular is focused a lot on garage bands and musicians.
- Some filmmakers say they **migrate away from the big sites like YouTube when they start getting more serious about your movies.** In niche sites you can get seen by people who care about watching movies rather than just gags and recycled TV clips.
- Some filmmakers say you are more likely to **find your creative "soul-mates" on niche sites,** rather than on mass-sharing sites. Niche sites like Vimeo are more likely to net you a bunch of close collaborators, or like-minded people who give you well-thought out feedback.
- **Ratings mean more on niche sites.** Five star ratings dominate mass sharing sites but viewers to niche filmmaker sites are more careful in how they rate your movie.
- **YouTube and other sites let you upload anything, even if you didn't make it,** so there are too many copies of other clips online. Niche filmmaker sites like Vimeo say you have to have made the film yourself to upload it, assuring viewers that only original videos get shown.
- **Commercial videos are more likely to get a showing on bigger sites like YouTube.** Filmmaker sites tend to sniff them out more quickly on niche sites and flag them up. YouTube hates them too, but these ads sneak in more easily because of the sheer volume of videos uploaded.
- **... And undercover viral films (commercials pretending to be real homemade movies) have a free rein to get spread around on mass-sharing sites.** Companies that sell links to bloggers, aiming to get over 100,000 hits for a commercial about a new product that looks just like a regular video, are more likely to succeed on mass-sharing sites.
- **Niche sites have a global spread** of viewers and users evenly around the world. Vimeo, for instance, is in the top 500 sites in a more diverse range of nations than mass-sharing sites.

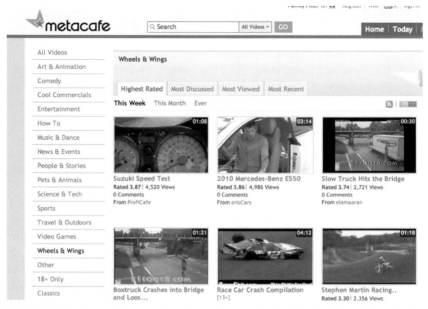

FIGURE 28.6 Metacafe has similar video categories to YouTube but its smaller upload rate means your movie gets a bigger chance of being watched.

Experts' Tips

Luke While, film student, UK

"Try creating an interactive storyline on a video sharing site, using related videos to link a bunch of clips together. Shoot multiple storylines, letting the viewer click on the next clip they'd like to see in the story. For instance, a man reaches a set of doors, so you click on different clips to find out what happened if he passed into each room, then more clips to find out various outcomes inside each room, and so on."

Experts' Tips

Liam Daly, film student, UK

"Vimeo is the best by far. You get a much better quality of viewer so you get a better quality of feedback. And it looks more professional with better content. It has a more creative feel to it. Vimeo now is the way forward."

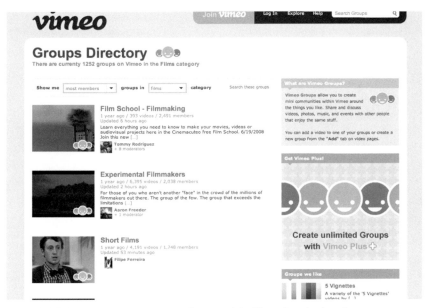

FIGURE 28.7 Join a group or community on a niche filmmaker sharing site.

USING FACEBOOK FOR YOUR MOVIES

- Facebook has **relatively poor upload times** and a lot of filmmakers say it crashes often as you wait to upload.
- **Facebook is ideal for keeping in touch with friends and crew.** It's more personal, and lets you create a strong team. You've got your close collaborators, other people you work with occasionally, and still other people you never meet but who like to talk about your movies and offer ideas.
- But **Facebook isn't professional enough for your movies.** It's more like a scrapbook, to enable people to check in and then link on to another site where they can watch your movie in better surroundings.
- Although it's great for creating groups surrounding your projects **try to keep group size manageable.** If it gets too big, friends lose interest and don't get their voice heard.
- Facebook is **excellent for increasing your circle of contacts,** especially on the next rung of the ladder above you. Get yourself attached to groups of people who are where you'd like to be a year or so down the line.
- **Use Facebook alongside business networking sites like LinkedIn** to have a more business-like side to your work. LinkedIn is good for keeping contacts live, even months after you last met them.

FIGURE 28.8 Facebook is great for keeping your team of people you like to work with in touch with each other. It also hosts opportunities like this 48-Hour Film Challenge in Pittsburgh, USA.

Chapter | Twenty-Nine

Social Networking

> **OVERVIEW**
>
> Make your movies better by linking up with other people to work on your movie, act in it, or just share advice and tips.

Social networking sites don't replace face-to-face meeting, they add to it, increasing your chances of meeting like-minded people and getting your movies out there.

First, decide what you want from a networking site.
Which of these do you need?

- Create your own profile to promote yourself
- Meet other people
- Get jobs and contracts by RSS or email
- Search for cast and crew
- Solve problems in your movie
- Create a group of like-minded people
- Keep interested people in touch with your movie as you make it
- Find out about screenings
- Buy and sell equipment
- Find out about events
- Find out about courses
- Join in with discussion boards

The bigger sites cover all of these. Others give you information but no way to post questions or profiles; others still are almost completely peer-to-peer, acting like a virtual media center you can drop in on to post questions, and recruit crew.

The most useful kinds of network sites are what's called "vertical" ones.
That means they are a thin slice of the web population who join for just one sort of common interest. The other kind are "horizontal" where one member may not

have anything in common with any other member, like MySpace which is host to any number of groups, communities, and individuals.

Vertical ones have very specific aims. For movie makers they are more than just resources to help you – they are at the center of your production, from recruiting crew, to getting advice while you shoot, to spreading the word about your finished movie. And of course they help put you face-to-face with people just like you.

Take a look at Shooting People (www.shootingpeople.org), based in the UK but expanding into the US. It has daily bulletins you can sign up for, on topics from general filmmaking to scriptwriting and animation. You can get daily news about directors needing crew, or items for sale, or events coming up in your area. It all depends, however, on the right people uploading the right stuff, so always add this with other bulletins from other places, such as your local arts funding board, or national screen commission, or city arts center. Subscribe to more than one bulletin from other sites and you increase the chances of getting the right news as it happens.

US network sites are more localized. This works better than big networks in many ways because they know the region, what the particular challenges are there, and how they can help. Take San Diego, for instance (www.sdfilmmakers. org). It has an energetic group running monthly workshops for local people, from acting to makeup. It also links up the San Diego Film Festival, the local media center, a women's filmmakers group, a student film festival, the film school, an editing group, plus the city's movers and shakers.

Horizontal sites such as Facebook, MySpace and others have their uses too. Everyone knows them so it is a good way to form a small community to track your movie as it gets made, or follow the progress of several filmmakers who link themselves together as a group. You can upload production stills, storyboards, blogs, and news about the film to build a profile for it. It makes you look serious and can increase your chances of getting funding or other help later on. It becomes an archive of your commitment. (Check out Chapter 28, Your Web Plan for more about Facebook.)

Table 29.1 Social networking sites

Networking Site	What It's Good For
www.flock	Use it to bring together the most notable networking sites, including Flickr and Twitter, plus your blog, and for bringing together your preferred RSS feeds and posts from your friends.
www.twitter	Great for keeping your tight circle of supporters and crew in touch with your movie as you make it. Send everyone regular updates and you smooth relations with those involved. Small messages like this help keep everyone in the loop.
www.deviantart.com	Vibrant site going since 2000, bringing together visual artists and filmmakers; it's a good base if you are into video art, super 8 and weird stuff. No peer-to-peer elements. USA focused.
www.studentfilms. com	USA site for film students, also big in India. Create a profile, upload your movie, get tutorials.

Continued...

Table 29.1 Social networking sites (Continued)

Networking Site	What It's Good For
www.linkedin.com	This site works like Facebook but is mainly for business users. Use this if you want to create a more up-market, professional profile for your movie, or to link up with investors.
www.tv.oneworld.net	A global site raising the green and social change agenda. Good for political or campaigning movies, or Michael Moore-style rants.
www.quarterlife.com	In a converged art world, where you make movies, take photos and write songs, this site brings it all together and helps you create your own community.
www.ryze.com	Primarily for business, this aims to network members face to face. Free to join.
www.taltopia.com	Mainly designed for actors and crew, you can post on this site to find cast or collaborators. Almost entirely US-based.
www.student.com	General networking site for students – mostly in the USA and India.
www.productionhub.com	Business to business site, for the guys with budgets. Use it for real paying jobs or when you need to recruit from the professional end of the industry.
www.indiewire.com	USA-based community for highly active independent filmmakers and crew. Good for news and up-to-date events and jobs.
www.creativecow.net	One of the oldest and most established communities for media people. A good vibe to it and it's got some of the best tutorials on every aspect of making a movie. Plug into it.
www.filmmaker.com	News and events, plus limited advice, focused on Los Angeles.
www.postforum.com	The only place you need for peer-to-peer (P2P) advice on editing, effects and everything post-production.
www.reelshowint.com	Film school and film students site, sharing videos, news and competitions.
www.xixax.com	Help site, centered on forums and P2P, and fairly active.
www.commonfilm.org	Small but neat idea – to share ideas, footage, storyboards, anything you've got. It's like open source software – just upload and see what other people make out of your stuff.
www.indietalk.com	P2P site for help, advice and tips.
www.indiefilmla.com	Los Angeles-based filmmaker community, useful for getting the skinny on how it works in the city.
www.talentcircle.org	Small, UK-based P2P site, excellent for film students and no-budget makers.
www.shootingpeople.org	Big P2P and resource site for the UK, also with a few bulletins in the US. Long-established and easy to use, but it charges for immediate bulletins; free members have a three-day delay in receiving them.

FIGURE 29.1 www.postforum.com is a great one-stop editing advice centre. Post all your problems here for quick responses.

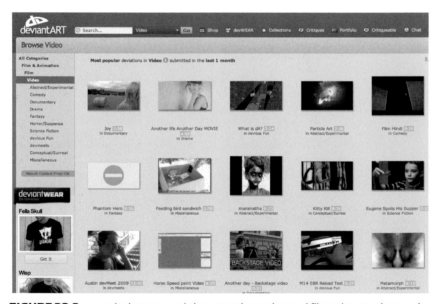

FIGURE 29.2 www.deviantart.com brings together artists and filmmakers to show and share their work.

DOS AND DON'TS: ETIQUETTE IN ONLINE COMMUNITIES

Whether you join or set up a community online, there are many ways to ensure you become popular and avoid virtual gaffes.

- **Look out for users who are not what they seem.** Corporate PR teams scour the web looking for ways to get their ads into community sites. If you don't like these hijackings, report the film as an abuse.
- If a community is open access, **avoid uploading films which seem out of place** against the rest of the clip list. If it's not your party, don't crash it.

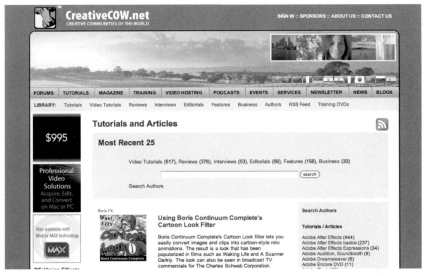

FIGURE 29.3 www.creativecow.net has been supporting filmmakers since the 1990s, with tutorials, forums and reviews.

- **Always get permission from friends before you upload a video that shows their image.** Also anything with children needs the permission of parents or carers.
- If you create a group, **invite members individually,** rather than via a group email. They are more likely to join if it seems like a select invitation.
- **Use non-copyright material wherever possible.** The age of free-use video is fast coming to an end. Stick to out-of-copyright footage such as that found at www.archive.org.
- Comment is free – **always add comments and ratings** to the films you watch. The thrill of seeing thousands of hits for your latest film is a real morale boost.

Experts' Tips

Lee Philips, director, London

"For me [social networking sites] have proved invaluable for recruiting supporting artists, and gaining public support for projects. I set up a MySpace for my last film, and gained seventeen thousand friends. That kind of publicity would never usually be possible with a micro budget."

R. Gesualdo, film director, Miami, Florida

"Because of where I live at the present moment, these sites are another tool for filmmakers. Here we don't have a big film scene like say New York or Los Angeles so those sites help a lot, from looking for talent to putting together your crew, getting equipment through people, and finally to showing your finished work."

Benjamin Rutkowski, film student, USA

"Last year I competed in the Insomnia Film Fesitival – a 24-hour film competition sponsored by Apple. Thanks to sites like www.studentfilms.com, YouTube, Facebook, Digg and Metacafe, our team won the grand prize which was decided by the number of votes and the quality of the votes. Many of our votes were absolutely recruited from those sites."

Derek Flagge, filmmaker, Florida, USA

"I use YouTube, www.studentfilms.com and even blog sites to get my shorts seen. Social networking is very important to me because that's how you make or break your career. You have to get out to an audience and sometimes it takes a long time."

Chapter | Thirty

Create Your Own Web Series

OVERVIEW

Why stop at one video? If you've got a great idea, create a series and build a bigger audience.

FIGURE 30.1 Aaron Yorkin's *Chad Vader* series of videos has built up an audience that any network show would settle for.

Many people now watch TV online, or via streaming players (like the BBC's iPlayer or ABC's www.abc.go.com) or as segments on YouTube. TVs have widgets which enable them to hook up to the web, letting you watch what you want when you want it. And anyway **TV schedules just don't fit with everyone's lifestyles.**

Cue webisodes, or "'sodes": short videos that link together just like regular TV serials. We may not watch TV so much but we still want to follow long-running storylines, with snappy dialogue, realistic sets and strong acting, and you never have to miss it because it sits online waiting for you to tune in when it suits you. As a result, webisodes get a big audience, and build up loyal followings.

The best webisodes don't quite conform to the stereotypes you see on most TV shows. To get big viewing figures, TV has to stick to the conventional ways that most people look, talk, and what they wear, staying with an urban or suburban setting. Prime time mostly avoids minorities, youth groups and special interest communities and – as any TV producer will testify – network bosses quickly drop shows they don't understand.

Webisodes fill the gap left by mainstream TV, and give it to you when you want it. And there are some groundbreaking 'sodes out there to rival the bigger-budget serials on TV – like the award-winning *The West Side* (www.thewestside.tv).

FIGURE 30.2 Award-winning webisode *The West Side*, made on a small budget at nights and weekends.

The rewards can be good, especially if you get a name for yourself as the maker of *that* hit webisode series. A lot of other people have the same idea, but not many have your drive and steady doggedness. With enough commitment you can build up a loyal audience who watch each episode and spread the word to friends.

Your target audience depends on the series you make, but you need to identify who you think would love your show. Describe the perfect viewer, how old they are, what they wear, what they drink, the music they like and so on. This imaginary person becomes Viewer One: the person you hope to attract to the show.

MAKING A WEBISODE

You might not need as much time for each webisode as a usual five-minute short film demands. **After a few webisodes you get good at working more quickly,** your characters fit their roles more and can talk more convincingly, and you need less rehearsal time.

Some webisodes take less than a couple of hours to shoot, and about the same to edit, but the more high profile ones, such as *Kwoon* (www.webisodes. org/items/Kwoon "the misadventures of five kung fu students in Silicon Valley") spend time on one-liners, visual gags, and each setup is lit and recorded with care.

Others are more improvised, such as the literary road trip *Catching Salinger*. This 2009 series was a weekly update on an avowedly fruitless search for the reclusive author of cult novel *The Catcher in the Rye* (www.catchingsalinger. wordpress.com).

Or try *Dead Patrol* (www.quietearth.us), a seek-and-destroy mission in post-apocalypse America where zombies outnumber the living.

But also take time to develop the network of your audience. Facebook, or other network sites, create ways to spread the word.

Your series needs you to think about it night and day, constantly moving it forward. You ditch what doesn't work and add new ideas, never quite satisfied with the shows. But once you find your groove, and feel totally at home with what you have created, it can run and run. If you have reliable characters who are closely acting themselves, then you have the potential for a self-sustaining series that just keeps getting better. The key to this success is spending time evolving the show, and working closely with your actors. Expect the first eight or ten to be testing grounds for the way you eventually want it to be.

Start here:

- You'll need to **create ideas that are different,** and not clichéd.
- Make sure you are **comfortable working to regular schedules,** with script meetings, rehearsals and shooting sessions planned in advance.

03:08 / 08:17

FIGURE 30.3 *Cerealized* is a long-running online series based on three friends who share an apartment.

- **Start working with networking sites** and other ways of viral marketing to create a buzz around the series.
- Since this series is designed wholly for the web, **look at Chapter 27, Web Your Movie.**
- **Take your overall plans from the genre chapter that suits your movie in Section 5,** making sure that it fits into a series of quick, mini-films in sequence.
- **You need a regular, dependable space.** It can be your apartment (as in *Cerialized*) or garage, but it has to be easily accessible and not subject to sudden changes.
- **Legally, you'll need to make sure the series is covered on all angles,** so get permission forms from location owners; release forms from actors, crew and anyone else in the series. Get music clearance forms signed (avoid the hassle by using unsigned local bands or copyright-free music online, though ready-made muzak like that can be a little cheesy).
- **Get the rights to your characters and story lodged and copyrighted.** Email a copy of the script or other documents to yourself or to a lawyer, to prove that you had this idea when you said you did.
- **Aim for straightforward narrative continuity editing.** Check out Chapter 21, Editing Methods: Narrative Continuity.

FIGURE 30.4 Kwoon has built up a loyal following with off-the-wall storylines and strong production values.

Experts' Tips:

Ryan Bilsborrow-Koo, maker of *The West Side,* Los Angeles
On webisodes:

"With *The West Side* we set out to try to create something that held up to the standards by which motion pictures are traditionally judged – suspension of disbelief, narrative continuity, quality performances and craft, emotional involvement of the viewer – and while I don't claim we succeeded on all of these levels, the interesting thing we've found in the process is that very few people in the industry judge internet video on any of these established metrics. Instead, they're concerned with number of page views, partnership deals signed, press exposure, ancillary opportunities, time spent on the site... it's a very Silicon Valley way of looking at things, as if everyone's trying to be the next Facebook. But we weren't trying to go viral with *The West Side*; we just wanted to create something of quality that would draw a quality audience, and we approached the project as filmmakers, not entrepreneurs. If we've learned anything in the year since, it's that we're going to need to fill both roles if we want to get anything made going forward."

On schedules for making a webisode series:

"We were both employed full-time at MTV (myself as a graphic designer, Zack [Lieberman] as a producer), so we had only nights and weekends to work on *The West Side*. Additionally, because all the actors were unpaid, we knew we couldn't press too hard in terms of hours worked to try to hurry episodes out the door; we'd burn out ourselves or our actors early in the series.

"In terms of actual hours spent on each episode, we could've gotten them done fairly quickly had we been without day jobs. But essentially our process was to write the entire script first – which took roughly eight months – and from there the challenge was to scout locations and schedule the actors based on their availability."

"In general it took us a few months to complete each episode. In the end the series did open doors to the film industry proper, so in that sense it served its purpose as a 'calling-card' type of project, even if we weren't able to finish it as we would've liked."

Chapter | Thirty-One

Your Online Publicity Kit

OVERVIEW

All movies are created equal. But when it comes to getting hits for yours, you need an advantage as you spread the word and help it find its audience.

FIGURE 31.1 Sports movies get a high hit-rate on video sharing sites. (Photo courtesy of iStockphoto, ©Polar-Media, Image# 4095378)

PUBLICITY FOR YOUR SHORT FILM

You made your movie, and despite all the faults you spotted it's a gem you are proud of. But, like a meal you took time over to cook, **it isn't complete until it has been served up and found its audience.** Every film has its own unique audience – the people who connect with it, who see the world your way. Just like there are infinite combinations of people in crowds, so there are infinite combinations of audiences – and there is one out there waiting to see your film. They don't know it yet but they are in the queue, ready to take their seat. Your trick is to track them down and tell them about what you did.

But hurry, you have one to two years after you finish the film to get it out there – after that its shelf life ends.

You need to do three things:

1. **To have stuff ready for people who are interested in your movie.** This is practical – you need a collection of images and documents ready to email out to people who liked your movie, or who are interested in selling/showing it. See below for how to create a press kit.

2. **To be smart about how to spread the word about your movie on the web.** The web is a viral medium. Money isn't enough to get your film known – it's what you do and where you place it that gets you seen widely. Use social networking sites (see Chapter 29), video sharing sites and local or national filmmaker bulletins to spread the word that you have made this great movie. And use filmmaker communities (see Chapter 29 Social Networking). People like rating movies – ask your email group or bulletin-board to click to your movie and rate it for you.

3. **To know what your aims are.** Decide what success means to you. What do you want? Is it, for instance, to get 100 million hits on YouTube, or to get 1000 hits by people who really understand your movie, or do you just want to raise your general profile and help get other jobs?

CREATE YOUR OWN PUBLICITY KIT

Use this chapter alongside Chapter 28, Your Web Plan and Chapter 26, Create a YouTube Hit.

FORM A COMPANY

Create a production company for your movies. Think of a name, create a logo, even make a quick Flash animation for the opening credits of your movie. Make **headed writing paper, banners for your emails,** and a postal address. JJ Abrams (*Star Trek*, *Cloverfield*) called his own production company Bad Robot, while Robert Rodriguez (*Sin City*) set up Troublemaker Studios to cover all his work.

SET UP A WEBSITE

Create a website for your company and a linked or subsite for each movie. Many filmmakers start a blog way back in preproduction. Include movie synopsis, cast and crew background, production stills, clips and background notes about how it was made. Enable some way for people to contact you without delay. If an opportunity comes up you need to be able to act on it immediately. Add your press pack (see below) to the site as a PDF, but make sure the images are accessible in a high-res format – at least 300dpi. Avoid excessive intros or other elements that slow the site.

SET UP A CHANNEL ON A SHARING/SOCIAL NETWORK SITE

Many networking sites let you group several films into your own mini-site. Try linking up with other filmmakers to form a small online TV company, drawing together anything that is common to you all, like you all work in Austin, Texas; or you all do extreme sports; or you all made a movie for under $10. Once you have a shared network of films and filmmakers, you can gather friends to support your channel, and set up viral campaigns: everyone who's joined your network group sends the film to two other people and asks them to pass it on. But make this stand out from the usual spam-like drive by adding in a request – for instance, that everyone emails you one plot idea for your next film or a real-life story that would make a good film.

FIGURE 31.2 Whatever the genre of your movie, there's a place to get it seen if you aim at the right audience. Shown here, two filmmakers at San Francisco's International Black Women's Film Festival.

PRESS PACK:

Your press pack is an online resource which anyone who wants to know more about your movie can access, from journalists to fans.

It should include:

- **Images from your movie** including stills and portraits of cast and production stills. These need to be large files, at 300 dpi (print quality), saved as TIFs or JPEGs, and zipped for quick download. Add a note that they need to credit the photographer who took the shot.
- **Interviews** with you and the cast and some crew. Create a covers-all-questions interview which could save the journalist time, with usable quotes if they can't talk to you direct. Most journalists won't use a complete interview unless it's their own, but the quotes can help flesh out a feature.
- **Synopsis** of the movie in about one paragraph.
- **Background to how the film was made,** including a brief summary of where and when it was made. Include production notes and storyboards, designs and sketches.
- **Clips from the movie**, plus a trailer if it's a longer film (upwards of 45 minutes).
- **DVD ready to mail out.** Have a screening disc (for festivals and events), plus a preview one that has the words "preview only" written permanently across the screen.
- **Email and telephone contacts** for you, the producer and any other collaborators.

Chapter | Thirty-Two

Online Screenings and Festivals

OVERVIEW

Whatever kind of film you make, there is an online festival waiting for it right now – comedy, experimental, zombie, wildlife, documentary and maybe even all of these together. The trick is to know what kind of films get accepted, how to apply and then how to use the screening to pole vault your way in to bigger things.

Use this guide to help you get accepted for online and real-world film festivals, and get a slot on TV.

Experts' Tips

Kerry David, producer, *My Date with Drew, Agent Cody Banks, College Sucks,* Los Angeles, USA

"Certainly for short filmmakers the internet is a Godsend. Also there are plenty of short film contests to showcase your work (we have one at IndieProducer now in its seventh year!) and with mobile phones and similar equipment actively looking for entertainment to transmit, it's a wonderful time to be starting out as a filmmaker."

www.indieproducer.net

ONLINE FESTIVALS

If you want to reach a real movie audience, just like you get at film festivals, check out online film festivals. It's a growth area, replacing real festivals because costs are tiny, organization is not too tough, and you get potentially bigger audiences. Many of them are aimed at new filmmakers, and try to encourage

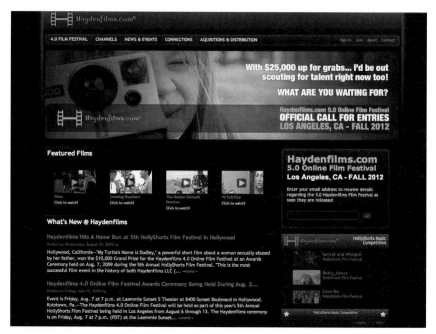

FIGURE 32.1   This online film festival based in Los Angeles shows movies by emerging and student filmmakers, and has an awards evening.

short films to get seen more widely. They also make more use of new way to view, getting even more exposure for your film. The Babelgum Online Film Festival uses phone and web viewing to gather public votes for films, creating a buzz for your movie, as well as showing it. There are festivals aimed at niche genres, or ones catering for filmmakers at different stages of their careers, like www.studentfilms.com.

Many regular festivals also have an online element, usually aimed at less established filmmakers or first-timers, but also showing parts of the festival schedule too. For example, the Los Angeles International Short Film Festival (www.lashortsfest.com) uses LA Shorts TV to encourage viewers to watch and vote for their favorite short movies.

Check out some online festivals and submit your movie. More festivals appear often, so Google to find out new ones.

www.filmfights.com – Running since 2003, a lively, active place to show your movie based on the concept of a shared title, theme and genre each month.

www.haydenfilms.com – A Los Angeles-based festival with some real cash prizes and probably the most authentic festival vibe.

www.babelgum.com/online-film-festival – An international festival with strong indie background, including an award in honor of Spike Lee.

www.coff.newmediafest.org/blog – European festival aimed at linking real festival locations with an online version.

www.newenglandfilm.com/festival – Regional festival in Boston, but open to submissions from anyone.

www.rebfest.com/ – A Twitter-based film festival popular among emerging filmmakers.

www.bestfestamerica.com – Large student film festival regularly attracting over 500 student entries. Look for BestFest festivals in other countries too.

www.cultureunplugged.com/ – Online festival emphasising films on social issues and global problems.

www.nyfa.com – New York's Film Academy hosts an online festival with UK site www.PutItOn.com.

Table 32.1 Improve your chances of getting selected for festivals – online and off.

Area	What to Do
Presentation	A good DVD cover, **excellent publicity stills** and a web presence can all help your film get accepted. "If you are intending to submit your film to any festivals **make sure that your presentation lives up to the standard of your film.** A little bit of effort in promoting your film will go a long way," says Andy Roshay, director of the Signals Film Festival.
Film length	If you are planning to shoot a film for the festival circuit and it is your first attempt, **keep it short:** between thirty seconds and one minute. It's always better to leave the judges wanting more. TV commercials squeeze stories into seconds, so try to steal ideas on how to compress a film into less than a minute.
Produce a press pack	Make publicizing your film easy for the festival's organizers. **Give them a movie DVD and CD with production stills,** director quotes, resumes, background trivia, and anything they can dish out to the press. If yours is packaged and ready to go then you get the headlines in the write-up.
Music and rights clearance	This will be in the application form, but **if you use music in your film check that you have written clearance** from the performers. And many festivals now prefer it if you have not sold the film already – to a DVD collection or short-films buyer – so they can attract industry sales people.
Use www.withoutabox. com	Many festival judges find films in this one-stop buyer's, seller's and judge's site. It allows you to access festivals around the world and send direct to the organizers. **You'll look professional and reliable.** The site has huge clout after merging with Film Finders, a US indie bulletin board. "We work with submission service Withoutabox," says Andy Roshay, of Signals.

Continued...

Table 32.1 Improve your chances of getting selected for festivals – online and off. (Continued)

Area	What to Do
Originality	Avoid clichés, and be true to yourself and your own vision. "What makes a film successful with an audience is when they can see **drive, passion, innovation and enthusiasm on screen,**" says Adele Hartley, of Dead By Dawn Festival. Mick Etherton, judge at the Two Days Later Horror Film Festival, says, "We have found that there are always entries that surprise us with their quality and originality, in terms of production values and script. "We've set our judges definitive areas to consider for judging: Concept: The degree to which the production has an original idea and fresh approach to its theme and/or use of technique(s). Communication: Does the production express its theme/key issues and ideas/emotions clearly. Production: The overall quality of script/storyboard; camerawork; editing; music; special effects and direction. Entertainment: The degree to which the production manages to be interesting and/or enjoyable and/or engaging."
Keep it simple	Avoid a messy film or one that spreads itself too thinly. John Wojowski, of Manchester's Kino Film Festival, says: "Keep to as short a story as possible; many people make the mistake of making what is essentially a 10-minute short drag out to 20 minutes. [You need] a beginning, a middle and an end, and a precise and clean edit."
Make a great opening scene	A festival favorite will have an opening scene that people. Change your story so that the best shot, with the weirdest angle, and the most impossible outcome is right at the front.
Go to festivals	Attend as many festivals as you can, any size, anywhere. "Try to see lots of short films, of all kinds of genres, go to festivals so that you can see films within the context of a program and in front of an audience, meet as many people as you can, get inspired and collaborate," says Alice Bennett-Leyh, of the Encounters Festival, Bristol, UK.
And if you don't get in…	Only start to fret over it if after 25 entries you fail to get into any festival. "A rejection does not necessarily mean you have made a bad film, there are other factors which many filmmakers, particularly starting out, don't consider. So, same old story – persistence is everything! Always ask for feedback on a rejection if you genuinely feel that your movie should have been picked, and not just because your ego is bruised. When you get your feedback, listen to what it is saying," says Adele Hartley, Dead By Dawn Festival.

COMPETITIONS AND CHALLENGES

You'll see a lot of open competitions aimed at new filmmakers, where you go along and pick up an idea to make a film about, then spend a certain amount of time making it, before returning to show your film to an audience. It's a great way to make films in a supportive atmosphere; people tend to be appreciative and want to help you succeed. Often the films you make are better than ones where you've had weeks to work on them, maybe because you have an aim in sight, an audience already booked in and the desire to make it work.

The **most popular events are 12, 24-hour and 48-hour film challenges.** Typically, in a 48-hour challenge you turn up at the start to collect a few key ingredients that have to be in your film, like a word, a prop or a place. You then incorporate these into your movie, spending the first day shooting and the final day editing, before a final audience screening.

Online competitions are becoming popular too, with people linking up via the web to watch and share their videos across continents. For instance, one Film in a Day event (1-hour movie) saw filmmakers who made their movie in London later watch responses to the same challenge in Moscow that night. Sometimes theaters or arts centers are linked via the web so large audiences get to watch each other's movies.

Experts' Tips

Walter Murch, filmmaker, editor *Apocalypse Now!*, *The Godfather*, *Cold Mountain.*

"It's amazing how varied [a film challenge event] is. Some people will have an idea they like to do before coming to the event and they shoehorn it into the ideas we give them. It's very enjoyable to watch, how they add in these extra criteria. I was speaking with a popular feature film director and I said that seeing all the constraints you have to go through, the producers who want certain things, and you take a year and a half to make these big things. And he said no, making a film with constraints like [the 12-hour film challenge] is very much like making a feature film. It brings out things you didn't really think about.

I want everyone to have a great laugh, and to see representations of what other people have thought of given the same criteria. When you see people come running in with their tapes you get these very varied films, and a sense of fun. There's no sense of competition. For me it's amazing to see what people will do. It's lovely to see people having a brilliant time, and it's very low-key. It's a very supportive atmosphere."

(Walter Murch was instrumental in setting up a 12-hour film challenge, to encourage filmmakers and students to make a film in a day.)

FIGURE 32.2 Berlin's International Short Film Festival. Go to short film festivals and meet other filmmakers, watch movies and improve your chances of getting selected.

FIGURE 32.3 New York's Tribeca Film Festival helps new and independent films get seen, helped by the festival's founder, Robert De Niro.

OFFLINE SCREENINGS

If you are aiming to get the film seen in the real world as opposed to online, you need to **seek out small opportunities locally, then go bigger and bigger as you move on.** But if you prefer to risk all on getting your film into some high-profile festivals then avoid every stop below that and instead head directly for the top. A-list festivals won't show your movie unless it's a premiere.

Table 32.2 Local, national, and international screening

Type of Screening	What to Do
Local and regional screenings	Look for arts centers, or local filmmakers' groups or collectives in your town. Seek out the independent film scene in your area and find out where shorts are being shown. For instance, in the UK, bars show shorts as part of the Future Shorts agency (www.futureshorts.com), which selects shorts and sends a new program out for screenings once a month. Look out for squat screenings – vacant buildings taken over by artists and DJs, where films are shown in group screenings. Check whether your local cinema has occasional slots for shorts by local filmmakers. For example, the Southern Ohio Filmmakers Association (SOFA) meets once a month to show local films from Cincinnati. It also runs Underneath Cincinnati, an occasional festival exclusively for local filmmakers.
National screenings	Look for debut screenings running alongside major festivals, where you can show your work on the fringe. Also check out network TV slots where new filmmakers can show shorts to a national audience (see Table 32.3). Or try US network PBS: www.pbs.org/independentlens/getinvolved which runs national screenings across over 50 US cities.
National online screenings	Some countries have online players for filmmakers from that country to upload their films. For example, Scottish filmmakers can show their films on a shared BBC/Scottish Screen online player.
National and international festivals	Check out www.filmfestivals.com to get the latest information on festivals and how to apply. Always use www.withoutabox.com to apply – it's an essential resource for any filmmaker.

Table 32.3 Get your movie on TV.

Name of TV Slot	About	How to Apply
Movieola	Canadian quality short film online channel.	www.movieola.ca and download their submission form and wait to see whether they like your movie.
Sundance Channel	Branch of the Sundance Festival, a TV and cable showing the best of indie shorts and movies for US viewers.	www.sundancechannel.com but you have to email a description and wait to hear back.

Continued...

Table 32.3 Get your movie on TV. (Continued)

Name of TV Slot	About	How to Apply
IFC	Independent Film Channel was the first US channel devoted to features and shorts on 24-hour scheduling. Regular open contests (with cash prizes), and open submissions.	Go to www.ifc.com and look for signs to Media Lab.
CBC Reflections	Canadian broadcaster with regular slot for new filmmakers' shorts.	Go to www.cbc.ca/reflections and download the submission form from the Producers Guide section.
Flickerfest	Australian cable show for short films and interviews.	www.flickerfestonextra.com.au

ALSO TRY

Many broadcasters also finance shorts for prime-time screenings. Channel 4 UK pay £4000 for a 3-minute short for its "3 Minute Wonders" series, and Canal Plus in France financed a number of animated shorts for its pay-per-view channel.

Also check out agencies in your country that buy "interstitials" or short fillers for mainstream movie channels.

Section Five: Make Any Movie

MAKE ANY MOVIE

This section takes you through the movies you want to make, and introduces some you might want to try out. These movies are the ones with the most to offer you – some have a big history of cinema to get inspired by and have become the most fertile places to stop at and hone your skills at moviemaking. Others are newer, are big online and are exciting and sometimes challenging movies to try out. A few are just for your downtime, designed to help you make movies whatever your mood and whatever time you have.

Each chapter has the essentials you need to know to make your short stand out, avoiding anything that makes it look dated or random. Find out who watches this movie, what could inspire you, how to use the camera, or edit or create the right theme.

To create something truly different, pick and mix from a few chapters to create fusions of different movies.

Chapter 33: **Genre: Drama**

Chapter 34: **Genre: Horror**

Chapter 35: **Sci-fi**

Chapter 36: **Comedy**

Chapter 37: **Drama: Noir/Thriller**

Chapter 38: **Documentary**

Chapter 39: **Music Promo**

Chapter 40: **Citizens News/Video Journalist**

Chapter 41: **(Extreme) Sports Movie**

Chapter 42: **Drama: War Film**

Chapter 43: **Freecording**

Chapter 44: **Road Movie**

Chapter 45: **Drama: Western**

Chapter 46: **Howcast**

Chapter Thirty-Three

Genre: Drama

FIGURE 33.1 Actors get ready to shoot a scene from a drama by Armen Antranikian.

WHAT IS IT?

A movie about relationships, people and life.

The Drama is **the mother of all genres,** bringing into the world a whole family of film genres. The bad boys grew up and became the Gangster films, the wanderers left home to become the Westerns, the weirdos became the Comedies, and the sickos became the Horror films.

So with the other genres all grown up and moved away, the Drama genre simply grew to fill the space left behind, with serious movies about people, loss, love, life and death.

Today's drama movies have probably the biggest and most fertile range of subjects to choose from: the things we experience and the things we remember in life:

- Families, what happens when they go wrong
- People who fall through the cracks of society, through alcoholism, drugs or abuse
- Injustice and inequality
- Poverty and wealth
- Corruption by people in power
- Oppression or violence toward women
- Mental turmoil
- Class inequality
- Loss and death

It has a huge hit rate, and packs a powerful emotional punch, leaving the audience wiser, more aware and sometimes wrung out to dry. But every drama has the potential, if handled right, to give the viewer an experience that chimes with their own life. That's what keeps them coming back for more.

MY KIND OF MOVIE?

You like people, you hate people. You don't know why people can't just get on with their lives, and why things get so tough sometimes. You've been on the inside of one or two stories of your own, and you see those times as a chance to learn more about life and people.

You can't help but eavesdrop on conversations around you, to hear what other people go through, and you wonder how to put all that into a movie that affects people just like that conversation affected you. The drama movie can distil all that into one short film, creating an emotional rollercoaster.

WHAT'S IT FOR?

Drama is the staple of most places we watch movies: TV and cable depend on it, the web has a wealth of webisodes centering mostly on people and lives, and most Oscar-winning shorts tend to be serious dramas. It might lack the instant hit that extreme sports or music promos have but it's a slow-burn type of movie, and as such builds up dedicated followers. If you can move an audience with your drama, then you have got friends for life.

HOW LONG WILL IT TAKE ME?

Expect to spend roughly three times as long on the script as on any other part of the production. It's not a quick project and you will find it easier if you let the ideas gradually hatch over a longer period of time, so you can toy with the ideas, adding some and taking away others.

FIGURE 33.2 In Jon Gunn's drama *Like Dandelion Dust* (2009), a couple's idyllic life is shattered when the father of their adopted son is released from prison and lays claim to his son. Mira Sorvino with Maxwell Perry. Credit: Mike Kubeisy.

HOW HARD IS IT?

Difficulty level:

★ ★ ★ ★ ★

Drama tests you on all aspects of moviemaking, so expect this to be an upward learning curve. Just about every aspect of the technical side of the craft is used, from clear sound, to expressive lighting, to location shooting, to continuity editing.

Download the free PDF Ten Start-Up Exercises from the website for this book to cover most bases before starting.

You need to:

- Be able to keep a clear vision of your movie in your mind
- Develop characters as real people
- Work well with actors
- Get good technical results from your crew
- Enjoy writing and coming up with realistic dialogue

WHO ELSE DO I NEED?

- Producer
- Writer
- Sound recordist
- Camera operator
- Editor

WHAT KIT DO I NEED?

- Camera
- Tripod
- Boom mic
- Set of lamps or low-budgets alternatives
- Lavalier mic

IF YOU LIKE THAT WATCH THIS

One Flew Over the Cuckoo's Nest (1975) is a powerful blend of the funny, cruel and the heart-breaking, with Jack Nicholson as the unwilling mental patient. For racial dramas, check out *Bad Day at Black Rock* (1955), *To Kill a Mockingbird* (1962), or Spike Lee's tense *Do the Right Thing* (1989).

Political dramas have become paranoid conspiracies since the 1970s such as *All the President's Men* (1976), *Michael Clayton* (2007), or *The Insider* (1999).

Meanwhile, smaller-scale urban dramas include Mike Leigh's *Naked* (1993), Sam Mendes *American Beauty* (1999) or Todd Haynes *Far From Heaven* (2002).

You could also burrow into the genre to get at the subgenre of melodrama, popular in the 1950s in films by the great Douglas Sirk. Related to melodrama, family dramas can have a big impact, such as Robert Redford's Oscar-winning *Ordinary People* (1980), or Alan Parker's *Shoot the Moon* (1982).

GET INSPIRED

Read supermarket people/gossip magazines to get real-life stories that seem beyond fiction such as *National Enquirer* (USA), *Closer* (UK), or *That's Life* (Australia). Check out Chapter 9, Law and the Movies for tips on how copyright works for real-life stories.

Or talk to friends and family about what they have been through, creating stories from their experiences, changing names or places to preserve anonymity.

PREPRODUCTION ESSENTIALS

Storyboards; script; location photos; release forms; backstory; treatment; lighting designs; budget; permission forms for locations; health and safety sheets; contracts; copyright release for music; shot list; shooting schedule.

See Chapter 11, Brief Directory of All the Paperwork You Need.

WRITING

The script is everything for the drama. It lives or dies by the strength of its lines, how real they sound and most of all how believable and three-dimensional its characters are.

But you don't need to be a seasoned writer to create an Oscar-winning script – Diablo Cody wrote the hit teen drama *Juno* in her 20s, part of a group of young all-women writers nicknamed The Fempire who took Hollywood by storm with their up-to-date, savvy and cringingly true-to-life scripts.

TRY WRITING WITHOUT WRITING

If you get stuck trying to get ideas flowing, try another approach, rejecting actual writing in favor of **improvisation with actors.** Start by discussing the characters of each person, and let the actors develop the backstory, the likes, dislikes and hopes of their character.

Create a dramatic situation as a starting point (like a divorce, or the loss of a job) and then play around with the ideas that come from your actors. You'll need a few more problems to throw their way, things from their backstory that lurk in their past and then cause problems, and you need to keep up the pressure constantly. Give actors a situation and ask "how would you react to that? What would you say?" UK director Mike Leigh has perfected this process in his movies, like the Oscar nominated *Secrets and Lies* (1996).

You can then slowly create a few believable characters who react like real people, talk like real people and make a great drama.

USING THE CAMERA

The focus of this movie is the people, so you need to let the camera linger, tracing every expression of the face and following every word. Take your time, keeping the camera steady, like it's an all-seeing eye, looking right into the soul of the people. Use wide shots and place the characters center frame when you want to isolate them, or push them further to the sides when you need to show heightened emotion. Extreme depth – putting some parts of the scene close to the camera and others much further away – can increase a sense of drama, more so if you place the camera at a slight angle.

Also try a constantly roving camera to make us uneasy, using the camera hand-held but with a steadying device like a Hague support.

EDITING

There are a lot of tried and tested tips which can increase the drama and crank up the tension where needed.

- Try using **juxtaposition** – where you cut between two scenes or places to reveal more about them both, like showing the very different reactions of two people to an event.
- Wherever you can, use this idea of **opposites** to quickly cut between funny and sad, up and down, giving more impact to these emotional scenes.
- Delay a big moment by **using suspense** – pausing on the action to keep us waiting, and creating anticipation while we imagine what will happen.

- In other places, too, **let the audience imagine** a scene before you actually show it. Pause, linger, then go for the dramatic moment. The quiet before the storm makes the storm seem louder.

Music can be over-used, especially in high-drama moments, so go easy and use it sparingly. Check out bittersweet dramas like *Little Miss Sunshine* for how to use music without dominating the show.

LEGALESE

Make sure you have done the following:

- If you use music tracks in your movie, check with the copyright owner.
- Get release forms from every actor stating that they agree to your use of them in the movie.
- Agree how everyone wants to be credited in the end titles.

Upload it

Best site to upload to:
Vimeo
Best communities to join:
Short Narrative Films group at Vimeo:
   "This group is for short films that are narrative driven, character filled and anything else that makes cinema compelling. Humor is hard, drama is risky, suspense can be a bust. But they're all basically people doing things on screen."

Cinebarre Short Films at Vimeo:
   "You've spent countless hours, all of your savings and poured your heart and soul into your film. But now what? Isn't our goal as filmmakers to get our work seen by a mass audience that will appreciate our efforts?"

Best channels to watch:
   The Storytellers at Vimeo, or Independent Films at Vimeo

DRAMA FILM SCHEDULE

This movie works on any length of schedule, but benefits from a longer period in the writing stage. Allow extra time to spend with your actors, rehearsing and improvising lines.

Go to Section 6, Make It Happen: Schedules for more help.

Chapter Thirty-Four

Genre: Horror

WHAT IS IT?

A movie designed to cause fear or a sense of revulsion or dread, with serious and graphic storylines.

There's no escape. Horror movies know what spooks you and they abuse this knowledge mercilessly. Like sci-fi, they tap into the *zeitgeist* and figure out what really keeps you awake at night – the next plague, total war, zombies, scientific breakthroughs backfiring on us – and get inside your head. And that's why we love them so much. Call it therapy, but we love getting together and sharing what scares us, hoping that a nightmare shared is a nightmare halved. If sci-fi takes the zeitgeist and messes with your head, horror does the same but gets you in your gut.

Horror films are unique in the way they affect you physically, manipulating your body through the terror of imagining yourself on screen. You get short of breath, your heart rate goes up, your head hurts – no small wonder then that with this sort of suspense we need a big release, whether it's gore or laughs. The audience is on a small piece of string and the horror movie can tug them at will to feel this or that. The movie gets under your skin and then crawls about.

With so many horror festivals, making a horror movie can be a rewarding project. And most festivals like to have a horror on show somewhere, so high is its audience rating. It's a crowd-pleaser, combining laughs, shock, the yuck factor and has strong word of mouth, making distribution easier.

MY KIND OF MOVIE?

You're sick – no, really. You can spend time recording a watermelon being hacked as Foley for a head dismemberment, then chat through your latest recipe for blood, and you look for body counts like other people check the football scores.

You have a gothic sense of drama where everything is high-octane emotions, live or die decisions, winner takes all. You are mischievous: your movie is like a voodoo doll, using it to create pain and terror in the viewer, and you don't shrink from the task.

In your day job, you are also highly organized, able to work with a team and get everyone on your side so the movie is shot just the way you want.

WHAT'S IT FOR?

Viewers find horror films like zombies returning to the mall. Just put your film out there and they will come and find it. To help you, there are TV horror channels and numerous online channels. If you make a good one, you might get it sold – sales companies roam the festival circuit seeking new movies, and you could land a distribution deal, though it won't make you rich. Or why not sell direct to the viewers? Make DVDs as you need them and let viewers buy or download direct from you.

Try to spot your ideal viewer as you walk around town. Think of who you are aiming at and keep that in mind. Horror film audiences are wholly committed to horror – they have an encyclopedic love of the genre and total recall of a movie's every scene. That means they'll notice every continuity glitch and blooper. But if you treat the fans with regard, horror audiences tend to be loyal and steadfast in their devotion to a movie, relentlessly spreading the word.

If features put you off, try horror Webisodes (see Chapter 30, Create Your Own Web Series) where this genre is very popular, or short horror virals, which get a good showing on phones.

HOW LONG WILL IT TAKE ME – WHAT SORT OF PROJECT IS THIS?

Take your time. You might be chewing over the idea and script for some months before you finally get to work on it. Or you could reasonably create, shoot and edit the movie in a weekend, following one of the many 48-hour film challenge competitions (see www.halloweenchallenge.com).

HOW HARD IS IT?

Difficulty level:
★ ★ ★ ★ ★

Like comedy, horror is easy to do badly. Spend a long time working on the script, running through the lines so they sound real, and honing the story so it runs at a sprint. Set a standard for yourself where you weed out any cliché, turn any horror convention inside out and upturn expectations. Go further and borrow from other genres to create a fusion in a new sort of horror – horror audiences love weird mutations.

You need:

- Good skill in lighting
- A focused team
- A clear vision of the movie – you're almost able to close your eyes and watch it play
- To work under pressure
- To handle visual stunts, effects and post-production tricks
- To avoid cliché and never underestimate the audience

WHO ELSE WILL I NEED?

- Producer
- Sound recordist
- Camera operators × 2
- Editor
- Makeup

WHAT KIT DO I NEED?

Shoot on HD unless it's just for the web. You'll need a good lighting package with at least one **heavy-duty key lamp** (see Chapter 16, Lighting) and at least **two smaller fill lamps.**

For sound, use a **boom,** but you will also need directional mics for recording sound effects.

IF YOU LIKE THAT, WATCH THIS

For the weird look of the movie, try *The Cabinet of Dr Caligari* (Robert Weine, 1919), built with slanted sets, painted shadows and crooked houses.

And you can't bypass *Night of the Living Dead* (George R. Romero, 1968). The movie is year zero for modern horror, taking the genre into political territory: dumb cops, quarreling human hostages, and a shock ending. By the end it's the zombies who get our sympathy.

To see where the slasher subgenre started, watch *Halloween* (John Carpenter, 1978) – the killer on the loose, the pretty teenage targets, the questionable morals of sex leads to death. Also check out Spanish and Latin American horror such as *The Orphanage* (2007), and *Let the Right One In* (2009) and fantasy crossover *Pan's Labyrinth* (2006). East Asian horror, meanwhile, is a cool and shocking law unto itself, serving up sushi nightmares that erupt into gore.

GET INSPIRED

Check out graphic novels and comics such as Alan Moore's *From Hell; Arkham Asylum*, from the Batman series (1986); and *The Walking Dead* series by

Robert Kirkman. For creepy short ideas, go direct to the master storyteller HP Lovecraft.

Or go way back to Greek myth tales such as *The Labyrinth*, used to maximum effect in *The Descent* (2005).

PREPRODUCTION ESSENTIALS

Storyboards; script; location photos; release forms; style sheets/designs; costume designs; backstory; treatment; lighting designs; budget; permission forms for locations; health and safety sheets; contracts; copyright release for music; shot list; shooting schedule.

See Chapter 11, Brief Directory of All the Paperwork You Need.

USING THE CAMERA

The problem with shooting horror is to **catch out an increasingly switched-on movie audience.** When we see a character on screen we now read the signs and expect someone to jump out, or an axe to fall. So far, so bored. Horror director John Carpenter's trick was to keep us guessing, using the entire camera frame, so we never quite know where danger will come from. With "peripheral misdirection," he deliberately shot crucial action at the edge or back of the frame. Without the standard film "signs" to read, we are as in the dark as Mike Myers' victims, unsure about where is safe and where not. To do this kind of shot well, treat the camera as yet another actor, and who hasn't seen the script. When something jumps out, it takes the camera by surprise.

If your story involves people getting hurt, then you shouldn't ignore the two essentials for this sort of scene: a killer getting its victim, and a way of letting us see what it's like to kill. The point-of-view shot (POV) does this perfectly. It goes to the heart of right versus wrong, asking us to briefly empathize with the monster, hitching a ride with him as he does what we ourselves shouldn't.

EDITING

In horror, suspending disbelief is everything. Remind us it's just a movie and we come crashing down to earth with a bump. So use classic continuity editing. See Chapter 21, Editing Methods: Narrative Continuity for help.

CLOSE-UPS

When you edit, choose close-ups whenever possible, for their dramatic value and for the way they control what we see. You can disorientate the viewer quickly, keep danger hidden until the last moment, and create the right atmosphere of claustrophobia and clamor to build tension. And viewers always want to forensically inspect gory scenes.

FIGURE 34.1 Use close-ups to capture tension and claustrophobia. (Photo courtesy of iStockphoto, ©clintspencer, Image# 6655407)

CUTTING FOR ACTION

Maintain the fluid transition of shot to shot, helping rhythm and pace by trimming the end of clips on the timeline to make sure every clip ends in mid-action. Don't let a clip show a complete sequence of actions, instead rely on several which partly show it.

RHYTHM

For tension and suspense, treat the sequence just as if it were a piece of music, building tension through a series of quickening beats. Start a sequence with long (say, four second) shots, and steadily shorten the length as you build tension. Hold fire suddenly, lingering on one image for a while, before launching into an even quicker set of clips.

If you want to add special effects, apply subtle color casts for particular scenes where needed, in dream sequences or when you need to unsettle the viewer's sense of time or space. For slasher moments, sound effects are a cheap and effective way of creating a gory finale, so opt for gooey sounds layered with animal noises. Mess up the whole thing further with three or four frames of blurred shots interspersed into the narrative.

Experts' Tips

Dewi Griffiths, film director, UK

"Have a great story, and good actors – and build from there. Try to make it as simple as you can so you spend your time working up what you have as opposed to moving from place to place or dealing with other logistical problems. Make it an audience pleaser, and it should be successful – but know that audience, what they want, what they like: research. Horror films follow rules – know which ones to break."

Ray Gower, director, *Dark Corners*(2006), USA

"Never stop believing. Find ways to shoot, whether it's using a camcorder and a couple of friends, or selling your house and shooting with a fullblown crew (not recommended, but how I started out!) – gain as much experience as you can, watch movies (good and bad!) and never give up. And if you can't shoot, then write. And write. And write. It is the most important aspect of filmmaking and the cheapest. Despite shooting hundreds of commercials, short films, corporates, you name it, it took me twelve years to get into movies – and my first real break came through my writing.

"[In *Dark Corners*] I tried to do something a little different. A kind of art-house, psychological horror. I like the look, the weird ambience, Thora (Birch) and Toby (Stephens)'s performances – but would I change anything? The honest answer would be yes – but then no director is ever happy with their work. Truth is we had a tiny budget, an extraordinarily tight shooting schedule plagued with problems and I had to lose and adjust scenes constantly. In an ideal world I would go back and create the perfect film I had originally pictured in my mind – but then filmmaking is all about managing compromise."

LEGALESE

STORY COPYRIGHT

For classic stories, copyright laws mean that most of the horror classics are free to use, such as most of Edgar Allen Poe, *Dracula*, and *Jekyll and Hyde*. If an author has died more than 70 years ago then in most cases copyright will have entered the public domain and you are free to use the work for your movie.

Make sure you have done the following:

- Checked with the copyright owner if you use music tracks in your movie.
- Before you shoot – get permissions from any location you want to shoot in. Some owners of locations are resistant to horror films, such as churches or schools.
- Get release forms from every actor stating that they agree to your use of them in the movie.
- Make sure you and your close collaborators all agree – in writing – where you want to show the film, so no one objects later.
- Agree how everyone wants to be credited in the end titles.

Upload It

Best site to upload to:
Vimeo
Best communities to join:
Horror/Thriller Movies at Vimeo:

"A place for Vimeans to post horror or thriller movies they like or created! Let's use this as a forum for constructive criticism on our works, discussions of techniques to improve suspense or to just talk about movies you like!"

Scare Me at Vimeo:
   "All things scary! Muaaaahahahaha…"
Best channels to watch:
At Dark Junctions at Vimeo:
   "A channel dedicated to the macabre, the phantasmal, and the unexplored."
The Horror Channel at www.Metacafe.com

HORROR FILM SCHEDULE

This movie will fit any length of schedule, from 48 hours to 28 days. See Section 6 for a guide to schedules.

Chapter | Thirty-Five

Sci-fi

WHAT IS IT?

It's like *The Matrix*: take the red pill. Sci-fi is the truth genre, letting you see the world as it really is. Sci-fi isn't really about the future at all; instead it shows us the present, revealing the real world beneath all our own Truman Show-like lives. Sci-fi just can't hold back from the truth.

Or you can take the blue pill and carry on watching rom-coms and stay smiling. Like Neo, the choice is yours.

Like Spielberg's Department of Pre-crime in *Minority Report*, sci-fi alerts us to what might happen around the corner, just a few years down the line – and it's done this since the 1950s. It's like an x-ray of the zeitgeist, telling us what really freaks us out, whether that's nukes, getting mutated by radiation, drowned out by climate change, or suppressed by corrupt governments.

But it's more than that – the reason it has the top slots in biggest box-office of all time charts is that it does all this with thrills, a hint of philosophy, action, and plots you can stand behind and shout for. It's the only genre where you are not restricted by any of the normal rules of life, or time, or space. Anything goes, anytime, anywhere. The only proviso is: it has to have its own logic, and make sense in its own way, so spend a while figuring out the back-story to your plot, so it has its own believable universe. If you get quizzed about your movie, you'll know it inside out.

MY KIND OF MOVIE?

You have your finger on the pulse. You watch the news, hear what goes on and what can go wrong in the world. Just like Sarah Connor, this means you might not sleep too well, but when you find other people who share your ideas, it's like a meeting of the faithful. To make a movie about your ideas seems just a small step: part therapy, part thrill-ride.

You have mapped out the prequel and sequel, and fleshed out the characters with real motivations. You're going to find this movie easy to make – it's already fully formed inside your head.

You like sci-fi but are very particular about your top 10 and you know enough about what you don't like to make sure it doesn't happen in your movie.

WHAT'S IT FOR?

Sci-fi has a big loyal fan-base, with a wider range of ages than horror, but like horror fans they are intelligently able to connect the dots in your movie and see the next plot turn coming. These people pay real attention to the film, they don't slouch in the quiet bits, instead seeing every section as potentially having the key to the movie. These people pay real attention.

Seven out of the top ten highest-grossing films of all time are sci-fi (the three others in the list are fantasy movies). Sci-fi has a lot of dedicated film festivals, comic conventions, and cable channels. Even decades-old TV shows get constant re-airing; at any time an episode of *Star Trek* is said to be showing somewhere in the world.

FIGURE 35.1 Use locations and props to create a futuristic feel for a scene, as in this image using an existing Geisha costume and a store room. (Photo courtesy of iStockphoto, ©nuno, Image# 8322770)

HOW LONG WILL IT TAKE ME?

Like other genre films, take your time in planning and reap rewards later. Sci-fi is a more thoughtful genre than most, requiring a strong idea followed through by detailed research. The only sure way to avoid a story that gets shot down by the fans is to expand your story and ideas into a much larger world, where you have thought about the background to the events in your movie, going back years, and the backstory of your characters. Use index cards to cross-reference events and people.

HOW HARD IS IT?

Difficulty level:

★ ★ ★ ★ ★

Sci-fi needs particular handling. You need two antennae fixed to your head – one to intercept and zap any extravagant or over-the-top plotlines or dialogue, the other to stop any possibility of patronizing the audience. The challenge with this genre is in making it believable and real (without spending big bucks), and coherent. It has to stand up to close scrutiny by fans and friends.

You need:

- A complete vision of your imagined world
- A complete back-story of your characters, and events previous to those in your movie
- The ability to make sci-fi it look like it's made now, not twenty years ago. It has to strongly relate to events in today's world
- Ideas that fit into today's visions of the future
- To be a good organizer and planner
- To re-imagine our world as a world of the future; use everyday places and use your ingenuity to make them appear from the future

WHO ELSE WILL I NEED?

- Producer
- Sound recordist
- Camera operator
- Editor
- Designer – or someone able to create your imagined world from few props

WHAT KIT DO I NEED?

- Camera
- Tripod
- Boom mic
- Set of lamps
- Lavalier mic

IF YOU LIKE THAT WATCH THIS

For inspiration try low-budget sci-fi such as the angst-ridden *Dark Star* (1974) by John Carpenter, and fan movies such as *Batman: Dead End*, by LA's Sandy Collora (www.collorastudios.com), made to fit into the franchise but on a fraction of the budget. George Lucas' *THX1138B* (1971) shows you how to use just a bunch of students plus a metro train system to create a weird vision of the future. *Alphaville* (1965), meanwhile, also manages without lavish sets, creating a paranoid future in everyday Paris, and apparently the inspiration itself for the later classic *Blade Runner* (1982).

GET INSPIRED

IDEAS:

To create your own sci-fi movie, avoid space operas in favor of ideas based firmly in the believable near-future. This allows you maximum room to include whatever futuristic wildcards you want to insert, but within the context of a familiar environment. Avoid a reliance on effects, since a tiny budget can't compete with the FX-laden blockbuster.

THEMES FOR LOW BUDGET SCI-FI

Stuck for ideas? Try these themes that have made classic sci-fi movies.

- **Body shock**

Crossing over into horror, this theme sees aliens, bugs, or disease take over or attack the human body. But it also takes a positive view of mutations, as in *X-Men*, using the theme to reflect racism and genocide.

Seek out: *The Fly* (1958 or remake 1986).

- **Technology**

This idea says that technology will get smarter than us and eventually turn on us, like *Terminator*, or *The Matrix* trilogy.

Seek out: *2001: A Space Odyssey* (1968)

- **Memory**

This theme goes with the idea that in a technological world all that we have left that machines can't do is our personal memories. Not for long, says the writer Philip K. Dick, who reckoned that our memories can be wiped or changed like any hard-drive disc. Dick singlehandedly created this theme in short stories and novels, leading to films like *Blade Runner* (implanted memories), *Minority Report* (foreseen events); and *Total Recall* (memories for sale).

Seek out: *Eternal Sunshine of the Spotless Mind* (2004).

- **Society**

A lot of sci-fi themes since 2000 have been about future society becoming totalitarian, like the Nazis. A lot of ideas about prejudice, race, civil war and corruption have been played out in some great sci-fi moments. *District 9* (2009) is a movie trying to figure out apartheid in racist South Africa, instead using a separate alien section of South Africa to create a gripping action movie.

Experts' Tips

Kole Onile-ere, director, *The Virus*, UK

"[For my story] I very much remember when President Bush said 'if you aren't with us you're the enemy.' There was no free speech – it was like there had to be one way or no way at all, there is no alternative. All of us in the West here, even if we wanted to disagree or even question anything, we were the enemy. So out of that I wrote this story."

PREPRODUCTION ESSENTIALS

Storyboards; script; location photos; release forms; style sheets/designs; costume designs; backstory; treatment; lighting designs; budget; permission forms for locations; health and safety sheets; contracts; copyright release for music; shot list; shooting schedule.

USING THE CAMERA

Sci-fi includes a wide range of ideas so no single method covers all. But if you are working on a zero-budget then you may need to **use existing locations** and make them look stranger or more futuristic. **Use wide angle lenses** and try to enhance the visual depth of the image – that means having stuff up close and other stuff far away at the back. It makes the picture look surreal and slightly disorientating. Check out surrealist painters like Salvador Dali or Giorgio de Chirico to get ideas. UK director Michael Winterbottom shot his movie *Code 46* in present day Shanghai and Dubai, using the camera to create a futuristic look.

FIGURE 35.2 Modern buildings make ideal no-budget sci-fi locations, as in this city library, shot using a fish-eye lens. (Photo courtesy of iStockphoto, ©Nikada, Image# 6291774)

EDITING

When you edit your sci-fi movie, spend time looking at the script again to remind yourself what you had intended. What was the overall atmosphere you wanted? **Sci-fi shorts can get away with being a little more weird, so be bold**, be adventurous and don't fall into the trap of thinking the viewer needs fast action right from the first moment.

Good sound editing can make a low-budget movie seem like it cost much more to make. Create a big, wide sound environment, using several layers on the timeline. Add sounds of what we can't see. You can conjure up a busy, dense city street with layers of traffic noise, audio advertising, and a range of machine-like sounds. This is the moment to think big and make us imagine a broader world – and pretty soon we'll think we saw it too.

Experts' Tips

Kole Onile-ere, director, *The Virus*

"Sci-fi is a very hard genre to get off the ground. Nowadays it has to be a hybrid, like a horror/sci-fi such as *28 Days Later* which some might say is almost not sci-fi. What I like about the genre is it allows people to just be who they are – black, white, whatever – and also it is a smarter way to talk about things. You can do that in sci-fi, you can talk about issues in the wider world and you can do it more cleverly. If you think of *1984* or *Blade Runner*, even *The Matrix*, they talk about things. It allows you that freedom to do that."

"If you want to make a sci-fi film, the first thing is you have to have something to say. For me sci-fi films like *Solaris* really talk about real issues so I would ask people to think about what they want to talk about and then to get together with a group of like-minded people. You don't always need a load of money as long as the story is strong, and the structure is right."

LEGALESE

Fantasy movies like sci-fi will have less to worry you about offending people here in the present, but beware of how you use real names and especially corporations – if your story is a *Matrix*-style future where computers took over, don't say it's all Bill Gates' fault.

You'll need:

- Release forms from all cast and crew
- Permission from the owner of each location to agree filming, and remember to contact city authorities if shooting in a city center or on busy streets

Upload It

Best site to upload to:
Vimeo
Best communities to join:
Art, Music, Sci-fi and Comicbook Group at Vimeo
Best channels to watch:
Live Action Sci-fi at Vimeo:
  "Live-Action Science Fiction Themed Videos."

Experts' Tips

Blanca Escoda, film director, *The Arrival*, London
  "The purpose of sci-fi movies is to make people think about the universe and humanity. These films have to bring the most basic philosophical questions to the audience's mind: who are we and what are we doing here. If the premise of a sci-fi film is good and original you might have a potentially interesting film even if you haven't got a great amount of money to shoot it. You should aim at having striking visuals in the film as well, but that doesn't mean you have to have expensive special effects. If you are going to shoot a genre movie but you use visuals of a different genre you will already be doing something different that might just intrigue the audience. The film *Let the Right One In* by Tomas Alfredson is a fantasy movie but some of its visuals seem to be more characteristic of a social drama. This mixture gives depth and interest to the film and makes it stand out."

SCI-FI SCHEDULE

This movie fits into any length of schedule, from 48 hours to 28 days.

Chapter Thirty-Six

Comedy

FIGURE 36.1 Jason Korsner's *2 Hour Parking* (2007) in which a date gets continually disrupted by Los Angeles' parking enforcement rules.

WHAT IS IT?

A movie designed to make you laugh, smile or see the funny side.

Bad times need good laughs. Comedy is huge business now and more comedy clips go viral than any other, with phone to phone sharing a great way to pass on an original, funny or plain stupid clip. The craft of hitting the right note in a comedy is still as elusive as it ever was – so when you see something that makes you laugh you have to pass it on. Quick skits, funny visual gags, TV rip-offs or street performers, all get around the world faster online than in a prime-time broadcast.

But comedy is not just laughs – it's also a place to get angry, to yell about what matters, to provoke new ideas and make yourself heard. Comedy is like a loaded weapon, ready to take you hunting on a big safari of smooth shysters, corporate scammers, political whitewashers or good old fashioned hypocrites. More than other type of movie, you make your point a hundred times stronger when the audience laughs.

MY KIND OF MOVIE?

You have a leftfield point of view, you were born to see the world in a different way. Before you could read you were a seasoned observer of the weird things we all do. You watch, you see all, you notice everything, you eavesdrop on the bus, and it all goes into the big mill that is your imagination.

Just like a stand-up comic, the best of your observations are of the Martian variety – hey, do you know what these humans actually do? When we watch your movie, we'll see the world your way, and understand why you have that occasional mock-scared expression when you look around you.

WHAT'S IT FOR?

You're going to make friends from this movie, make no mistake. You'll find it easier to get crew, and to be downloaded widely to get the movie seen. And, if you shoot in higher quality, you can be a contender for sales companies, selling your short movie to cable channels, airlines and other slots.

Even better, film festivals almost always like comedies. They like to kick off the first night with one, sprinkle them throughout the proceedings and use as dessert to close the festival. Distribution should be fun.

HOW LONG WILL IT TAKE ME?

The work starts here – the script needs your loving care and attention. It needs redraft after redraft, reading through with a few friends, and you'll be ready to take it on the chin when no one laughs at your favorite parts. Expect to spend a couple of weeks honing the script, working both on the dialogue and visual gags.

Then check you're not going to get sued by anyone if it's a satire or spoof, so check Chapter 9, Law and the Movies for more guidance on defamation.

Shooting might need more takes than other movies, as you try to get exactly the right timing and comic effect. Get multiple takes so you can decide which one you want later in the quiet of the edit room. The trick is to make it look easy, casual and relaxed, but just like a drama, it needs careful rehearsal and shooting.

Edit at your leisure but run through the movie at a small screening for friends – pre-drinks.

HOW HARD IS IT?

Difficulty level:

★ ★ ★ ★ ☆

Challenging, but more rewarding. Comedies need to be governed with an iron fist, as it's all too easy to let it go off into wild, funny-to-make-but-not-to-watch territory. As a rule of thumb, the more sober you are making it, the more you can keep us laughing later.

You need:

- Good sense of humor
- To have an eye for observing and remembering the weird stuff people do
- To be able to see the movie just as an audience would
- To love writing
- To enjoy working hard to get the movie right
- Being original and unusual in your ideas
- To work as part of team

WHO ELSE DO I NEED?

You need to be freed up from technical duties to focus on the movie. What is in the script won't always appear as you thought it would, and you need to be on a state of high alertness to make changes as you go.

- Sound recordist
- Camera operator
- Producer

AND:

Test your script on other people way before you shoot. In comedy the writing is everything – even if there are no spoken words and all gags are visual.

WHAT KIT DO I NEED?

- Camera
- Tripod
- Hand-held mic
- Lavalier mic × 2
- Basic lighting kit for indoor shooting

IF YOU LIKE THAT WATCH THIS

Funny to some is dull to others, and comedies only thrive when they find their own bespoke audience. Some of the best comedies have taken a while to find their own elusive audiences of fans, but they have lasted longer, like *Withnail and I* (1987), *Clerks* (1994), *Fargo* (1996), or *Napoleon Dynamite* (2004).

For indie laughs, in the so-called "mumble-core movies" (where people don't talk like actors), laughs are at the expense of the hero and even then are more of the quiet chuckle variety. Try *Garden State* (2004), *Little Miss Sunshine* (2006), or *Rushmore* (1998).

Dark humor plays well to festivals and gets you the acclaim of the seen-it-all variety of viewer. Try *Dr. Strangelove* (1964), Peter Jackson's *Braindead* (1992), *M*A*S*H* (1972), or *Shawn of the Dead* (2004).

GET INSPIRED

Ideas for comedy tend to come from anywhere except funny situations. If something hurts, then it can be funny. Look at events in your own life and your friends' lives; pick the very worst times and use them as the basis of your comedy. Many great comedy classics tend to be rooted in a kind of cathartic humor which releases tension, like *Little Miss Sunshine* or *Dr. Strangelove*.

PREPRODUCTION ESSENTIALS

Storyboards; treatment; script; location photos; release forms; budget; permission forms for locations; health and safety sheets; contracts; copyright release for music; shot list; shooting schedule.

USING THE CAMERA

Shooting comedy won't demand any single approach for using the camera. But funny moments can be undermined by using the camera in a way that deflates the joke, so it helps if you have a general awareness of the effect of each type of camera angle or movement. Sometimes, the camera angle itself is enough to make the moment funny, such as creating pathos by showing a character alone in a wide shot.

EDITING

- Sharp editing is essential in this kind of movie; comedy needs **precise timing and a confident style.** Timing means knowing how long to show a clip for maximum effect. If you leave a shot too long on screen it can fall flat, but too little and we miss the gag.
- A lot of independent comedy films **avoid jokes in favor of images.** A situation is set up and then we watch as the elements of it collide. In **Napoleon Dynamite,** the hero of the title has to feed the pet llama. It's a great edit – the shots are slow, with 6 to 10 seconds each, making it all look awkward. The framing is big and wide, so we see Napoleon in center frame, looking pitiful and embarrassed. Unlike most films, there's no cut on movement (see Chapter 21, Editing Methods: Narrative Continuity), leaving some awkward pauses in the sequence. It's comedy because the

viewer gets embarrassed, because the shots are so long, and because Napoleon is so totally incapable of filling the screen. It's not belly-laugh comedy, but you remember the clip long after – YouTube hits for this scene exceed ratings for some network comedy shows.

LEGALESE

Treat this with kid gloves – some people get a little crabby when you poke fun at them so be careful to mask the target of your comedy. Screen a disclaimer if you are too close to reality, and if they have bigger lawyers than you.

Aside from a target, get release forms from all cast or others who appear.

Upload It

Best site to upload to:
YouTube or **Revver**
Best communities to join:
Web Comedy at Vimeo:
   "A chance for comedians to showcase their web series, stand up, or sketch comedy. Everyone is welcome . . ."
Best channels to watch:
Derrickcomedy Channel at YouTube

COMEDY SCHEDULE

Comedy movies need extra time honing the script but if you are happy with that then it suits any length of schedule.

Chapter | Thirty-Seven

Drama: Noir/Thriller

FIGURE 37.1 *The West Side*, a powerful web series with hints of thriller, noir and western in its setting.

WHAT IS IT?

A dark, psychological, and bleak drama often based around urban crime.

Noir isn't just a genre, it's a genre-for-hire, instantly lending a simple plot-driven B-movie the chance to become a work of art, to give it a philosophy. Sure, it tends to be fatalistic, downbeat, menacing, and you won't form lasting attachments with noir characters – in fact, you'll want to lose them soon after the credits roll. But these are movies that leave their mark, evident in the many noir films still being made. In *The Bourne* trilogy, the title lead is a typical noir antihero – a mysterious past, no fear and no hope, all set in a cynical and corrupt world.

Forget the fact that noir films tend to be *visually* dark, the real point of them is that they are *psychologically* dark, they have a kind of inner darkness of the soul. Writers like Paul Schrader *(Taxi Driver)* prefer to label these movies "dark expressionistic cinema" or "psychological melodrama."

The genre even creeps into places you wouldn't expect – inspiring Clint Eastwood's *The Man With No Name* in the *Dollars* trilogy or Sean Connery's police marshal in sci-fi thriller *Outland* (1981). In fact, once you think of noir as a psychological movie, it becomes a fertile place to create deep and dark characters and detailed plots in any location and any period in time.

MY KIND OF MOVIE?

You'll enjoy drama, but are drawn to the more extreme, dark and almost gothic stories. You are fascinated by finding out what goes on beneath the facades of people and everyday life, and generally believe that what you'll find is not too clean, or honest. There's dirt on those streets.

If glossy Hollywood happy endings or cheery moral tales leave you unconvinced, noir seems more realistic to you, like it lifts the rock of society and shows you the teeming low-life underneath. It may not be pretty but to you this is the truth, and underneath that tough exterior of yours that's something you can believe in.

WHAT'S IT FOR?

Noir and thrillers have a high audience rating – people know what to expect and they enjoy the grown-up mix of thrills plus psychological undertones. They like a strong plot, driving forward at a fast pace.

Noir also exports well – try clashing it with other genres, updating it or moving it to unexpected settings.

Aside from traditional audiences, noir fits well into short webisodes, with enough action and dialogue to make a quick hit in just a few minutes.

HOW LONG WILL IT TAKE ME?

It's heavily dependent on script and ideas, so take a long while to develop both. Characters need to be fully developed, with a full backstory to refer to, but at the same time avoiding regular clichés you tend to find in genres that have been around for a long time.

Expect to spend three times as long on script as on shooting, just like with dramas.

HOW HARD IS IT?

Difficulty level:

★ ★ ★ ★ ☆

Noir and thriller movies demand a lean, clever script, honed into good shape over time. During shooting, the camera can't be an innocent bystander – it has to show a lot of the meaning in each scene by the way you frame the action. So spend time working on your camera technique, especially how to create atmosphere and mood using lighting. Editing is less taxing than some genres, since it needs to be led by the action and dialogue.

You need to:

- Be able to write good dialogue and create believable characters
- Shoot expressive images
- Work well with actors
- Keep a plot-driven movie managed well – making sure you get the shots you need, and stick to the plans
- Organize and work well with teams
- Believe in your own vision for your movie

WHO ELSE DO I NEED?

You need all the usual suspects:

- Producer
- Sound recordist
- Camera operator
- Editor

WHAT KIT DO I NEED?

- Camera
- Tripod
- Boom mic
- Set of lamps, including large key lamp, and any improvised lamps you can get hold of
- Lavalier mic

IF YOU LIKE THAT WATCH THIS

Check out anything by the German wave of directors who fled to America in the '30s and '40s and brought with them a dark style, a pessimistic plot and a low budget – Fred Zinneman (*High Noon* – a kind of western noir) Billy Wilder (*Double Indemnity*) and Otto Wilder (*Laura*) Preminger.

For a crash course in how to get expressive lighting, try *Mildred Pierce* (1945), by Michael Curtiz, another mid-European director.

Into the twenty-first century, noir thrillers have found a new lease on life in the retro *Kiss Kiss Bang Bang* (2005) and in the unlikely shape of high school noir *Brick* (2005).

GET INSPIRED

Go back to basics with the writers who inspired the movies, like James M. Cain, Ed McBain, Jim Thompson (*The Killer Inside Me*), or James Ellroy.

Check out the very noir-like graphic novels created by Alan Moore and others such as the sci-fi series *Watchmen*, and the *Dark Knight* Batman series.

PREPRODUCTION ESSENTIALS

Storyboards; script; location photos; release forms; style sheets/designs; costume designs; backstory; treatment; lighting designs; budget; permission forms for locations; health and safety sheets; contracts; copyright release for music; shot list; shooting schedule.

See Chapter 11, Brief Directory of All the Paperwork You Need.

To make sure that your themes are coherent, **try writing the subtext first,** leaving spaces between each line to add in dialogue later. You'll have explicit lines saying what the real underlying theme is (the subtext – see Chapter 1, Ideas) in each scene. Then later you can write the best way of showing this more subtly.

When you are certain you have this core theme watertight, and that no scene happens that doesn't push this theme forward in some way, then is the time to **turn this subtext into dialogue – with hints, innuendo, and symbols.** For example, in one scene in *Double Indemnity*, the seen-it-all hero Neff realizes that he has not quite seen everything coming and that the culprit of a murder is right under his nose, as femme fatale Phyllis. If that is the subtext, then the spoken text has to be more interesting to hear: "How could I have known that murder could sometimes smell like honeysuckle?" he says.

Also try these ideas that crop up in noir movies:

THE NONHEROIC HERO

Your main character rejects heroism, and is flawed after realizing the futility of bringing order to a chaotic world. They should be people who have been through bad times, who've suffered, and who now fear nothing but also hope for nothing.

ALIENATION AND LONELINESS

This is a great theme to use in a noir. It's every man for himself, in a world where community is lost and no one trusts anyone else. Think *Swamp Thing* meets *Shawshank*.

FATE

The gamble of the dice plays both ways: blind chance helping produce a clue to reveal a crime or instead sealing a death. In *He Walked By Night* (1948), an escaping man is shot by police in the sewers all because a parked car blocked his escape via a manhole cover.

VIOLENCE AND PARANOIA

As in *Taxi Driver*, keep the audience guessing whether the seemingly paranoid delusions of the hero are to be believed or not. Use a voiceover to help us identify with the hero. And when the violence starts, don't hold back.

USING THE CAMERA

Visually, **noir movies tend to be overwhelmingly dark.** All those shadows create a sea of darkness in which the characters seem to risk being submerged in what lurks there. Look for shots that make the most of the shadows you create on location, and which emphasize the psychological tone of the movie.

Elsewhere in the frame **you can represent chaos and fragmentation by having jagged lines of light or half-revealed objects.** It's a powerful effect: it leads the viewer to the crucial parts of the frame, creates a composition with impact and the high contrast heightens the drama in a big way.

Noir lighting is about how little you can get away with, but also has a lot to do with what the camera can contribute. Make sure you have manual settings on your camcorder – with both the iris and shutter speed ready for adjustment to darken the image or increase contrast.

LIGHTING STEP-BY-STEP

- In a darkened location, **arrange the set so you have total control over lighting,** closing curtains and if necessary working at night.
- A **slide projector or overhead presentation projector** is an even better no-budget solution as the light it throws is sharply defined. And it allows you to place gobos, or paper masks, to imitate shadows.
- Next up, **arrange the action so that strong lights illuminate the crucial parts,** but try masking wherever possible, to cut down light further.
- Many noir films succeed by using deep focus in a shot, where objects are seen further away in the frame to add interest and exaggerate the sense of drama, as seen in *Citizen Kane* (1941). Once you have the main action lit, **pick out occasional details further back with smaller lamps,** or throw long shadows against back walls. Or you can point lights right at the camera itself, the glare helping further to reduce the surroundings to black.
- **Why keep the light stationary?** Bounce it off a shallow puddle of water to create Ridley Scott-style rippling, or cast it through a rotating fan.
- **Next, arrange the camcorder settings manually**. Turn down the iris so that the aperture is letting less light through the lens. After a few stops (shown on the LCD monitor by numbers prefaced with the letter 'f') you should notice that the grey parts of the scene are now black, and the bright areas are now isolated puddles of light.

EDITING

Use Chapter 21, Editing Methods: Narrative Continuity but also experiment with more unusual editing moments, so try Chapter 22, Editing Methods: Montage to get us inside the heads of your characters. Don't just give us the plot, instead give us their minds and their feelings right up on screen.

Take a deeper look into montage editing and **try out some other branches of montage** such as *accelerated montage* where clips are cut together at shorter and shorter lengths to create a heightened emotional moment or *parallel montage* where two separate locations are cut together to create links between the two, or with flashbacks for flash-forwards.

Many noir thrillers **mess up the editing deliberately** now and then, to make us feel uneasy. Try breaking a few rules like adding in jump cuts, cutting erratically without rhythm or making big leaps in time or between places – anything to throw us off balance as we watch. Go to Chapter 13 Shooting and break a few rules.

Voiceovers are a useful, and kind of retro, tool. They tend to be used in documentaries to clarify what's happening, but in the noir thriller, it's the opposite – they can be used to confuse us or give us the wrong information – or even speak from beyond the grave, as in *Sunset Boulevard* (1950).

Experts' Tips

Simon Phillips, producer, *Jack Says* (2007)

"Noir film was all about characters and mood – which they created with some fantastic, now almost formulaic, shots. They also had a wonderful mix of iconic characters that are so recognizable in many films today. But the question here is not 'how to create a film noir'; it's a contemporary film noir that our audience crave, so how can this be delivered? You've still got to take the raw ingredients of characters (the femme fatale, the pure-of-heart love interest, the street wise guy pushed from pillar to post) and put them in surroundings that are foreign to them. For *Jack Says* we have given our leading man amnesia – which allows a certain artistic license for a slightly surreal picture to be painted. But it's characters and quick-delivery that allow the audience to be reminded of a film genre that won't die."

LEGALESE

Make sure you have done the following:

- Checked with the copyright owner if you use music tracks in your movie
- Before you shoot, get permissions from any location you want to shoot in
- Get release forms from every actor stating that they agree to your use of them in the movie

Upload It

Best site to upload to:
Vimeo
Best communities to join:
Film Noir and **Dystopic Sci-fi** at Vimeo:

"This group is dedicated to the still growing community of creators of the modern Film Noir, Dark Fiction and dystopic Science Fiction Movies and Videos. Most material of good quality is welcome."

Best channels to watch:
Film Noir Channel at Vimeo:

"A Vimeo Channel to showcase cinematic Hollywood crime drama style films known as film noir."

NOIR THRILLER FILM SCHEDULE

Make this movie in any schedule length, from 48 hours to 28 days. See Section 6, Make It Happen: Schedules for more help.

Documentary

Anne Aghion, documentary filmmaker, New York

"I make creative documentaries. I'm sometimes tempted to make fiction films, but the truth is it's *much* more fun to make docs. You can improvise and go with the flow, whereas in fiction, you have to have everything planned out right from the start."

WHAT IS IT?

Any movie filmed for real with real people in real events, but could also include dramatizations and reconstructions.

Documentary is not what it used to be, and that's good. It has evolved into a type of movie that contains every other movie within it – you can use bits of animation, music promo, drama, montage – just about anything except probably the old-school documentary where a guy looks at the camera and talks with news clips.

On a low budget this is a great option, as you don't need actors, just the gift of talking your subject into letting you film them. And most situations seem to lend themselves to scrutiny once you get deeply involved – from a day in the life of a taxi driver, to the inside story of a tattoo parlor, to the story of your friend who survived a car crash.

Documentary – or nonfiction to give it a common name – has now become one of the most interesting places a filmmaker can work. They break new ground, can be totally original, and potentially make big names for their creators. Many nonfiction directors go on to become fiction directors, using the skill of creating a realistic fast-moving story and bringing it to action thrillers like *The Bourne Supremacy* (Paul Greengrass), or *State of Play* (Andrew Macdonald). It's a great school to hone your storytelling crafts and avoid big costs and the headache of organizing actors.

MY KIND OF MOVIE?

You'll be fascinated by stories, and by what is hidden from view. You are intensely interested – even nosy – about other people, and love to get inside other people's lives. You'll want to get to the truth, but you are smart enough to know that when you find it, you can't always rely on it. You often work alone, are well-organized and can handle sound, camera and editing with ease.

Top of your list is to get people to listen to you – and you know that for people to tune in to your movie you need to make it entertaining, so you are going to grab your viewer's attention by any means necessary.

WHAT'S IT FOR?

Documentary is for everyone. It's made by the average Jo/e and always trying to tilt at "the man" or puncture the bubble which big business, or the authorities, or simply the plain ignorant, choose to live within. It's the closest the movie world has to Knights of the Round Table, and like any good jousting session, documentary filmmakers know when to put on a thrill or two, but also how to keep their target in their sights. It's information and entertainment, with high standards of both. It has big ambitions – to tell the truth and nothing but, and it doesn't matter whether that's a corruption scandal or a simple tale of life in a small town.

Since the big blockbuster documentary movies by Michael Moore, Morgan Spurlock and others, documentary is now a perfectly acceptable Saturday night movie, so why not aim for a big audience? There are many more nonfiction cable channels than ever before, and online there are many dedicated channels looking for new documentary material. Citizens journalism is bigger than ever, so you can upload a movie on an issue important to you and get it seen on news sites around the globe.

HOW LONG WILL IT TAKE ME?

Your documentary movie is whatever you want it to be. It might take a day, a week or a year to shoot, depending on what it's about, but whatever you choose, be prepared to get wholly involved in the project – you can't always predict when you need to shoot, and your work hours will vary widely. But as a ballpark figure, give yourself a fixed period to shoot the movie, keep the energy for the project flowing, and avoid getting sidetracked.

HOW HARD IS IT?

Difficulty level:

★ ★ ★ ★ ★

Documentary is tougher in things like organization and preparation, but easier to shoot. If you like working solo, and don't always get on with teams, this could work for you.

You need:

- Self-reliance so you need to be good at organizing yourself
- The ability to think of several things at once (call it a four-track mind)
- To be a little cynical
- ... but also optimistic about carrying on when things get tough
- More skill in sound and camera but less needed in lighting or effects
- The ability to talk your way into (and out of) trouble

WHO ELSE DO I NEED?

It works well solo but it's also good to be able to chew it over with other people, so it suits a small and highly mobile team. But draw the line at any more than three people.

A sound operator is crucial, and if you want to be freed up to talk and investigate, then another person on camera would be good.

Practice working with sound a lot before you get into real situations. Make sure that when it comes to the big moment, you can get the mic rigged up, shoot and ask questions, and still get quality sound. Viewers will forgive you almost anything except bad sound.

FIGURE 38.1 Director Franny Armstrong filming from the back of a motorbike in New Orleans for her 2009 documentary *The Age of Stupid*. The entire film was shot on Sony's HVRZ1U HDV camcorder. (Credit: Chris Graythen, www.ageofstupid.net)

WHAT KIT DO I NEED?

Not much. Practice making do with very little: just a camera, tripod, a shotgun mic and a tie-clip mic. When you can, get a radio mic.

IF YOU LIKE THAT WATCH THIS

Check out anything by **Nick Broomfield:** his movies on Aileen Wournos, or *Kurt and Courtney* (1998), his bio-pic of Kurt Cobain, or *Biggie and Tupac* (2002). Quietly persistent, he doesn't take no for an answer, and prefers to hunt alone.

Michael Moore is an acquired taste, and you may prefer not to acquire him, but he has shifted gear in the whole documentary medium in films like *Fahrenheit 911* (2004) or *Bowling for Columbine* (2002).

James Marsh's *Man on Wire* (2008) blends thriller with documentary and got an Oscar. But track down his early movie, *Wisconsin Death Trip* (1999), to see an original talent do something extraordinary.

PREPRODUCTION ESSENTIALS

Release forms; budget; health and safety sheets; crew contracts; copyright release for music if used; shooting schedule.

USING THE CAMERA

- **Your camera has an ego even if you don't.** You might fall under its spell and start to show off how great it is, playing around with effects, manual controls and lenses. Better to play it cool, and restrict yourself to just point and shoot.
- **Keep the camera steady** – hand-held doesn't have to mean shake 'n' blur.
- **Film for longer:** point the camera and keep it drilling its gaze at your subject. Let the camera stay still and you'll get some fascinating moments as your subject forgets the camera is there and starts to relax.
- **Record everything, every step and moment.** Keep the camera running throughout – as you get out of the car, as you take a crucial phone call, as you ring a doorbell. It gives us a bigger picture of what's happening, but also makes you look more honest as we get to see all the "behind the scenes" stuff surrounding each part of the film.
- **You are a part of the movie.** Telling the truth also means coming clean that this is a movie and, yes, the person behind it also has an opinion too. Like it was tough to get that interview or maybe you felt uneasy talking to that other person. Don't over-do it and dominate the movie but your insight of what's going on is as valuable as the person you talked to.

EDITING

Documentary movies play it straight. If you get too flashy in the editing you risk making your movie look like it was too manipulated. People will think you are trying to mess with their heads and lead them to think a certain point of view. So just edit in a low-key way, with no tricks and no post-production effects.

- **Avoid music promo-style fast cutting** for the main part of the film. Keep the clips a few seconds or more.
- **Music works well to focus your main ideas.** If you have an idea you are trying to get across in the film, take some time out and use a montage with music midway through to really make that point strongly. Get clips we have seen or were missed, use a different style of editing – either faster or slower – and give us something different.
- **Even if a clip doesn't look great, keep it in if it helps tell the story.** Focus on what the movie needs to show, not whether a shot looks nicely framed.
- **Take time out.** If you are showing a lot of stuff happening, a lot of action, take some time to slow things down and give us time to think about we have been watching. This consolidates the movie and reminds why we are watching, like those catch-ups before a weekly TV drama, but without the cheesy voiceover.
- **Use subtitles or on-screen text** to make clear what is happening, and what we need to know. Tell us what city we are in when we cut to a new interview. When we cut back to a previous interviewee give us their name again. Use opening text to set the scene. Maybe even use ticker-tape scrolling words across the foot of the screen to add more information.

Experts' Tips

Nick Broomfield, director, *Battle for Haditha, Kurt and Courtney, Aileen: Portrait of a Serial Killer*, London/Los Angeles

"I think that in many ways the world is more complicated now than ever and documentary is a way that people get information into areas of the world and life that they don't know anything about. Documentaries give you that knowledge, they give you an inside story, an experience of being with those people and spending time with them and learning how they think, how they view the world and their reality. But then you understand their thinking and in a way documentary can do that better than a newspaper article or anything else. What a first-time filmmaker should look for is a story that they feel people don't understand a lot about, that they can get access to."

"Documentary is so informative and I think it's always fascinating to look into another world that you don't know anything about – particularly if it is character-led, not the filmmaker putting all his opinions in, which is less interesting. It's something that documentary can do and it is very hard for drama to compete with. Drama is very good for certain subjects, thrillers, comedies, or love stories; documentaries are amazing for looking at the world of reality."

LEGALESE

Permission to shoot in the places you need to go: get a written or emailed response to allow you to shoot if that place is not open public space.

Release forms from all participants: that goes for all interviewees, and anyone else who appears in image or just by voice in the film. They sign the form and you keep it.

Responses: if you are shooting a documentary that shows one side of a controversial event or incident, get hold of a statement from whoever the bad guys are and put it in the movie. If they won't respond, put up a few words saying that you gave them the chance to respond but they declined.

Upload It

Best site to upload to:
Vimeo and OneWorld TV
Best communities to join:
Documentaries group at Vimeo
Best channels to watch:
Documentary Film at Vimeo:

"A place for Vimeo's documentaries including full documentaries, single chapters, or extended trailers, over 3 minutes in length."

DOCUMENTARY SCHEDULE

This movie suits any length of schedule, particularly a 14-day shoot.

Chapter Thirty-Nine

Music Promo

WHAT IS IT?

A short movie designed to promote a song or piece of music.

Everything about music promos screams "look at me" – this is the movie to make if you love images and think that dialogue just slows everything down. Music promos used to be about seeing the band in action, goofing around. Now we expect something to project an image that suits the band – with or without them on screen.

A promo pushes the boundaries, inventing, experimenting, making do with no cash, stretching what you can do with very little. Anything goes, everything rides on the visuals – so that means you get to make the kind of movie you always wanted to make, freed up from the constraints of story, or even having to make sense. You only have two aims: it has to be cheap to make, and it has to grab the viewer constantly. You'll need a lot of ideas, but it has to all hang together. It can't be self-indulgent, and it must be memorable. Use that box of tricks on your PC, creating effects in editing and messing around with the colors. Just remember to please the viewer with the shortest attention span.

MY KIND OF MOVIE?

You wanted to study art but couldn't draw, or spent your time doodling images like **Donnie Darko**. Maybe you did some DJing, and loved the projections behind the band, and maybe you enjoy editing in a weird way. You believe rules are there to be ignored without negotiation and everyone else just gets in the way of you and your extraordinary ideas. You wouldn't want to make anything else – the thought of making a movie with a story makes your heart sink. All that narrative, plodding on and on, stopping you from the real fun of taking your imagination out around the block.

WHAT'S IT FOR?

Music promo is an industry like none other. It's big, has a fast turnover of new promos, and it needs new talent constantly, people who can come up with new no-budget ideas. Meanwhile, promos are being shown everywhere, as background wallpaper, but rarely watched in the same way you watch other kinds of movies. Sure, they are there to promote a band, but they are also used to create an ambience, with screens in bars and clubs.

Start local by seeking out bands in your town that need a promo. You can also take a sideways move into working in live visuals, producing images to project behind a band on stage, or as a VJ in a club.

Meanwhile, some cash-strapped record companies, hit by a revenue downturn from illegal downloading, are looking toward students and new filmmakers to make promos. Don't assume that promo jobs get handed to established hands – you stand a chance of getting paid for your work if you can prove you can generate a neat idea on a low budget. Form a small group of artists and filmmakers, think up a name for yourselves, and start pitching for work.

HOW LONG WILL IT TAKE ME?

Try to keep energy flowing by keeping preparation down to a minimum. Make the film more instinctively and intuitively than others, relying on just a strong feeling that you are doing the right thing.

Promo directors tend to work quickly, so aim for a shoot lasting just a day or two, with the whole job lasting about a week.

HOW HARD IS IT?

Difficulty level:

★ ★ ★ ★ ★

You've got the freedom to just do what you want to do and answer to no one else. You don't need to make your movie resemble others in the same genre because music promos succeed by how much they *don't* resemble each other, unlike, say, noir films or action thrillers, which succeed largely through conformity and similarity. It means the spotlight is on your ideas. If you get inspired often and get original ideas coming to you like fireworks, then this is an easy project for you.

You need:

- To be able to think up simple ideas
- To make them for almost no money, so they don't rely on big costs
- To quite possibly be a control freak
- A sense that every idea is not quite good enough yet until you have twisted it slightly, given it a new slant that no-one else has tried yet
- To work quickly
- To enjoy editing

WHO ELSE DO I NEED?

- One camera operator, preferably two
- Lighting
- Designer

WHAT KIT DO I NEED?

- High-definition cameras
- Tripod
- Lighting kit consisting of at least one large lamp (300 W or more) plus two smaller ones
- Good post-production software such as Adobe After Effects and Flash

IF YOU LIKE THAT WATCH THIS

Michel Gondry does it for real – try his collected music promos, shot without resorting to expensive digital effects and instead using on-set tricks and sleight of hand to create stunning visuals. Gondry perfected this technique in the movie *Eternal Sunshine of the Spotless Mind* (2004).

Or try anything by **Spike Jonze**, the Gollum of the music promo: low-tech, mischievous, and with a restless, roaming imagination.

And check out **Hype Williams, Daniel Levi, Lynn Fox, Chris Cunningham, David Wilson** and anything on **Onedotzero** DVDs (www.onedotzero.com), Warp Records or Zen TV. Watch the latest directors direct from the stable at Ridley Scott's company RSA (www.rsafilms.com) or www.anonymouscontent. com or www.colonelblimp.com.

FIGURE 39.1 RSA Black Dog has produced some of the best music promos, including this image for Florence and the Machine, directed by Dawn Shadforth.

GET INSPIRED

Limit how much you look at other promos. Instead, check out viral films on the web where a great low-budget idea gets passed around quickly. Also look at classic montage sequences in films such as the training scene in *Rocky IV*; or an ironic sequence of news footage edited to Louis Armstrong's 'What a Wonderful World' in Michael Moore's *Fahrenheit 911*.

PREPRODUCTION ESSENTIALS

Style sheets; lighting designs; budget; permission forms for locations; health and safety sheets; contracts; copyright release for music; shooting schedule

See Chapter 11, Brief Directory of All the Paperwork You Need.

USING THE CAMERA

The idea is everything with promos. That means that every other part of the movie has to relate back to this idea, from the lighting to the camera, to the color and design.

LIVE PROMOS

Live performances can be used as part of a promo where you might record other stuff later. If you record live, use two camcorders – one to catch the overall set, from the mixing desk (usually midway down the auditorium) and another to catch a range of close-ups, more diverse angles, looser and wilder than the main camera.

Use the main camera to record the sound, or if possible ask to get a direct recording from the mixing desk as a digital audio file (.wav). You'll easily be able to sync the images on your cam with the sounds from the audio file on the timeline. Record some crowd noise too using the main camera.

NON-LIVE PROMOS

These are promos without the band, or where the band acts or takes part, without performing. Anything goes here so use other chapters to help according to what sort of movie you are making – Chapter 34, Horror if the promo is dark and weird; Chapter 44, Road Movie if the promo is centered on a journey, and so on. Take a look at Chapter 27, Web Your Movie to get some tips on working for the ultra-small screen.

EDITING

Montage could be the most useful style for your promo so use Chapter 22, Editing Methods: Montage to help you. Montage means you can be creative, try out more experimental ideas, and it's more rhythmic.

When you have a lot of shots edited roughly on the timeline, look at the rhythm of the shot lengths throughout the film, judging by the length of the clips on the video track. For instance, you could have some shots half a second long, followed by three wide shots lasting longer, say four seconds each. Then you return to the faster shots and so on. Have a structure to the length of the clips – it should look like a regular repeated pattern on the timeline.

At some point in the film you can look for a point where the promo changes direction – like in a song where it moves up a key to get a fresh impetus of momentum. You could change tack here too – perhaps up the pace of the editing, or try some new effect.

LEGALESE

Music clearance. You'll need to get written clearance from the owner of the music track you used. The hassle-free option is to make a promo for a band who are not yet signed and still own the rights to all their music – but even then get a written form which gives you the right to use the promo in festivals or online.

Check you also get **release forms** from anyone in the promo.

Upload It

Best sites to upload to:
www.veoh.com, www.revver.com, and www.blastronetworks.com
Best communities to join:
We Love Music at Vimeo
"Do you love music? Join us! Share your music and music videos."
www.vimeo.com/groups/100
Best channels to watch:
Future Shorts at YouTube or try videos uploaded on **We Love Music** at Vimeo

MUSIC PROMO SCHEDULE

This movie works best on a fast turnaround, at 48 hours to 7 days.

Table 39.1 Add these extra jobs to any of the template schedules in Section 6, Make It Happen: Schedules.

What to Do	Who Needs to Do It	How Long This Will Take	Chapters in This Book to Help You
Choose music to use for promo	Director		
Work on ideas for the promo; meet with the band to discuss ideas and options	Director	90 mins	
Previz: start turning the ideas you and the band discussed into actual locations, places, people, and images for the promo	Director	2 hours	Ch 7 Previz

Continued...

Table 39.1 Add these extra jobs to any of the template schedules in Section 6, Make It Happen: Schedules. (Continued)

What to Do	Who Needs to Do It	How Long This Will Take	Chapters in This Book to Help You
Budge	Director	2 hours	Ch 4 Budgets
Designs: work on the overall style of the promo; choose a limited number of colors and use them throughout; think about the way you are going to use the camera, and the lighting you can use; choose ideas that fit into the main theme for the promo and stick to them	Director	Spend as long as you need; allow a couple of hours at least	Ch 5 Designing Your Movie

Citizens News/Video Journalist

FIGURE 40.1 (Photo courtesy of iStockphoto, ©Nikada, Image# 4629603)

WHAT IS IT?

A news piece made by you, uploaded and shown on the web.

You can make the news every night. TV news companies have lost money as we change our news habits: more people now switch to online news, catching the latest events via word of mouth from their social networking sites, and seeing the essentials on YouTube. The difference is that the big news clips that get swept around the world are the ones made by someone with a camcorder who happened to be at the right place in the right time. If you want the job, that's the future of the daily news – *you* are now the anchorman, the producer and the viewer.

But how can you take advantage of this? Suppose you want to get more involved in exposing injustice, showing real events as they happen, and actually go seek the news rather than just wait for it to land in your neighborhood? If so you need to get prepared to take on the mantle of "citizens journalist." Find stories, shoot, share them, spread the word via network sites such as Twitter, and become one of a powerful posse of people looking for real stories that need telling. It's become a big part of the protest movement, like in a series of protests in Iran in 2009 where people found they could get real events on the web in hours, while the regular news guys were still stuck at customs. The images uploaded showed what was happening, and provoked an outcry around the world.

A citizens news video will be short, less than five minutes and ideally 60 seconds, perhaps with a voiceover or text. It is usually part of a stream of news clips on an event, and linked to a blog, or Twitter.

MY KIND OF MOVIE?

You have one ear to the ground, often looking for events going on that affect you. You distrust everything you hear from those in power, and most of what you hear on the news; you believe only what you see and hear for yourself, rather than from big-business media. You might be interested in conspiracy theories, but you know that even they are just another spin on the news.

You like drama, and to you it's crucial to put together a story in a way that people relate to it, just like narrative movies. The bottom line, though, is seeing the truth, and sharing the truth.

WHAT'S IT FOR?

People trust you, like they don't trust the news corporations. You can show events as they happen and present real life as it unfolds. This movie tends to be focused solely on the facts from your point of view. Unlike the news companies, you don't have to worry about showing all sides of the story – if there is another side to be told, someone else will pick a camcorder and get to work. You only have to be true to what you know, what you see and what happened around you.

This movie is for global or local consumption. Anywhere, anytime, by anyone – your clip will travel as far as it can, but you can help it on its way by using blogging or social networking sites to spread the word. Expect to sell a clip if it is picked and used by major TV news stations.

HOW LONG WILL IT TAKE ME?

The key to the success of this project is working quickly. The more practiced you are with filming, the more you are certain that you can shoot, edit, and upload within a few hours.

FIGURE 40.2 Activist sites such as www.undercurrents.org are popular places to show videos. BeyondTV is a festival which highlights the best of these.

Viewers will sit up and take notice of videos made quickly. The longer you take to edit it, the more likely it is that people will think it is tainted with the possibility of digital manipulation, so avoid anything that seems to add gloss to the video, such as music or excessively designed text.

HOW HARD IS IT?

Difficulty level:

★ ★ ★ ★ ★

You will be working solo, controlling the camera and sound, so be prepared to use your mics in situations where you have had little time to practice or run through what is happening. Good quality sound is crucial here. Use a tripod when you can – the images will be shown on small screens on the web or phones, so avoid shaky movement of the camera, and use close-ups wherever possible. Practice using the camera under low light conditions, opening up the iris to let more light in.

You need:
- To feel OK about working alone, but also able to talk to people to get help
- Have a strong nose for a story
- To be fast – when events are taking off you need to get to the heart of the action quickly
- To be undeterred by the people who want to stop your story getting out there
- To work in a tight, efficient way, able to shoot what you want without wishing you had time to rehearse

WHO ELSE DO I NEED?

You can work entirely alone, but it might be good to get in touch with people who have done this kind of thing before so you know how to handle the situation. Also, get involved in networks of other news gatherers, so that when events take off you have your pathway already in place to get the video out there.

WHAT KIT DO I NEED?

- Sturdy camera
- Tripod
- Hand-held mic
- Extra recording cards/discs/tapes

IF YOU LIKE THAT WATCH THIS

Tune in to **Undercurrents.org (www.undercurrents.org), OneWorldTV (http://tv.oneworld.net),** plus particular sites relevant to your own interests such as campaigning groups or charities. Check out online videos of other news events where videos shot by people on the streets were right at the heart of the action – more than the networks – such as the 2009 G20 protests in London.

For features, get inspired by watching how the truth can be uncovered through images, video or sound. Francis Ford Coppola's *The Conversation* (1974) centers on a surveillance expert who finds out more than he bargained for, while Michelangelo Antonioni's '60s movie *Blowup* (1966) does the same but with a photographer.

Closer to the present, try *Burma VJ* (2009), a powerful movie shot by undercover Burmese people showing what they see as their country's brutal regime.

PREPRODUCTION ESSENTIALS

Release forms—anyone you interview needs to agree to you using them in the film.

USING THE CAMERA

- Find out about your rights if you are detained during your news gathering. Go to www.aclu.org or www.liberty-human-rights.org.uk.
- Shoot while staying safe. Avoid working alone.

FIGURE 40.3 VisionOntv (http://visionon.tv) is one of many video sharing sites that show uploaded clips from protests and other events.

- Protect your equipment – some public control forces use flash guns or strobe lights to repel video recording. Look out for use of water or gas to control crowds.

SHOOTING TEMPLATE (thanks to VisionOntv)

This will take you 10 minutes only. No editing needed.

It's all about where, what, when and why.

Start recording with your camera/phone pointing at you and say your name (or tag) and location and what the date is. Then have a wide shot of the situation or place and start talking. You've told us where and when you are, now tell us what is happening, and why. Get close-up shots of the action or events. Then end on a detail or close-up to get a human angle to what is going on. Keep the camera ultra-steady throughout this whole shoot.

EDITING

No need to edit with really short news clips. Just upload to news sites or social network or video sharing sites as soon as possible. If you send it to YouTube tag it with the name of your preferred news network (for instance, "VisionOntv"). Getting it seen on the same day the event happened guarantees maximum viewing. Some TV news networks will buy your footage of an event if it is newsworthy enough.

If you are doing a longer report with several parts like interviews and action shots, follow this template (thanks again to VisionOntv):

- Open with an establishing shot showing the whole scene or situation
- Cut to an action shot showing people doing stuff
- Then cut to some interviews you recorded, interspersed with cutaways of more action
- End with a summary of what has happened

Edit tips:

- Edit with long cuts rather than short; 3–4 seconds per shot is a good length to see what's happening
- Don't use effects
- Avoid use of music
- Use your steadiest shots
- Keep voiceover or taking loud and clear

LEGALESE

You are pitting yourself in the firing line so make sure you are joined up to like-minded people. If you attend an event where you think you might be vulnerable, link up with others and work in small groups.

If you do interviews, always get signed permission from the interviewee.

Upload It

Best site to upload to:
YouTube for immediate events or http://tv.oneworld.net for other videos
Best communities to join:
Join the site community of **VisionOntv** showing activist and news videos
Best channels to watch:
Various channels at **www.undercurrents.org**

CITIZENS NEWS SCHEDULE

There's no specific schedule to a citizens news video, since you are responding to a sudden event. If you do get the chance to plan in advance, do a recce of the location to check out the best places to shoot from. Also, research into previous similar events.

Chapter Forty-One

(Extreme) Sports Movie

FIGURE 41.1 A skater does a trick while being filmed. (Photo courtesy of iStockphoto, ©deanmillar, Image# 4077913)

WHAT IS IT?

A movie of a sporting event. Extreme sports involve some danger or risk.

Sports movies are big business, attracting huge viewing figures. Most video sharing sites have large sections with extreme sports movies – skating, freerunning, biking or other high-risk sports. But they almost never capture the thrill of the action, instead making do with a distant spectators-eye glimpse of what happened, or a first-person white-knuckle ride where you can't make out too clearly what is going on. Extreme sports movies go further; they tend to get right to the heart of the action, resembling real action thrillers, but the element of actual risk makes it an even more tense viewing experience.

Sports movies mix a range of shots so we get to experience the action, while also seeing the overall picture from several angles. These movies are widely seen online, but there is a thriving TV market for all extreme sports, from kite surfing, to zorbing to base-jumping.

MY KIND OF MOVIE?

You love the thrill of speed, and just want to share your enthusiasm for it. Why shouldn't everyone get a taste of the adrenalin rush you feel when you pull off extreme feats on the waves, up a sheer wall, or out of a plane? If you don't take part yourself, these real-life stunts are what you have been waiting for – they are what movies should be about. You'll enjoy having to play around with extreme camera angles, catching speed, depth, height and movement. You don't mind the challenge of not knowing where the action is going to lead, and adapt quickly to new situations.

You're addicted to the outdoors, you know where to meet extreme sports devotees, and you can gain their trust in activities that are just about legal.

WHAT'S IT FOR?

This is pure escapist fun, designed for sheer spectacular enjoyment, the wow factor embodied in video. And it has the history to back it up; this sort of spectacle movie has been around since the earliest days of cinema, when shorts of fast trains, horseback acrobats and death-defying stunts were the norm in movie theaters, way before sound and color took hold.

Expect to see your clips shared widely – viewing hits for extreme sports are far above many other tags. If you shoot on higher-quality cameras you might want to start pitching your movies to cable or satellite TV channels such as Extreme Sports Channel (www.extreme.com).

Extreme sports attract diverse audiences, from participants to spectators. Assume you will be watched by thousands, and remember to use commonly used tags as part of your movie title to aid browser searching.

HOW LONG WILL IT TAKE ME?

You can create a simple record of the events in just a half-hour session, but for the stunning footage you are seeking, you need to allow some time to make a movie that hypes up the stunts, builds up slowly, and allows a degree of mystery to get into the movie. Put aside a few hours, but then return to the project the next day to tweak it some more, increasing the cutaways, and checking that it's clear what is happening.

HOW HARD IS IT?

Difficulty level:

★ ★ ★ ★ ★

Simply freecording the whole thing is OK (see Chapter 43, Freecording), but drains the action of real adventure when you watch it on a small screen – too much shake and not enough editing. Instead, take a moment to plan out the shots you need, and improvise heavily on the day you shoot, gathering cutaways to add in later.

You need:

- To use the camera for action and speed – using shutter speed and iris controls
- To be fast – you'll be confronted with a moving target and need to be able to follow it wherever it goes
- To be able to see the events from the view of the bystander – is it actually clear what is happening at all?
- To think ahead, gathering the right shots to use later
- To be physically adept at moving around and following the action
- To know your camera well so you work with it quickly

WHO ELSE DO I NEED?

You can work solo, but your movie will step up to a whole new professional level if you can share the shooting with another camera operator. Find someone to shoot from a distance, gathering master shots of everything. Get someone else to get into the awkward places, allowing you to get the action shots.

WHAT KIT DO I NEED?

- Camera × 2
- Tripods
- Shotgun mic

Practice making do with very little: just a camera, a shotgun mic and a tripod. To avoid heavy gear, try a monopod, and you could try a long range parabolic mic. These have a semispherical collar which helps pick up sound from a hundred meters away or more. You can build your own version for less than \$10£20. Google "build your own parabolic mic" and you'll get several cheap ways to do it yourself.

IF YOU LIKE THAT WATCH THIS

EPIC America is a TV series from 2004 which followed various extreme sports enthusiasts; off air now but still available on YouTube. For paragliding, try *Into the Wind*, a feature-length documentary from 2006.

Weirdo director of *Being John Malkovich* (1999), **Spike Jonze** codirected a hugely inventive and unmissable 40-minute movie of skate stunts, *Yeah Right!* (2004). Also check out National Geographic's *Extreme* (1999), a collection of on-the-edge stunts by the world's top extreme athletes, from snowboarding, to surfing to climbing. It's available in IMAX, but also on DVD. Online, tune in to www.extreme.com for up-to-date clips.

PREPRODUCTION ESSENTIALS

Release forms; budget; permission forms for locations; health and safety sheets; copyright release for music.

Go to Chapter 11, Brief Directory of All the Paperwork You Need, for help with all of these.

Check out the scene before the event kicks off. Use the camera to view how things look at the aspect ratio you are shooting in. Take a range of shots to figure out how the camera responds to light in the location. You may need to have sudden pans of the camera, from ground level to mid sky, or side to side, producing problems with light. Set up an aperture that works for all eventual places you need to point the camera.

Experts' Tips

Leo Dickinson, action sports filmmaker, UK

"If you are not sure when something is going to happen then leave the camera rolling. Having a camera off a tripod makes it more flexible but it starts to hose-pipe all over the place and a tracking shot gets the whole thing much more animated. Be aware that parachuting or base-jumping, where you fall at 125 miles per hour, causes problems with the video tape going round the heads because of the air pressure, so simply tape the case in with insulating tape."

USING THE CAMERA

- **Declutter the background,** leaving as much empty space as possible around the area where the action will take place.

- **Focusing on just the area of action will be almost impossible,** especially if you want to let it move around a lot within the frame, where it will go in and out of focus continually. So enjoy the blur and let it happen now and then – it will look authentic.

- **Check for problems with anything that can get inside the camcorder casing,** including damp. Most extreme sports and action shots tend to either thrive on or create their own mess in environments where dust, sand or other corrosives can cause havoc with your precious kit.

- **Check out your shutter speed.** Filmmakers vary in opinion about shutter speed but the general wisdom is that a high shutter speed is essential for high speed action. The standard 1/50 setting will produce blurred results, while an ultra-fast setting such as 1/1500 will not only produce strobed images but will significantly darken the image too, with less light getting past the lens.

- It helps if you can **shoot your footage using two cameras** – a master getting the overall show, including sound, and a more free-wheeling one gaining shots that will act in the edit room as the dynamic backbone to the film. Rules used to be that the master shot was the main one and the cutaways were cutaways.

FIGURE 41.2 Shooting public sports events means getting close to the action. Arrive early to test out the best places to shoot. (Photo courtesy of iStockphoto, ©mountainberryphoto, Image# 4634072)

Experts' Tips

Jason Bell, filmmaker, USA, www.vertical-visions.com

"**Light:** The light on your subject can't often be changed when shooting extreme sports. Therefore, recompose your shot to allow for the most possible light. Keep the sun and other light sources toward your back and carefully adjust your shutter speeds accordingly."

"**Framing the subject:** Learn when to center your subject and when to use the Rule of Thirds. Keep your viewers interested in your presentation and don't be afraid to try something new. If you're following your subject, don't concentrate on the shot too much to the point of risking your safety."

"**Following the action:** Practice, practice, practice. Hold your breath to minimize body movements. Learn to shoot video with both eyes open in order to track your subject better."

"**Shutter speeds/frame-rates:** If your camera supports higher frame-rates or shutter speeds, use them."

"**Using good tripods:** Spend the extra money on a good tripod with smooth panning and tilting fluid motion."

"**Camera protection:** Your camera is often a big investment, so don't skimp when it comes to protecting it. House it in a carbon fiber shell or waterproof enclosure if your activity is deemed hazardous to electronics from shock, vibration, or impact. If you don't have a lot of cash, bend some sheet aluminum into a protective housing or wrap a fiberglass repair kit over a foam replica of your camera to make a cheap but effective housing."

"**Be innovative:** Use high-speed cameras, and mount them in innovative locations. Everyone loves a unique, innovative camera angle. Mount cameras on your head, leg, wrist, or belly for unique POVs."

"**Backing up your work:** Make backup copies of your tapes or DVDs and keep them at a different location in the event of theft or fire."

"**Wide angle lenses:** Work with wide angle lenses because they reduce camera shake and provide amazing images with extreme sports."

EDITING

The action depends on seeing cause and effect, a stream of events going one after the other. Get this by **grouping shots together in patterns.** Each short event or part of the action, lasting around 20 seconds, can be a chain of five clips:

1. **Master opening shot** (e.g., group of cars approaching bend on the track)
2. **Closer shot** showing which part of that master shot we are going to home in on
3. A **succession of close-ups**, lasting less than a second each with a rhythm created in editing that matches the speed or pace of the event. (e.g., tires, hands on the steering wheel, shots from inside the car)

4. Intersperse the close-ups with **cutaways** from the action to elsewhere in the scene – keeping to close-ups (e.g., faces in the crowd, pit stop technicians)

5. End with a **suitable exit shot** (e.g., showing the skater exiting the bend and approaching the next corner)

You then create a way of signaling to the viewer that a new chapter in the event is happening, by starting and ending each section with wider, master shots.

SOUND

Unless you have dialogue involved, be prepared to record sound separately and add it to the edit later. But always record what you can using a catch-all boom or omni-mic to add to the track, to create a more natural track. Depending on the action being recorded, supercardioid mics can effectively pinpoint the sound. These mics are good at long distances but their sideways range is small, so any slight shifts in position and you suddenly drop out of range.

Go to Chapter 17, Sound Recording for more help.

LEGALESE

You'll need **permission to film** at the venue of the sporting event if it's indoors. If it's held at a beach, park or other outdoor location, check in advance whether you need permission. Large events will allow spectators to film on camcorders, but if you need to get among the action right at the frontline you'll need clearance first.

If you do interviews, get a signed **release form** for each interviewee.

Upload It

Best sites to upload to:
YouTube or **Vimeo** or **Metacafe**
Best communities to join:
www.vimeo.com/groups/extreme
Best channels to watch:
Sports Extreme Channel on YouTube
Sports and Extreme Channel at www.dailymotion.com

SPORTS MOVIE SCHEDULE

This movie is ideal to make in just 7 to 14 days.

Table 41.1 Add these extra jobs to any of the template schedules in Section 6, Make It Happen: Schedules.

What to Do	Who Needs to Do It	How Long This Will Take	Chapters in This Book to Help You
Before you shoot:			
Watch sports movies that are similar to what you are doing. Ask yourself how yours can avoid their clichés and how it can stand out.			Ch 4 Budgets
Practice shooting fast-moving objects or events. Try out how the shutter affects the image, and what shutter setting works best for you. Try 1/1000 for a start. But a bit of blur in the image can make it look more natural.	Director/ camera	Allow an afternoon session	Ch 13 Shooting Ch 12 Using a Camcorder
During shooting			
Arrive well before the event is due to start. Find the best places to shoot and practice working so you can check how the weather and light looks on screen. If there are warm-up sessions where competitors practice, take the chance to record sound for background tracks and cutaways shots to include in the edit.	Director/ camera	Throughout the warm-up session	Ch 12 Using a Camcorder
Check you get release forms signed by everyone involved as you shoot.	Producer	As long as necessary	Ch 9 Law and the Movies

Continued...

Table 41.1 Add these extra jobs to any of the template schedules in Section 6, Make It Happen: Schedules. (Continued)

What to Do	Who Needs to Do It	How Long This Will Take	Chapters in This Book to Help You
Get enough extra shots – close-ups, cutaways, shots of the crowd, shots of the preparation and if possible backstage or behind the scenes.	Director/ camera	Throughout filming	Ch 13 Shooting
After shooting			
Upload quickly to sharing sites or contact companies you can sell the video to. Mobile phone content providers buy short sports videos and sell them to phone networks.	Director	1 hour	Ch 26 Create a YouTube Hit Ch 28 Your Web Plan

Chapter Forty-Two

Drama: War Film

FIGURE 42.1 Close-ups capture the human drama in a war movie. (Photo courtesy of iStockphoto, ©Johncairns, Image# 8909261)

WHAT IS IT?

A drama based around events during a conflict – real or imagined.

The twentieth century was nonstop war, from Arnhem to Zagreb, Baghdad to Ypres, big wars and small wars, hot war and the cold war. No wonder then that the war film has become so popular as we try to get our heads around why all this goes on at all. But what about the twenty-first century, now that wars are kept hidden in far-off countries, with an invisible enemy? Rather than disappear in this fog, the war film is back with a vengeance and with a heat-seeking need to find and destroy – but this time it's not the Japs or the Vietcong in the cross-hairs. The twenty-first war film is about lies, deceit and global cover-ups.

As war has changed, the war film has found a new lease on life. Gone are the table-top tactics, missions and fanfares. Now it's about darkened torture cells, civil war and corporate killing: "a message from our sponsors" written on the bullets. Cynical, sharp and every bit as action-packed as war films from the

1960s, these new movies are hard hitting, politically savvy and not afraid to put their heads above the parapet.

For low-budget filmmakers, this means that the genre is more easy to make, with no need for huge fields of battle. It offers the perfect mix – a chance to grab the audience firmly by the throat with visceral action filmmaking, but also make serious political points and lob a few grenades at the powers that be. Good luck.

MY KIND OF MOVIE?

You don't seek the easy life. You know your own mind and although sometimes you go too far at least you say what you think. You like the idea of making films because you know you are right. For you filmmaking isn't about getting angry, but about getting even, a chance to see it like it is and shout it loud.

For you, the war film is the perfect blend of brain and guts. Action movies were too stupid and political movies were too talkative. But you wanted a bit of both and now the war film presents you with a movie that is clever *and* physical.

WHAT'S IT FOR?

War films are no longer the macho outpost of Hollywood. It used to be a dumb action spectacle, but now it's smart and gets good reviews. Audiences are big, and willing to make a war film their Saturday night. They might be put off by too much political stuff but are easy when it turns into conspiracy theory territory, and even better if you take aim at the lurking presence of big business.

There is less of a market on movie sharing sites like YouTube, but it does well on cable, DVD, pay-per-view and download sites, where it's seen as a safe bet.

HOW LONG WILL IT TAKE ME?

The war film tends to be heavy on locations, and needs some expendable props. Writing the war film takes time, so let your ideas gestate over months while you do other stuff. The actual dialogue needn't be too clever, but the overall story and structure has to be strong to support and compete with the action.

HOW HARD IS IT?

Difficulty level:

★ ★ ★ ★ ★

The war movie is demanding in terms of how you organize the production. It's likely you'll have a number of locations, more characters or extras than usual, and more props.

You need:

- To be a good organizer
- To enjoy working with a large team
- To prefer location shooting
- To be able to create strong and believable characters, avoiding clichés often found in the genre
- To be able to fuse strong characters and plot with action

WHO ELSE DO I NEED?

A full squad:

- Two cameras would be ideal
- Sound
- Producer
- Runner
- Plus any other help you can get for the logistics of the production

WHAT KIT DO I NEED?

- Two cameras (of the same format and quality)
- Boom mic
- Lavalier mics, or radio mics
- Lamps if shooting interior scenes
- Reflector boards for increasing or bouncing light on location

IF YOU LIKE THAT WATCH THIS

Any sprint through the genre has to stop at *Apocalypse Now!* (1979), not least to catch the surreal dialogue and car-crash story of the making of the movie itself. Since then, war films sobered up, in the horrifically real *Saving Private Ryan* (1998), *Platoon* (1986) and the gut-churning *Black Hawk Down* (2001). Take a look too at Terence Malick's *The Thin Red Line* (1998) for a peek into the dark abyss and a lesson in how to make a war film with poetry as well as bullets. Also try the dark comedy of *Three Kings* (1999) just to hear the Beach Boys *I Get Around* as a war movie song.

For twenty-first century wars, there are a stream of powerful low-budget war thrillers from *Redacted* (2007), to *Body of Lies* (2008), to *Rendition* (2007) and *The Hurt Locker* (2008).

GET INSPIRED

Read the newspapers, diary accounts of wars, and magazine features from war zones. Tease out the stories that people forgot like a piano player who carried on playing nightclub standards during the Iraq war, in Sean McAllister's

The Liberace of Baghdad (2005). Documentaries work well as war films, and the drama-documentary has been one of the most successful of the war genre since the early 2000s.

PREPRODUCTION ESSENTIALS

Storyboards; script; location photos; release forms; style sheets/designs; costume designs; backstory; treatment; lighting designs; budget; permission forms for locations; health and safety sheets; contracts; copyright release for music; shot list; shooting schedule.

See Chapter 11, Brief Directory of All the Paperwork You Need.

WRITING THE WAR FILM

- **Characters and story**

The best war films **focus on a small human tragedy set against a vast backdrop.** Whether it's the ruined streets of a Balkan city, the villages of Vietnam or the beaches of Normandy you'll need to find a microcosm of the larger devastation within the lives of a few characters. Create characters that are deep enough to hold the themes you are trying to get across.

- **The protagonist**

Central to this is the protagonist: the person we identify with in the movie. Memorable war films like *Apocalypse Now, Platoon, Jarhead* or *Full Metal Jacket* all have **a quiet observer who offers us a neat way into the film.** This person might be a drifter in life, or been overlooked by the officers, or court-martialed. They would be a whistle-blower if they cared enough, but are more often an intelligent but detached presence – a witness, like Sean Penn in *The Thin Red Line.* This character makes it easy for you to navigate around a series of scenes, linking by voiceover perhaps the thoughts of us all as we watch the events play out.

- **Structure**

To structure your war film, avoid the obvious. War films used to fall into a simple join-the-dots style of moviemaking, where the first reel laid out the mission, the middle saw the build-up and action, and the final section showed us the fall-out with mission accomplished. Instead, **throw the viewer straight into chaos and confusion.** Look out for too much exposition, like telling the audience too much too soon. Just a simple subtitle on screen giving location and date can be enough to give the viewer a foothold in the movie.

- **Locations**

Locations are crucial to the war film: **find the right places to shoot.** Look for open spaces or derelict industrial areas (Kubrick shot *Full Metal Jacket* in England, at an old factory site.)

FIGURE 42.2 Locations are crucial for a war movie. Abandoned factory buildings can be ideal settings for conflict. (Photo courtesy of iStockphoto, ©gremlin, Image# 3326061.)

USING THE CAMERA

Hand-held camera can work especially well in the war movie. It's the opposite of the tracking shot, in which the camera moves like a train along a track telling everyone where it's going. Hand-held camera makes a powerful message by itself, even without the actors – the camera is a loose cannon; no one knows where it's going, it's out of control and it might just cause an accident.

If you use this method, **avoid messy "hose-piping"** where the camera just goes wild, by using a steadying device. Fig-Rigs are a great compromise, giving you freedom with a little stability, while Hague camera supports are a cheap way of getting the steady-cam look for less than $100 (www.b-hague.co.uk).

EDITING

In your war film, editing is a way to take the viewer off guard, reflecting the reality of war. Even shooting a simple dialogue scene can be enhanced if you **opt for a style that avoids the sureness of normal life and replaces it with a nervous energy.** Use a lot of fast shots, changing rhythm to keep us guessing. In the iconic opening sequence to *Saving Private Ryan*, the camera seems as much in danger as the soldiers, having to dodge bullets, recording the action against the odds.

Edit like no one is in control, like there's no plan or reason to events. Avoid build-ups to big events, or suspense – avoid any warning about what is going to happen. Use a quick succession of good shots, bad shots, get-anything-you-can shots. Try to edit like you yourself don't even know what's going to happen next.

Trawl through your footage while editing to include out-of-focus images, flashes, sweeps of the camera; in fact, look for the bad shots – they give the movie some life.

COLOR

When you have finished editing, reduce the color of the movie to create a more moody and grim effect. Try taking saturation down by 60% to make a washed-out and hard-hitting look.

MUSIC

Music sequences can be a chance to open up the theme of your war movie, delivering the message you are making louder and clearer. Use these parts as mini-music promos, using montage to take a break from the hectic style used so far (see Chapter 22, Editing Methods: Montage).

SOUND

ENHANCING THE SOUNDTRACK

Take royalty-free sounds and beef them up using basic sound software: many sites offer war sounds for free (try www.partnersinrhyme.com for a range of good effects). Foley experts then advise adding a few extras to create a more realistic effect, for weapons and explosions:

- Add more whistle and lead-in to the bullet sound. In a battle scene there should be at least as much sound of bullets whizzing past as of bullets being fired.
- Add more reverb to bullets and explosions, but don't overdo the echo.
- Pitch the sound down slightly toward the end of the sound effect, so that it appears to flatten, giving the weapon a more dangerous edge.
- Add more bass.

Location sound

- Don't record dialogue and sound effects on the same mic at the same time. Actors just end up having to yell too much. Always add sounds of bullets and explosions later, or dub the actors' lines separately, having recorded them moments later on location while they still have the right voice energy.

Experts' Tips

Preston Randolph, film director/writer of war film *Proud Sins* (2008), Los Angeles

"Every film has its hardships. You will have times where you are stressed and may even feel like giving up. Never give up. Keep your head high and act like a professional. You are a filmmaker so prove it. At times you will get frustrated, but fight through it. If you are destined to make films than you will overcome the adversities that come with it and learn from your mistakes.

Enjoy what you do. You have the privilege to make art and nothing compares to that capability."

LEGALESE

Make sure you have done the following:

- Checked with the copyright owner if you use music tracks in your movie.
- Before you shoot – get permissions from every location owner, especially if you think there's a chance you might cause damage.
- Get release forms from every actor stating that they agree to your use of them in the movie.
- Agree how everyone wants to be credited in the end titles.
- If you plan to make a noise while filming, contact the neighbors to let them know – and always contact the police to tell them your guns aren't real.

Upload It

Best sites to upload to:
YouTube or Vimeo
Best communities to join:
FH Internship Programme at Vimeo
War Room Collective at Vimeo
Best channels to watch:
Humanity Productions at Vimeo:

"Humanity Productions exists to produce and support media that celebrates the inherent dignity of human life. We work to inspire a courageous, compassionate and authentic response. We want people to act on what they see."

WAR FILM SCHEDULE

This genre works best at longer schedules, at least 21 or 28 days.

Use the plans in Section 6, Make It Happen: Schedules but also add these extras:

FOUR TO FIVE WEEKS BEFORE YOU SHOOT
Research into the setting and background to the movie. Find oral history books or online resources to get the soldier's view of a conflict rather than rely on the history books. Try www.bbc.co.uk/ww2peopleswar.

Also find views from civilians caught up in the conflict.

Chapter Forty-Three

Freecording

WHAT IS IT?

An improvised video involving you and what you did, like a place, a situation, a journey, a party.

Musicians call it jamming – playing without knowing where you are going to end up, responding to where the music leads you. In video, this sort of fast-footed improvisation is now easier with camcorders that are light to carry and make shooting as natural and effortless as sketching or strumming a guitar. Just like jamming, sometimes you get a great melody going, other times it just goes nowhere. But once you start using video in this way it becomes liberating – and the more you do it the better your hit rate in getting unique mini-movies.

Freecording is about letting the camera roll and seeing what happens. You watch what you are recording, and make immediate decisions about what to do next. You notice the footage is going a certain direction – like toward comedy, or a journey – and you move with it. Just like jamming where you listen out for the changes in key or tempo, so you keep one eye on what is on the LCD monitor and one eye on where it might all be heading.

Probably the most attractive thing about freecording is the way it is immersive. Usually when you shoot you are an observer, sitting it out and watching the action unfold on the camera screen. Instead, you are the participant as well as the camera operator. You *are* the action.

MY KIND OF MOVIE?

You like chance, fate, serendipity, and are willing to film far and wide to stumble across a hit, where you shoot while being a part of the action. You take your chances, thinking of filmmaking as a little like surfing – one good wave, 99 duds, and all worth it for that single good one. You think filmmaking must be natural and you don't get hung up by shaky cameras or messy shots. It's physical, led by chance but not always pretty to look at.

WHAT'S IT FOR?

It's your party and the door is open to anyone, but this movie is for you and yours. This is not for cinema-style viewing and you are never going to sell it or see it hurtle around cyberspace. Instead, this is going to be the way you bond with your camera, incorporating it into your daily life. There's no "movie world" separated from "your world"; instead everything is potentially a slice of video.

Upload it to social network sites or link it to other films you have made. Apart from those involved in the movie, it doesn't need to interest many other people. However, there is a strong free-running element to many freecording films, and these get a good airing on free-running or Parkour sites.

HOW LONG WILL IT TAKE ME?

If you are going to the beach, or to a party, or just loafing around, prepare what you can by arranging a rough idea of how to shoot in your mind. But limit it to just a broad, overall view, and avoid trying to make it look like a genre movie.

The big moment comes when you switch to record, and from then on your mind is on a loop: seeing, shooting, thinking and watching, and round again, the whole process taking place in seconds. You need to be in a heightened state of awareness so you are able to think quickly on your feet.

HOW HARD IS IT?

Difficulty level:

  ★ ★ ★ ★ ★

It's probably the easiest way to shoot, but what it lacks in difficulty it makes up for in agility: you really need to think quickly and trust your decisions.

You need:

- To think that all life is a potential movie
- To put ego aside and go with the flow of what you shoot
- To always have a charged battery or two in your pocket, plus tapes
- To be unobtrusive, able to blend in and shoot without trying to control what you see

WHO ELSE DO I NEED?

Just incorporate your camcorder into your everyday life. Films with people are better on camera than just places or objects, so hook up with your friends and include them in your video jamming session.

WHAT KIT DO I NEED?

- Your camera
- Spare batteries
- A lot of SD cards/tapes

IF YOU LIKE THAT WATCH THIS

Try movies that unravel a story in video footage regardless of how many glitches it has. *Cloverfield* (2008) and other imaginary narratives such as *Paranormal Activity* (2009) show how the fictional characters responded immediately to events and composed a narrative. For the real thing, watch freecording hits online, but steer clear of corporate examples in favor of real jamming from no-budget filmmakers.

You could also check out *Zidane: A 21st Century Portrait* (2006), a hypnotic multi-angle movie about the football superstar shot by UK art-movie director Douglas Gordon.

Try Parkour videos at www.3run.co.uk.

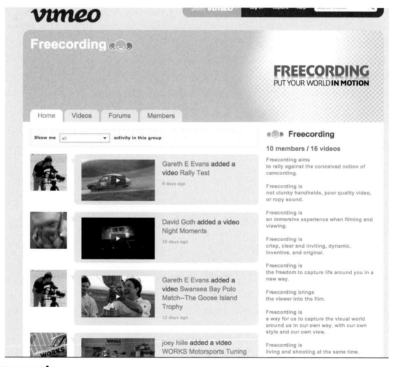

FIGURE 43.1 Freecording groups are popular in video sharing sites such as Vimeo.

USING THE CAMERA

You have to be able to hang back and allow the action to unfold. Avoid trying to impose what you think should happen. Just record and think constantly about what the film is becoming and what shots you are getting. Roll with it. This is not for control freaks. Just get the images in shot and avoid camera-shake.

EDITING

Who said there was editing? Sure, you may need to assemble the footage later, but this is the film to bypass audience attention spans and create as long a film as you need. If you want to work within a pre-set time span to fit online, you can try using long shots, interspersed with fast sections to create a rhythmic set of sequences.

When you get home, edit it but don't assume you have to take out all the long shots where nothing seems to happen. It isn't that sort of movie. Edit in just the way you shot it – responding to the footage you have rather than trying to impose another sort of movie on it all.

Go to Chapter 22, Editing Methods: Montage to get help with this.

Upload It

Best sites to upload to:
YouTube
Best communities to join:
www.flickr.com/groups/845251@N24
   Discussion and sharing tips on freecording
Best c.hannels to watch:
Freecording Channel at YouTube

Chapter Forty-Four

Road Movie

FIGURE 44.1 Elliot Bristow on his epic car journey across the United States for his movie series *Road Dreams*.

WHAT IS IT?

A movie of your trip or journey. Any length, any place, any time.

Movies have the ability to make us see the world entirely in a fresh way, as if for the first time. Journeys are kind of the same – the constant flow of new things to see, smell and hear wakes up your senses and, just like a good movie, you are in a heightened state of alertness. You get switched on to the smallest details and notice everything around you.

Car journeys themselves are like montages – a stream of images slipping past your widescreen windscreen, and all in 3D high definition. They make fascinating movies, drawing together music, sound and a rich variety of images, constantly avoiding boredom. They don't hang together as stories, and there is no real end to them – they just reach a critical mass when the effect of all those images builds up. Road movies tend to be unmistakable metaphors too – you can't help but think of them as being about life itself with the detours you take, the stops you make, the people you meet.

It's also the movie which is most like gaming. Video games let a story unfold in a spontaneous way, with no big build-up to a finale, and you explore the narrative possibilities over weeks or months as you encounter different parts of the game. Your road movie can be just like that.

MY KIND OF MOVIE?

You like stories, but don't like the artificial way regular movies do it. You want action, but not guns, events but not contrived, you prefer not to plan a movie, and believe in luck, chance and being in the right place at the right time. You follow your instincts with ease, you trust the road and you get restless if you are stuck in one place too long. Like a nomad you thrive off movement, and feel oppressed by settlement. You think movies should show this, instead of trying to make those stories tie up in such a neat and tidy way. It's more real, isn't it?

WHAT'S IT FOR?

The travel movie is going to travel well – naturally. Its absence of dialogue and plot means it can be seen without subtitles in other cultures. It's part National Geographic, part comedy-party, part meditation. The overriding factor is that it's great to look at – the sunsets, the speed, the spectacle, all the things that bring out the best in moving pictures.

HOW LONG WILL IT TAKE ME?

Your trip determines the length of the project. A week-long trip is ideal, but longer is better. Less than a couple of days would probably not net you the sort of footage you need. You need time to slow down and get into the right groove to shoot this movie.

HOW HARD IS IT?

Difficulty level:

   ★ ★ ★ ★ ★

The travel movie is fun to make but figure out before the trip starts how you might want the movie to unfold. Try out some of the script methods in Chapter 3, Scriptwriting.

You need:

- A natural curiosity about the world
- To enjoy travel
- To be able to let go control of the movie – you are as much the subject as the maker

- To be open to new ideas as you shoot
- To be able to do most jobs in the production

WHO ELSE DO I NEED?

This is a solo project but will also work well with at most one other person.

WHAT KIT DO I NEED?

You need a camera that is sturdy, resistant to weather conditions and reliable. The Sony PD170 was a stalwart of the hard-bitten news guys, and could stand up to a few knocks. Solid-state of hard drive (HDD) cams might be a good option too, as they have no moving parts to get clammed up in difficult conditions.

If you are planning a long trip it might, on the other hand, be better to use a cheaper camcorder that you can replace easily when it breaks down. If you buy a camcorder in a country which uses a different TV system from your own, you may have trouble editing the mixed footage together – for instance if you mix UK camcorder footage (which is set to PAL) with US camcorder footage (which is set to NTSC).

You'll need a lot of storage capacity. Tapes are a safe bet but might succumb to extremes of heat and cold. SD cards and discs are more resistant. You could travel with a laptop and an SD card reader and simply upload footage from cards to the hard drive as necessary, transferring to an external hard drive for safekeeping.

IF YOU LIKE THAT WATCH THIS

Road Dreams is the quintessential road movie – a series of programs for UK television (Channel 4) shot from thousands of hours of Super 8 film in a long and winding trip through the States (www.retroroadtrips.com).

For features, check out *Wild at Heart* (1990), *Kings of the Road* (1976) or *Easy Rider* (1969).

PREPRODUCTION ESSENTIALS

Avoid documents like storyboards or scripts – they won't help you when you get on the road. Instead **focus on what overall idea** to have in your movie. Give it some idea, maybe even a really pointless one, to make it move forward:

- **A quest** – like having to taste every coffee stop on a 100-mile rural journey.
- **A pilgrimage** – to a place important to you or someone famous you admire.
- **Immersion** – to become a traveler or delivery driver.
- **By foot or cycle** – to sample the slow life at leisure.

FIGURE 44.2 For a travel movie, shoot a lot of footage, taking time to set up shots and record whatever comes your way. (Photo courtesy of iStockphoto, ©Petrichuck Image# 6831154.)

USING THE CAMERA

This movie demands you **slow down and take a chilled approach to shooting.** This isn't about seeking out the action, and it's not about the big moments. Instead it's about seeing what the landscape and the cities throw your way, responding to what comes along.

You need to be receptive and open to new ideas, able to be flexible about what happens and happy to change your views suddenly. You are like a lightning conductor – the land, the towns, the people, all strike you and your camera and you then convert this energy into a movie. You don't care what comes your way just as long as it keeps coming.

In practice, this means shooting a lot of footage, not jumping to conclusions too quickly, and to keep looking. Shoot with a still and steady camera to let us do the looking, with wide angles and panoramas. Use close-ups to catch small, seemingly irrelevant details. Use the camcorder like a stills camera, framing each shot as well as you can, pressing record and just seeing what you get.

EDITING

This is an editor's movie – if you enjoy editing you'll love getting to grips with a travel odyssey.

To start, look at the footage you got and try to spot common ideas or threads appearing. Imagine your movie is like a song, with a verse, then chorus, then verse, chorus and so on. You need to find that chorus – a few images which can come back again and again or which all resemble each other. For instance, it could be a certain moment where you sit and strum a guitar by the side of the road, the backdrop changing each day.

Edit more intuitively than in other movies. Expect to have long sections where not much happens – this is the sort of movie to be watched as you listen to great music, sip a drink and let the images wash over you. Don't hurry the action either, instead letting the pace slow to a slower, more long-distance rhythm.

Experts' Tips

Elliot Bristow, director, traveler, *Road Dreams*, UK

"Why did I make the journey and shoot it? Several different influences. The main one is that I had formed a romantic notion of the freedom that America had to offer from reading (in 1958) Jack Kerouac's book *On The Road*. I'm hardly the only one who has responded to this book. What may make me a bit unusual is that I found the fantasy I had, lived up to expectations."

"I tended to use the movie camera rather like a still camera, at least in the way I went about responding to imagery. This wasn't a film that had a storyboard and a shot list – the scenes in it are all found; they presented themselves."

www.retroroadtrips.com

LEGALESE

Keep careful track of **release forms** from people who appear in your film. It will be difficult to contact these people again when the trip is over.

Upload It

Best sites to upload to:
Vimeo and **YouTube**
Best communities to join:
Travel in HD at Vimeo:

"Add your Travel Video here and share places you've been, what you've eaten, travel tips, etc."

Best channels to watch:
Project Pedal at Vimeo

ROAD MOVIE SCHEDULE

This movie is a long-term project, perhaps 14–28 days or longer. Add these ideas to whichever schedule you opt for:

Table 44.1 Add these extra jobs to any of the template schedules in Section 6, Make It Happen: Schedules.

What to Do	Who Needs to Do It	How Long This Will Take	Chapters in This Book to Help You
Before shooting Check you have enough batteries to last a full 12-hour day. If you are using SD cards, make sure you have enough. A single 4 GB card will store between 40 and 90 mins of HD video depending on your camcorder setting (lower to higher quality). (See www. sdcard.org.)	You	Less than 30 mins	Ch 12 Using a Camcorder
After shooting Look for images or sequences you can use again and again, just like you have a chorus in a song. You can use the same kind of shot with something that happened a lot – lie watching the sunset each day in a different place.	You	Allow an afternoon to trawl through the footage	Section 3, Cut Ch 20, Pre-edit Footage Viewing
Editing: Work on the movie for two hour stretches. Limit the time you spend on editing to avoid overworking the movie. (Montage is a great tool in this movie, and possibly the only way to work.)	You	A few hours for the first draft	Section 3, Cut Chs 21 and 22, Editing Methods
Screenings: Show a finished draft to friends and crew.	You	Screening over one evening	Ch 25, Screening for Feedback

Chapter Forty-Five

Drama: Western

WHAT IS IT?

A narrative movie set among pioneers – often set in 1880s, in USA, Australia or Mexico.

Forget all other movies, the western is the original genre, the Native American of the movie world. Once upon a time, every film was made of shoot-ups about lonely heroes west of the Mississippi, north of the Rio Grande, south of heaven. But then the big-business corporate confederate hit town with his big-budget blockbusters and soon the western was reduced to its own reservation in small film festivals for the faithful.

So what did the western do then? Just like you'd expect, the genre went a-wandering – ending up with some great movies from Australia, Italy, Spain, Mexico, any place where the countryside was hostile, poverty beckoned and the lawmakers were no different from the lawbreakers.

What makes the western a great genre for a filmmaker is its sheer unrivaled capacity to carry just about any idea, any theme, in its desolate landscape. This desolation acts like a big blank stage, and you can have whatever combination of revenge, chasing, searching, losing or fighting you might want to drop into it. There are no distractions to dilute the plot – just the hero, the enemy and the big sky. Low-budget filmmaking doesn't get any better than that.

MY KIND OF MOVIE?

You have a sharp and almost cynical view of the world. You don't like frills and prefer your apartment basic, sparsely decorated but not neat. You might not have seen too many westerns and you certainly don't have any nostalgia for the old movies. You might prefer noir films, you don't mind if there's not much talking, and you don't care if there are long pauses – you just expect bad things to happen. In fact, you don't care if people are a little uncomfortable or get a few illusions shattered – that's the real world to you.

WHAT'S IT FOR?

Westerns have a huge fan base, mostly in countries where there is a history of braving the elements and taming the fierce force of nature. Film festivals and online sharing sites like the genre for a few reasons: it blends like Jack Daniels with just about any other genre to add a twist to it; film festivals like it because audiences have a kind of retro fondness for it; and it has managed to keep reinventing itself over the decades so it still doesn't seem dated.

HOW LONG WILL IT TAKE ME?

It's a narrative movie so expect to spend time on the script. Full-blooded westerns, or movies with even a hint of western in them, need a script that has been stripped down to basics, with **a simple plot but a complex character.** But this also means that shooting is simpler, without excessive props, makeup or sets. If you get the location right you could make this a quick movie to shoot.

HOW HARD IS IT?

Difficulty level:

★ ★ ★ ★ ☆

You need to be able to commit to the pared-down, sparse kind of movie this is. It thrives on a simple story, bare locations and yet the meaning in this sort of movie gets filled up by the intense emotional power of the primal themes it uses. It's going to be a great movie.

You need:

- To be able to do a simple, mean and sharp script
- To work with a team
- To resist making a flashy, MTV style movie – this is a brooding and threatening movie and needs to be edited that way, slow and menacing

WHO ELSE DO I NEED?

- **Sound**
- **Camera**
- **Producer** (or at least someone else who believes in the film as much as you)
- **Runner** for extra help

WHAT KIT DO I NEED?

Shoot on HD – the lens and camera will deliver a great-looking movie and make the most of your locations.

For sound, use a boom, but also try and get hold of a radio mic to enable you to shoot way back from the actors.

IF YOU LIKE THAT WATCH THIS

Sam Fuller's *Run of the Arrow* (1957) is way ahead of its time, while anything by Sergio Leone can be safely eaten whole – try *Once Upon a Time in the West* or the *Dollars* trilogy for all the ingredients you need.

And the western is not just about pioneer times: it's no surprise that the big days of the genre have been in turbulent times – with 1950 seen as the year zero, where *High Noon* brought America's fears about Korea and McCarthy to the screen. In the early 2000s, the brutal *3:10 to Yuma* (2007) added in a graphic prisoner torture scene to this classic remake, hinting at the Iraq war and the Abu Ghraib incident. Or there's *The Wild Bunch* in 1969 with its corrupt hunters, helping America figure out the moral confusion in Vietnam.

Other genres absorbed the western in the 1970s in movies set in modern cities but with real western themes, atmosphere and plots – *Dirty Harry* (1971), *Serpico* (1973), *Taxi Driver* (1976), and *Badlands* (1973).

Online, try the superb *The West Side*, an urban western that shows how to update the genre for today, winner of a Webby Award for Best Online Drama in 2008 (www.thewestside.tv). (See Chapter 30, Create Your Own Web Series.)

GET INSPIRED

Westerns succeed with strong plots. **The best westerns hinge on plots so tight they can be described in a dozen words.** Practice reducing your outline story down until you have sheered off the frills and detours, ending up with an austere plot unadorned with distractions. Then flesh it out with subplots, love interest, or backstory.

Learn from the past and take from the genre what works; sixty years of classics have given us enough traits to choose from, so cherry-pick the best ideas and sift them into a streamlined story. In the best westerns, landscape is more crucial than in any other genre. It isolates the hero and it switches from Eden to hell overnight – it's your extra enemy waiting to pounce.

Authorities get a bad press: invariably corrupt and immoral. The hero is self-reliant and pitted against the state as much as against the local bad guy. But don't make life easy for him or her; always push them further than other genres dare by isolating them from their community, with more deprivations and fewer weapons than the enemy. Above all, find the best enemy you can.

PREPRODUCTION ESSENTIALS

Storyboards; script; location photos; release forms; style sheets/designs; costume designs; backstory; treatment; lighting designs; budget; permission forms for locations; health and safety sheets; contracts; copyright release for music; shot list; shooting schedule.

See Chapter 11, Brief Directory of All the Paperwork You Need.

USING THE CAMERA

The western makes the landscape or cityscape a central attraction – almost an honorary cast member – so use it well. Have extreme depth in your shots, by showing something right up close to the camera and other stuff far away in the distance, producing a kind of flat vertigo. This depth of field, as it's called, makes the viewer feel uneasy, and makes the scene more tense.

Close-ups are essential, especially cutting from extreme depth to a close-up. They let you get right to the emotional heart of what's going on – showing the sweat of the forehead, the shaking hands, or the ticking clock.

Try **placing the actors center in the frame,** perhaps a few meters away, wide angle, and against an empty backdrop. This makes them seem isolated and apart from the world.

EDITING

Time takes on a different scale in the western, with the simple plots allowing a stronger suspense, build-up and shoot-out. But suspense is more than just a stay of execution; if handled well it can add extra layers of meaning to the movie, by reflecting a while on the film's themes. Also include cutaways to every element of the scene, from harmless spectators to close-ups of the props of the action.

Foley will be crucial, but to create sounds that feel authentic to the location you shot in, record the sounds in that location, rather than in a studio or back home.

Westerns use the landscape like musicals use the chorus line: echoing whatever point needs to be made about the story. Use strong sounds of wind, rain, storms and wheat fields to match the mood of your hero, bringing the landscape into an almost human role. In urban westerns, try the same idea but with city sounds. Make it sound sparse and empty.

Experts' Tips

John Francis, director, *Cowfusion,* UK

"Make it fun. If you're trying to get people to help you, make sure they enjoy it. Before you think about making a feature, make loads of short films. This is the best way of learning how to get a film made for nothing as well as giving you something to show people when you're persuading them to act for you, lend you their car, hold a microphone in the air for three weeks, allow you to blow up fruit in their house or just borrow their cat for five minutes."

"In terms of editing, I used some of the western conventions such as fast cuts to bring out the speed of action sequences when compared to the slower sections of the films. Shooting on a budget, it was my primary goal to keep the pace moving quickly. Effectively compressing time and space was integral to creating narrative momentum throughout the film. Each scene was deliberately concise and with as much action as possible to provide the audience with constant stimulation."

"Try and be original. It sounds funny coming from a guy who made a western but the idea behind *Cowfusion* was totally fresh. Take a look at what you've got that someone else hasn't. Keep it simple. A major attraction of the western genre is its simplicity."

"Don't take yourself too seriously. Your primary goal is to have fun and make something that people will enjoy. If something more comes of it, good for you."

LEGALESE

Make sure you have done the following:

- Music clearance – use original music or music from local bands to keep costs down.
- Before you shoot – get permissions from the landowner of location you want to shoot in.
- Get release forms from every actor stating that they agree to your use of them in the movie.
- Agree how everyone wants to be credited in the end titles.

Upload It

Best sites to upload to:
Vimeo and **YouTube**
Best communities to join:
Western X web series on Vimeo
Best channels to watch:
Westerns at Vimeo

WESTERN FILM SCHEDULE

Westerns rely on locations more than most genres, so if you have that sorted this movie should fit into either 7-, 21- or 28-day schedules.

Chapter Forty-Six

Howcast

WHAT IS IT?

A howcast is a short, usually online, movie which shows you how to do something.

Howcasts get used everywhere from universities to corporations to charities and campaigning groups. Usually, you have a presenter or demonstrator facing the camera, cutting to close-ups and examples.

We use them because everyone learns things differently; some people learn best through words, some through visuals. As you'd expect, a lot of visual people (like filmmakers and artists) learn better through seeing something explained visually or, like this book, prefer text broken up into chunks, allowing them to scan the page and gather what they want. Online movies are a great way to pass on knowledge and because they are so visual, they appeal to people.

MY KIND OF MOVIE?

You'll enjoy working in a calm, meticulous and ordered way, laying out the process just like a police procedural. You use the camera well – nothing flashy, just straight down the line and precise. You have the ability to see a movie from the viewer's point of view, so you'll know when the presenter is losing the viewer's attention, perhaps by going too fast or not being clear enough.

You enjoy editing precisely and pride yourself on shooting clean footage with clear sound.

WHAT'S IT FOR?

This movie is destined to make the rounds on the web as part of other information on a subject. Take moviemaking skills, for example. You might be part of a filmmakers group, and want to share a method you use for creating strong lighting. You can upload the movie and link it to your local film school, and share it in your networking and video sites.

Howcasts are a fast and easily shared way to get information across. Most people respond better to these than to complex, weighty manuals. Software use, filmmaking techniques or practical skills, such as drawing or cooking, all benefit from a video howcast.

HOW LONG WILL IT TAKE ME?

This project is short, but taking a few rehearsals will save time in the edit room. Before shooting, run through the demonstration to get a feel for how it looks on camera, seeing how close you need to be to focus on details, and whether there's enough lighting. Expect to shoot it a few times, mixing clips from each edit to get the right overall cut.

Editing is straightforward, with no effects, transitions or graphics to mess with. Use Chapter 21, Editing Methods: Narrative Continuity.

HOW HARD IS IT?

Difficulty level:

★ ★ ★ ★ ☆

Howcasts are a disciplined form of movie – but if you get it right you stand to get a decent paying job making them, since the skills they teach you are going to help in just about any movie you make. It's about good basic skills in moviemaking like clean sound, showing what's going on, and editing clearly.

You need:

- Skill in lighting
- To be able to shoot detail so no one gets confused
- To follow a series of actions so the viewer can make sense of it in the final cut
- To record clear sound and use mics well
- To look out for things that look weird on camera – the howcast can fall down if a strange angle or setup gives an unintentional moment of comedy
- To be able to work slowly and calmly

WHO ELSE DO I NEED?

This movie is great practice for working in corporate or public information films, which could become your subsistence money to help support your own personal projects. Try to rope in some more people to work with you, and maybe set up a small company to pitch for similar work locally.

WHAT KIT DO I NEED?

- **One key light**
- **One smaller lamp**

- **Tripod**
- **Boom mic**
- **Tie-clip mic**

IF YOU LIKE THAT WATCH THIS

Go to www.wonderhowto.com or www.ehow.com/videos.html for instructional videos on a wide range of subjects.

PREPRODUCTION ESSENTIALS

Script; release forms; budget; health and safety sheets; contracts; copyright release for music if used; shot list; shooting schedule.

USING THE CAMERA

Continuity is crucial to this sort of movie. Plan your footage so that you get every shot you need and that each one shares the same color, lighting, use of camera and sound. If any single shot looks like the odd one out, it will get harder to convey even simple information.

1. **Set up the camera at a distance from the action and keep it there** – two meters at most. This camera records the main master action. It looks at the subject and doesn't move.
2. **Use a tie-clip mic to record sound** from your subject.
3. **Use a second camera to record cutaways**. This camera can have more fun, moving around the subject and perhaps hand-held.
4. **Keep lighting constant throughout**. If you are interviewing several people, use a common background, or even greenscreen it so you can add your own background to each one later.

Run through the howcast with your subject. While they are doing their stuff, practice with the camera to get the right angle, set up the right lighting for maximum clarity (try a key light three or four meters away from the subject, softened by a smaller lamp on the other side, and avoid shadows if you can).

Bear in mind that most howcasts are destined for the web, so use filming techniques in Chapter 27, Web Your Movie.

EDITING

- The howcast depends solely on clarity, so the golden rule is, as with shooting, continuity. Edit to show step-by-step processes so there's no doubt about what happens and when it happens. The only aim is to convey information. If it's demonstrating something, use long cuts (a few seconds or more) and intersperse wider shots where we see the whole scene with close-ups.
- Take your time, don't hurry, and don't use gimmicks or effects.

- Use titles to enforce what's happening on screen.
- If you want to add some style to the movie try playing around with the hand-held cutaways, for instance using them as black and white.

Go to Chapter 21, Editing Methods: Narrative Continuity for more help.

LEGALESE

You'll need **release forms** from all performers, or demonstrators, or interviewees.

Upload It

Best sites to upload to:
YouTube
Best communities to join:
How to category on YouTube
Best channels to watch:
videojug.com on YouTube

HOWCAST FILM SCHEDULE

This movie is ideally suited to a 48-hour schedule.

Section Six: Make It Happen: Schedules

MAKE IT HAPPEN

You can make a 90-minute feature in a week or a 5-minute short in a month. The length of time you spend on your movie doesn't have to be related to the length of the movie. Your schedule is your business. The only thing that everyone has in common with all these schedules is that you have to prioritize, sorting out which jobs to do and in which order. Try out some of these schedules to find out what suits your project and your temperament.

Chapter 47: **Slacker Schedule.** OK, not really just for the slacker but for the slacker in all of us who wants to make the movie when it's right, not just because you have a deadline.

Chapter 48: **48-Hour Film Schedule: Make a 5-Minute Film in 48 Hours.** An ideal length for the weekend shoot, just long enough to shoot in one day, edit the next.

Chapter 49: **7-Day Schedule.** For projects a little more ambitious, or just for the perfectionist.

Chapter 50: **28-Day Schedule.** Ideal if you want to spend longer planning and editing, with a week to shoot in the middle.

Chapter Forty-Seven

Slacker Schedule

OVERVIEW

Forget planning, just get camera, go shoot, assemble and view.

Table 47.1 Make a movie on a slacker schedule.

Time	What to Do
When you get the urge	You've got an idea for a movie. Get a coffee and go through three questions: Who can I call to help me? What can I get for free (camera, lights, people, etc.) Where can I shoot with minimum hassle for free? Check batteries are on charge.
Later	Limit the movie to just a couple of locations close by. Go there and get inspired about the place. Create a quick movie based on what you find there. You might get to a disused house; there might be a ladder, a broken telephone, a beat-up car and a torn curtain. Think up a movie that involves these things and the people who turned up to help you.
When you are ready	Run through what you want to shoot. Check there's enough light. Use light reflectors, or lamps if you have them. It doesn't matter what you don't have, the movie will work regardless.
Soon after	Shoot. Make it quick, limit yourself to just a couple of takes for each bit. Don't stop or get bogged down with discussions. Play music to keep motivation going. Stop every 30 minutes for a laugh and a coffee. Let anyone argue who wants to. Listen if they have good ideas. *Continued...*

Table 47.1 Make a movie on a slacker schedule. (Continued)

Time	What to Do
While having a break	Check footage so far. Don't judge it, just a quick check to find out if the sound is OK.
After a break	Carry on shooting. Stop when you have what you need. Then shoot some sounds like effects, ambient noise and maybe some Foley if you need it.
Just before dusk	Wrap it up.
When you want to	Start editing. Look through the footage to get a feel for how it's looking. Then limit yourself to just a few hours to get a rough draft.
Later	Watch through the first edit.
When everyone turns up	Show the movie as a rough draft. Get some ideas about it so far.
If you need to	Re-edit if needed.

48-Hour Film Schedule: Make a 5-Minute Film in 48 Hours

OVERVIEW

You've got the creative bug; you can't hang around planning for weeks. You need a hit-and-run project and you want it now. Here's how to think up, shoot, edit and show your movie all in one weekend. Start Friday 6PM and finish Sunday 6PM – one film richer.

Check out www.instantfilms.tv – a company that makes movies in two days.

You need:

- Three people, plus however many actors you need (limit this to three main roles to make logistics easier)
- Camera; batteries; tripod; four × 60 minute DV tapes; one strong lamp; white reflector board or sheet; smaller lamp; shotgun/boom mic; tie-clip mic

Table 48.1 Make a movie in 48 hours.

Time	What to Do	Role	Chapter to Get More Help
Friday **6PM–8PM**	Brainstorm your ideas on what to shoot. Prepare a one-paragraph outline of the story. Spend one hour discussing and writing ideas for the script, including characters, the structure of the movie and the overall style. **Check you know:** • What's the **atmosphere/mood** of the film? • Who is the main **character**? • What is the movie **about** in ten words? • Describe the film in three **adjectives** or descriptive words (e.g., *warm, sparky and energetic;* or *dark, solemn and spooky*) • Describe one image that you could work as a poster for the film. Use this image as the defining **style** for the film.	Whole group	Chapter 1 Ideas Chapter 5 Designing Your Movie
8PM–10PM	Limit the movie to just two or three locations and keep these close to avoid lengthy travel times. Write complete script – aim for five pages, so one page equals one minute of the movie.	Whole group, or writer and director	Ch 10 Working with Locations Chapter 3 Scriptwriting
10PM–12MIDNIGHT	Create a breakdown of everything you need and when. Make copies. If you use tapes, stripe them now: simply press record while the lens cap is on and leave it to run the full hour of the tape. Means you'll get continuous timecode (those numbers that tag each bit of the tape) without errors.	Director/producer	Chapter 8 Script Breakdown and Shot List
Saturday **12AM–2AM**	Make sure batteries are on charge. You need at least three charged for tomorrow's work. Rest.	Camera operator	
2AM–4AM	Sleep and dream your movie.	Whole group	

Continued...

Table 48.1 (Continued)

Time	What to Do	Role	Chapter to Get More Help
Saturday **4AM–7AM**	Sleep (or pace the room with anticipation).		
7AM–8AM	Prepare for shoot: get crew together for an early breakfast meeting to make sure everyone is up to speed on what to do today.	Whole group	Chapter 15 Manage Your Production: Be a Producer
8AM–10AM	Travel to the first location. Shoot at least one scene. Aim to get a certain amount of finished footage on tape. A good target would be one to two minutes by noon. **Checklist:** • Have you shot some ambient sound tracks for each scene? • Make sure settings on the camera are left untouched within each scene, like white balance, aperture and so on.	Whole group	Chapter 13 Shooting Chapter 14 Continuity Chapter 16 Lighting Chapter 17 Sound Recording Chapter 18 Health and Safety
10AM–12PM	Shooting.	Whole group	As above
12PM–2PM	Take a break for one hour. Send everyone away to relax while you view the footage so far. Don't be too harsh on your footage – it's usual to not like everything you have shot. But just check how it looks compared to what you agreed in the quiet of the meeting last night. It's looking good. Note any reshoots you need to do. Check battery power. Resume shooting.	Director	Chapter 20 Pre-edit Footage Viewing
2PM–4PM	Aim to shoot another two to three minutes of finished movie by 6PM.	Whole group	As above (Shooting)

Continued...

Table 48.1 (Continued)

Time	What to Do	Role	Chapter to Get More Help
Saturday 4PM – 6PM	Shoot.	Whole group	As above (Shooting)
6PM–8PM	Take a break and meet. Get feedback on how it's going. Ask for views and figure out whether anything needs reshooting. Check sound carefully. Have any parts been recorded badly? Eat well.	Whole group	Chapter 17 Sound Recording
8PM–10PM	Everyone else goes home, but you and your editor or close collaborator stay with the footage and start assembling sections as a rough outline. If anything looks wrong now, this is the time to find out. You can shoot again tomorrow if necessary. By 10PM you need to have called anyone who needs to be back on set tomorrow morning to carry on shooting or do reshoots.	Director, producer	Chapter 20 Pre-edit Footage Viewing
10PM– 12MIDNIGHT	Start logging the tapes to show exactly where the good clips are. If you took lots of versions of a scene, you need to know which were the good ones, using timecode.		Chapter 20 Pre-edit Footage Viewing
Sunday 12AM–2AM	Sleep the sleep of the righteous.		
2AM–4AM	And more.		
4AM–6AM	And more.		
6AM–8AM	Wake early, eat well and get a clear head to tackle editing.	director	
8AM–10AM	If you are doing more shooting, aim to get together with cast and crew early. Limit how much time you have – set a time when you want to be back at your desk ready to edit.		

Continued...

Table 48.1 (Continued)

Time	What to Do	Role	Chapter to Get More Help
Sunday **10ᴀᴍ–12ᴘᴍ**	You're either editing, or finishing shooting.	Editor, director Or whole group if shooting	
12ᴘᴍ–2ᴘᴍ	Edit: Try simply starting from the beginning and piecing together the rest of the film. Or try assembling a crucial sequence in the middle and working either side of it, editing it in large chunks.	Editor, director	Chapter 21 Editing Methods: Narrative Continuity Chapter 22 Editing Methods: Montage Chapter 23 Audio Editing
2ᴘᴍ–4ᴘᴍ	Edit. Save the project regularly.		As above
4ᴘᴍ–6ᴘᴍ	Edit. Allow a lot of time to render and copy. Make a DVD, and create a master on DV tape.		As above
6:30pm	Screening at your place.	Everyone involved	Chapter 25 Screening for Feedback

Chapter | Forty-Nine

7-Day Schedule

Table 49.1

Task	Who's Job	How Long to Allow	Chapter to Get More Help
Day 1			
Work on ideas and possible stories, developing them out of people you know, or related to the number of actors you can get.	Director/ producer	Three to four hours	Ch 1 Ideas
Start to recruit crew.	Producer	One hour to email, plus several to discuss and reply	Ch 6 Cast and Crew Online
Recruit actors. Use social networking sites to find the right people.	Director/ producer	One hour to post emails; several hours to reply to responses	Ch 6 Cast and Crew Online
Budget: Work on lowering costs through using existing props and locations.	Producer	Two hours	Ch 4 Budgets
Day 2			
Meet with your actors and crew if possible, or continue to look at replies to your crew and casting call.	Director and cast		Ch 3 Scriptwriting

Continued...

Table 49.1 (Continued)

Task	Who's Job	How Long to Allow	Chapter to Get More Help
Locations: find the right places to shoot. Look for places that give you a lot of possibilities for framing – pillars, stairs, big open spaces, corridors and so on. Send emails or submit permission forms to let you film at locations.	Director/ producer	Look for two or three locations; allow a week or more to get permissions returned	Ch 10 Working with Locations Ch 9 Law and the Movies
Perform health and safety assessments	Producer	Two hours	Ch 18 Health and Safety
Schedule the production – who is due where and when.	Producer	Three hours	Ch 8 Script Breakdown and Shot List
Day 3			
Storyboard your movie if you need to. Use your location recce photos to help you.	Director/ designer	A few hours	Ch 7 Previz
Check equipment and budget. If you need extra actors, get hold of people now.	Producer plus all crew	Less than an hour	Ch 12 Using a Camcorder Ch 16 Lighting Ch 17 Sound Recording Ch 6 Cast and Crew Online
Check you now have signed or email permissions to shoot at your locations.	Producer	Allow enough time to send off new requests for permission if necessary	Ch 9 Law and the Movies
Look at the script again. Go somewhere quiet and check it's still what you wanted it to be. Make changes if needed.	Writer, director	A couple of hours	Ch 3 Scriptwriting

Continued...

Table 49.1 (Continued)

Task	Who's Job	How Long to Allow	Chapter to Get More Help
Day 4 and day 5			
Shooting Keep to two pages of script as your aim for what you achieve each day.	All crew	A five-minute film might take three to four days to shoot	Ch 13 Shooting Ch 15 Manage your Production
Check sound quality after each take. Make sure you get the right levels each time.	Sound/director	Five minutes	Ch 17 Sound Recording
Record sound effects while on location to get most authentic sounds. Always record an ambient track after every scene.	Sound	Up to three hours for a range of effects.	Ch 24 Foley Ch 17 Sound recording
Look at what you have shot each evening and look for problems you can avoid, such as poor sound.	Director, plus camera and sound	About an hour each evening	Ch 20 Pre-edit Footage Viewing
Day 6			
Finish shooting if you still have stuff to do.	Crew	Limit to morning only	
Look through your footage. Make decisions about how you can edit. Plan editing using an EDL once you have ideas you like.	Director, producer and editor	A few hours to log the footage	Ch 20 Pre-edit Footage Viewing

Continued...

Table 49.1 (Continued)

Task	Who's Job	How Long to Allow	Chapter to Get More Help
Start work on editing	Director/producer	For a short film allow two hours to complete one minute of finished movie	Ch 21 Editing Methods: Narrative Continuity Ch 22 Editing Methods: Montage
Day 7			
Carry on editing and aim to finish by evening.	Editor		Ch 21 Editing Methods: Narrative Continuity Ch 22 Editing Methods: Montage
Screenings: Show a finished draft to friends and crew. Be open about negative feedback – it all helps.	Director/producer	Screening over one evening	Ch 25 Screening for Feedback

Chapter Fifty

28-Day Schedule

Table 50.1

Task	Who's Job	How Long to Allow	Chapter to Get More Help
Week 1			
Work on ideas and possible stories, developing them out of people you know, or the number of actors you can get. If you base the movie on real-life stories, research more about it to get an inside view of what happened.	Director/ producer	Allow a day or so	Ch 1 Ideas
Write a treatment, putting the story into written form to show exactly what happens and when.	Writer	Allow several days to get it right	Ch 3 Scriptwriting
Write the script and test it on friends, enemies and family.	Writer/ director	A couple of hours	Ch 3 Scriptwriting
Find a producer or a close collaborator. You need someone who is a more creative producer rather than just a manager.	Director	Allow an hour for posting to film networking sites	Ch 6 Cast and Crew Online Ch 15 Manage your Production: Be a Producer
Research into the setting and background of the movie.	Writer	Allow a week or more	
Recruit crew: sound, camera, producer, plus someone to just help out if you can.	Producer	1 hour to email, plus several to discuss and reply	Ch 6 Cast and Crew Online
Recruit actors. Use social networking sites to find the right people.	Director/ producer	1 hour to post emails; several hours to reply to responses	Ch 6 Cast and Crew Online

Continued...

Table 50.1 (Continued)

Task	Who's Job	How Long to Allow	Chapter to Get More Help
Week 2			
If you are using actors, work within two sessions: one to create characters and come up with responses to your outline story, and another to develop the detail of the story. They'll need to rehearse a lot, especially if you have intense scenes between two or three people.	Director and cast	From four weeks right up to the shoot	Ch 3 Scriptwriting
Budget: Work on lowering costs through using existing props and locations.	Producer	Two hours	Ch 4 Budgets
Arrange a meeting for your crew. Read through the script. Agree responsibilities.	Director/ producer	Meet for 90 minutes	Ch 15 Manage Your Production
Locations: Find the right places to shoot. Send emails or signed permission forms to let you film.	Director/ producer	Look for two or three locations; allow a week or more to get permissions returned	Ch 10 Working with Locations Ch 9 Law and the Movies
Designs: You need to get the look and overall design of the film right. Get inspired by the script to give you the right ideas.	Designer/ director	Allow a day or less	Ch 7 Previz
Perform health and safety assessments.	Producer	Two hours	Ch 18 Health and Safety
Schedule the production – who is due where and when.	Producer	Three hours	Section 6: Make It Happen Schedules
Storyboard your movie, if necessary. Use your location recce photos to help you. You could try 3D storyboard software to get a clear idea of what your scenes will look like.	Director/ designer	A few hours	Ch 7 Previz

Continued...

Table 50.1 (Continued)

Task	Who's Job	How Long to Allow	Chapter to Get More Help
Check equipment and budget. If you need extra actors, get hold of them now.	Producer plus all crew	Less than an hour	Ch 12 Using a Camcorder Ch 16 Lighting Ch 17 Sound Recording Ch 6 Cast and Crew Online
Get a blog or other social networking feed going. Keep people involved with the film before and during production.	Director/ producer	30 mins to set up blog, less to register for talk feed sites	Ch 29 Social Networking
By the end of this week, check you now have signed or email permissions to shoot at your locations.	Producer	Allow enough time to send off new requests for permission if necessary	Ch 9 Law and the Movies
Look at the script again. It has to work even after several readings now. Work with your actors to run through the film from start to finish and get a few people to watch.	Writer, director	A couple of hours	Ch 3 Scriptwriting
Week 3			
Aim to shoot one and a half to two minutes of finished movie each day – out of probably two or three hours of footage.	All crew	A five-minute film might take three to four days to shoot	Section 6: Make It Happen Schedules Ch 15 Manage Your Production
Look at what you have shot each evening and look for problems you can avoid, such as poor sound.	Director, plus camera and sound	About an hour each evening	Ch 20 Pre-edit Footage Viewing
Check sound quality after each take. Make sure you get the right levels each time.	Sound/director	Five minutes	Ch 17 Sound Recording

Continued...

Table 50.1 (Continued)

Task	Who's Job	How Long to Allow	Chapter to Get More Help
Continuity is crucial in any plot-based film. Check each scene fits the rest of the movie. Pay close attention to the script and if you have a spare person, ask them to have the script checked against what the actors actually say.	Director/editor	Throughout filming	Ch 14 Continuity
Record sound effects while on location. Record an ambient track after every scene.	Sound	Up to three hours for a range of effects	Ch 24 Foley Ch 17 Sound Recording

Week 4
Carry on shooting into this week for a day or two if you need to.

Task	Who's Job	How Long to Allow	Chapter to Get More Help
Log your footage. Run through some of it to see how it looks. Most people don't like what they have shot at this stage. Take a break and you'll see it more objectively.	Director, producer and editor	A few hours to log the footage	Ch 20 Pre-edit Footage Viewing
Look at the footage to think about editing.	Director, producer and editor	Allow an afternoon to trawl through the footage and discuss what you've got	Ch 20 Pre-edit Footage Viewing
Editing: Work on the movie for two-hour stretches.	Director/ producer	For a short film allow two hours to complete one minute of finished movie	Ch 21 Editing Methods: Narrative Continuity Ch 22 Editing Methods: Montage
Screenings: Show a finished draft to friends and crew. Be open about negative feedback – it all helps.	Director/ producer	Screening over one evening	Ch 25 Screening for Feedback

Index

Note: Page numbers followed by *t* indicates tables; *f* indicates figures; *b* indicates boxes.